Thomas Boston

A view of the covenant of works from the sacred records:

Wherein the parties in that covenant, its parts - our father Adam's breaking of it, the imputation of that breach to his posterity, and the state of men under that broken covenant. Second Edition

Thomas Boston

A view of the covenant of works from the sacred records:
Wherein the parties in that covenant, its parts - our father Adam's breaking of it, the imputation of that breach to his posterity, and the state of men under that broken covenant.
Second Edition

ISBN/EAN: 9783337728571

Printed in Europe, USA, Canada, Australia, Japan

Cover: Foto ©ninafisch / pixelio.de

More available books at **www.hansebooks.com**

A VIEW

OF THE

TWO COVENANTS,

OF

WORKS AND GRACE.

A
VIEW
OF THE
COVENANT OF WORKS
FROM THE
SACRED RECORDS.

WHEREIN

The PARTIES in that COVENANT, its PARTS *conditionary, promiffory,* and *minatory;* our Father Adam's BREAKING of it; the IMPUTATION of that BREACH to his Pofterity; and the STATE of MEN under that broken Covenant, and under the Curfe thereof, are diftinctly confidered:

Together with

A particular APPLICATION of the Subject, for the CONVICTION both of *Saints* and *Sinners.*

By the late Reverend and Learned
MR THOMAS BOSTON,
Minifter of the Gofpel at ETTRICK.

THE SECOND EDITION,
With confiderable CORRECTIONS.

𝔈𝔫𝔱𝔢𝔯𝔢𝔡 𝔦𝔫 𝔖𝔱𝔞𝔱𝔦𝔬𝔫𝔢𝔯𝔰 𝔥𝔞𝔩𝔩.

EDINBURGH:
Printed by and for JOHN GRAY.
Sold at his Printing-houfe oppofite the City-guard.
MDCCLXXV.

PREFACE.

Though the doctrines and precepts of Christianity are unalterable in their nature, and must necessarily be the same in all ages and places; yet we find that the foolish caprice of men has made them appear in various shapes, in different periods and countries.

In the golden days of Christianity, before men had learned the art of making gain of godliness in a literal sense, and contracted the ridiculous humour of modelling religion according to their respective tastes and tempers, the religion of Jesus was then seen in its native simplicity, unadulterated with the unnatural additions and embellishments of human invention. In process of time, when it was found that religion was not unsubservient to worldly interest, some of its votaries, inclining to make the kingdom of Christ resemble the kingdoms of this world, stripped religion in a great measure of its native unadorned simplicity, and dressed it in garments of their own manufacture.

This dangerous spirit of innovating, when it once begins, knows no bounds or limits. It is like a river or flood whose current has been stopped, when once let loose, it will disregard its proper channel, and carry every thing down with its impetuous torrent. The rapid progress which this wild spirit has made, is clearly seen in those enormous corruptions which gradually crept into the church of Rome, until at length she arrived at the monstrous absurdity of a *wafer-god*, created by the benediction of a priest.

It had not however been so fatal to the interests of true religion, if the inventions of men had been confined to circumstantials, or things of lesser importance. Had this been the case, the blessed religion of Jesus would not have had so much reason to put on her widow's weeds. The Christian world was pleased to indulge some ingenious triflers, in forming refined theories of the creation of all things, and was not offended whether they chose a *volcano* or a *long-tail'd comet*, for the instrument of their dissolution;

folution; nor has the Chriſtian denied the ſame gracious indulgence to ſuch of the ſame kidney as have tried *to laſh their lingering moments into ſpeed*, by attempting curious calculations with reſpect to the prophecies in the book of the Revelation, nor will he laugh, I am perſuaded, when they outlive their calculations. A decent company will not readily quarrel with a conceited cook for garniſhing the diſhes with herbs that are not eatable; but if he infuſes theſe herbs into the ſauce, every one who regards his life and health, will immediately take the alarm, and refuſe to eat. In like manner, the friends of Jeſus, for the ſake of peace, will be diſpoſed to bear with mens foibles and humours, when they are, comparatively ſpeaking, harmleſs, and do not alter the ſyſtem or affect the eſſentials of our holy religion: but on the other hand, if men take it into their heads to new-model the ſyſtem of Chriſtianity, and to preſcribe a new plan of ſalvation, ſuch criminal liberty can never be permitted, and thoſe who regard the health and welfare of their ſouls, will neither taſte, reliſh, nor digeſt ſuch poiſonous unwholeſome food.

That ſuch attempts have been made, (and with conſiderable ſucceſs too), the preſent ſtate of the religious world is a ſufficient proof. The ruſty armour of *Pelagius* and *Socinus* has with unparalleled effrontery been buckled on, and the ſelf-flattering doctrines of *Arminius* have, with ſanguine hopes of ſucceſs, been furbiſhed up anew. Nor has the wild-fire ſtopt here. As *Pelagius* took away original ſin, another adventurer [*], determined not to be outdone by the arch heretic, at one blow rids us of actual tranſgreſſion. Strange hypotheſis! Sin, revelation as well as experience and fact tell us, has an actual exiſtence in the world. There are only two kinds of it, *viz*. original and actual: how then can any of theſe ſpecies of ſin exiſt, if man is guilty of neither?

One could ſcarce believe, that ſuch chimeras as theſe would ever enter into mens heads, to whom the uncorrupted ſources of divine truth are acceſſible. But the truth is this: Men have generally formed ſuch conceptions of the preſent ſtate of human nature, and the extent of its

[*] See the concluſion of Eſſays on the principles of morality and natural religion.

powers,

powers, as they wish to be true; and, wishing them to be true, have asserted them to be so; and after dressing her up in a gay attire of their own making, to complete her honour, and fix the crown of glory upon her head, have complaisantly enough given her salvation of her own working out. Hence it is, that human merit and personal righteousness pass so currently in this refined age, as the only conditions of our acceptance with God, and justification in his sight. The success of this modern method of Christian-making is easily accounted for. For as it ascribes the whole praise of his salvation to man himself, it is much more agreeable to the pride of the human heart, than the gospel-method of salvation, which resolves the whole into the free grace of God in Christ Jesus. But though such a scheme of salvation is greedily swallowed by the human heart, yet, if it has not the sanction of the infallible oracles of truth, it must be looked upon as *a cunningly devised fable.*

Whilst such unscriptural principles as these, with respect to the way of access to the divine favour, are assiduously propagated by some, and greedily swallowed by others, the following publication cannot be deemed an unseasonable one. It turns upon a capital article in the Christian system, upon our notions of which all our views of the method of acceptance with God must depend. For if one man maintains, that human nature, by proper culture and improvement, may acquire strength and integrity equal to that which it had in the days of primæval rectitude, salvation by works will to him appear quite practicable. But on the other hand, if another man, according to sacred writ, believes that the descendants of Adam are obnoxious to the curse of the law, and *dead in trespasses and sins,* he will clearly see the necessity of Christ's satisfaction to remove the one, and the power of the Spirit to raise from the other.

As the following sheets therefore are designed to give us the scriptural account of the original transactions betwixt God and the first parent of the human race, to express the nature and extent of the effects of the fall, and consequently to lead us to right conceptions of the method of salvation

salvation prescribed in the gospel; they will not, the Editor fondly hopes, be an unacceptable offering to the public.

As to the performance itself, the reader, when it comes into his hand, must judge of its merit. To attempt a character of it, would be too delicate a task for the pen of so near a relation as the Author's grandson. He only begs leave to inform the public, that the work is genuine, and is printed from the Author's manuscript, without any alterations or additions. It was preached in a course of sermons to his own congregation by the worthy Author, in the latter end of the year 1721, and in the beginning of the year 1722. And it appears from the following paragraph, extracted from his Diary, that he was led to undertake the subject, on account of the controversy agitated before several general assemblies of this national church, concerning a book, entitled, *The Marrow of modern Divinity*. " I was now led," says the Author, " for my ordi-
" nary, to treat of the two covenants, which lasted a long
" time. I began on the covenant of works, August 27th
" this year [1721]; and handling it at large, from several
" texts, I insisted thereon till May in the following year *.
" I studied it with considerable earnestness and application;
" being prompted thereto, as to the close consideration of
" the other covenant too afterwards, by the state the doc-
" trine in this church was then arrived at." N. B. The Author here alludes to the controversy above mentioned.

The Editor did not think himself at liberty to change its original form of sermons. He has however, for the ease of the reader, divided the treatise into heads, and added general titles to them, as well as to the subdivisions of each head, which he thought himself sufficiently warranted to do, as the Author himself has followed the same method in his *View of the Covenant of Grace*.

It would be unnecessary to offer to the public the reasons why this performance remained so long in manuscript, or why it now emerges from its obscurity so long after its

* The Author's manuscript bears, that the sermons on this subject were begun Aug. 27. 1721, and ended May 6. 1722; having preached on other subjects during that period. On the first of July that year he began his sermons on the covenant of grace, and ended them on the 14th of June 1724. So that this important subject, the doctrine of the two covenants, employed his public labours a considerable part of near three years.

reverend

reverend Author's death. Readers of a certain clafs will perhaps think that it has come to light foon enough, and thofe of another complexion will not relifh it lefs becaufe they have wanted it long. It now ventures out an orphan into the world; and as fome of the fame family [*The Fourfold State*, &c. &c.] have met with a candid reception from the public, the orphan hopes, even under the difadvantages common to pofthumous publications, that it will meet with fome regard for its parent's fake.

That this treatife may contribute, through the divine bleffing, to lead finners to a deep conviction of their guilty and defperate fituation under the broken covenant of works, fo as they may be induced to accept the remedy offered to them in the covenant of grace, as the only infallible means of everlafting felicity, is the ardent wifh and earneft prayer of,

MICHAEL BOSTON.

ADVERTISEMENT to the fecond EDITION.

THE firft edition of this treatife on the *Covenant of Works* was publifhed in April 1772. In it there are feveral things wrong. This fecond edition has been carefully compared with the original manufcript, and purged from the errors of the firft; and comes abroad along with a new edition of the Author's *View of the Covenant of Grace*. Thefe two treatifes, to which we may juftly apply the epithet of *twins*, being fo near akin, and taken up in their connection, the one it is hoped may ferve to caft an additional light upon the other.

The character which the *View of the Covenant of Grace* has long fince eftablifhed, the many editions it has underwent, and the extenfive fale with which it has been honoured, whilft they evince its worth, at the fame time fuperfede the neceffity of any encomium here. I fhall only beg

beg leave to transcribe a paragraph from the Author's Diary, in order to show with what solemn application to the Father of lights, and with what assiduity and diligence, the Author entered upon and prosecuted the study of it. Diary, MS. page 359. "It was with much fear and trembling that I entered at first on the subject of the covenant of grace: and being, after some interruption, to return thereto, I did, from a sense of my great unacquaintedness with the mystery, on October 25. [1722], being the day before my study day, spend some time in prayer, for the Lord's manifesting his covenant to me, and for some other causes. And soon after that, I saw, the Lord had been graciously pleased to hear me; and he gave me some sweet views of the mystery. And the truth is, that, notwithstanding of what light into the doctrine of grace I had by the divine favour reached, at several distant periods above marked, I was still all along dark and confused in my notions of that covenant, until I entered on it at this time to preach it: and in the progress therein, things were, by the good hand of my God upon me, gradually cleared unto me, endeavouring to study it with the utmost application, in dependence on the Lord for light thereinto." The Author adds in another paragraph, Feb. 10. 1723, That he then entered on Psalm xv. and for a considerable time dwelt on ver. 1. and 2. judging it meet to intersperse the doctrine of the covenant of grace with that kind of subjects, that he might jointly teach the people the doctrine of grace, and Christian morality *.

That both treatises may be more and more useful in promoting the design the worthy Author had in view in first entering upon them, is the sincere desire of

Falkirk, Aug. 30.   M. BOSTON.
1 7 7 5.

---

* The sermons here mentioned, are inserted in the volume, entitled, *The Distinguishing Characters of true Believers*, published in 1773.

THE

THE CONTENTS.

HEAD I. Of the *Truth* and *Nature* of the Covenant of Works.

	Page
Gen. ii. 17. *explained*	1
The covenant of works, betwixt God and Adam, a proper covenant	4
Confirmed from five considerations	5
The Parties *in the covenant of works*	8
God the first party in the covenant	ib.
Adam, as a public person, the other party	9
Considered under a twofold notion	9. 11
Christ not included in this representation	ib.
All Adam's posterity included in it	12
The equity of this representation	14
The Parts *of the covenant of works*	15
1. *The* condition *of it*	17
Man under a twofold law, natural and symbolical	ib.
The nature of the obedience due by man to the law	20
Perfect obedience	21
Perpetual obedience	22
Personal obedience	25
2. *The* promise *of the covenant of works*	28
A prosperous natural life promised	29
A prosperous spiritual life promised	31
Eternal life in heaven promised	32
The difference between innocent Adam's and the saints heaven, in four particulars	34
3. *The* penalty *of the covenant of works*	38
Legal death	ib.
Real death	ib.
Spiritual death	ib.
Natural death	40
Eternal death	44

The Seals *of the covenant of works*	46
The doctrine applied for instruction	48
——————— *for refutation*	51
——————— *for exhortation*	52

HEAD II. Of the *Breach* of the Covenant of Works.

Hosea vi. 7. *explained*	53
The fatal step by which the covenant of works was broken, of eating the forbidden fruit	56
The progress of this sin	57
The ingredients of it	58
The aggravations of it	59
How this fatal step was brought about	61
Of Satan's tempting to it	ib.
God's leaving man to the freedom of his own will	64
Man's abusing the freedom of his will	65
How the covenant of works was broken, by this fatal step	ib.
The doctrine improved as a memorial	67
——————— *as a watchword*	ib.
——————— *as a demonstration of the necessity of being united to the second Adam*	68

HEAD III. Of the *Imputation* of Adam's first Sin, of breaking the Covenant of Works, to his Posterity.

Rom. v. 19. *explained*	69
Of the extent of Adam's first sin	72
How Adam's sin, of breaking the covenant of works, is our sin	77
Proof of the imputation of Adam's first sin to his posterity, in five particulars	79
The ground and reason of this imputation	84
The doctrine improved for information	85
——————— *as a motive to stir up to several duties*	88

HEAD IV. The *State* of Men under the broken Covenant of Works.

Gal. iii. 10. *explained* 91
That there are many still under the broken covenant of works, proved 93
Those who are under it described 95
The effect of the broken covenant of works, upon those who are under it 101
  1. *It has a commanding power* ib.
  2. *It has a debarring power* 103
  3. *It has a condemning power* 106
  4. *It has an irritating power* 107
Why so many still remain under this broken covenant 110
The doctrine applied for information 114
———— *for exhortation* 115
Characters of those under this covenant 117
The vanity of some pleas offered by such, to prove that it is not to their own works they trust for salvation, but to Christ, discovered 122

The dreadful Condition of Men under the Curse.

A general view of it 125
What the curse is which natural men are under ib.
What it is to be under the curse 127
That man, being under the broken covenant of works, is under the curse, proven 129
A more particular view of the dreadful condition of men under the curse 132
I. *The condition of the natural man under the curse, in this life* ib.
  1. *Of his soul under the curse* ib.
  2. *Of his body under the curse* 144
  3. *Of the whole man under the curse* 149
II. *The condition of the natural man under the curse, after this life* 156
  1. *His condition dying under the curse* ib.
2. *His*

2. His soul's condition before the tribunal under the curse   159
3. The condition of his soul in hell under the curse   161
4. The condition of his body in the grave under the curse   164
5. His condition rising again under the curse   166
6. His condition compearing before Christ's tribunal under the curse   169
7. This world burnt with fire, in virtue of the curse   171
8. The condition of natural men, lying for ever under the weight of the curse in hell   172

The doctrine improven for conviction, 1. to the saints, in five particulars   176
——————————————— 2. to sinners, in seven particulars   181
——————— for exhortation, 1. to unbelievers   198
——————————————— 2. to believers   199

A

A

VIEW

OF THE

COVENANT of WORKS, &c.

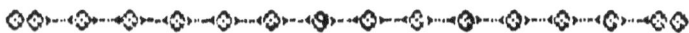

HEAD I.

Of the TRUTH *and* NATURE *of the Covenant of Works.*

GENESIS ii. 17.

But of the tree of the knowledge of good and evil, thou shalt not eat of it: for in the day that thou eatest thereof, thou shalt surely die.

INTRODUCTION.

MY defign is, under the divine conduct, to open up unto you the two covenants, of works and grace: and that becaufe in the knowledge and right application of them, the work of our falvation lies; the firft covenant fhewing us our loft ftate, and the fecond holding forth the remedy in Jefus Chrift; the two things which, for the falvation of fouls, I have always thought it neceffary chiefly to inculcate. And I think it the more neceffary to treat of thefe fubjects, that, in thefe our declining days, the nature of both thefe covenants is fo much perverted by fome, and ftill like to be more fo. And as I defire to lay a good foundation among you, while I have opportunity; so I entreat all of you, and particularly the younger sort, to hearken and hear for the time to come. I begin with the *first* covenant, to shew the *nature* of it from this text, *But of the tree of the knowledge of good and evil, thou shalt not eat of it*, &c.

In which words we have an account of the original transaction betwixt God and our first father Adam, in paradise, while yet in the state of primitive integrity. In which the following things are to be remarked, being partly expressed, and partly implied.

1. The Lord's making over to him a benefit by way of a conditional promise, which made the benefit a debt upon the performing of the condition. This promise is a promise of life; and is included in the threatening of death, thus: " If thou eat not of the tree of the knowledge of good and evil, thou shalt live;" even as in the sixth commandment, *Thou shalt not kill*, is plainly implied, " Thou shalt preserve thy own life, and the life of others." And thus it is explained by Moses, as the apostle observes, Rom x. 5.—*The man which doth those things, shall live by them.* Besides, the licence given him to eat of all the other trees, and so of the tree of life, which had a sacramental use, imports this promise.

2. The condition required to entitle him to this benefit; namely, obedience. It is expressed in a prohibition of one particular, *Of the tree of the knowledge of good and evil, thou shalt not eat of it.* There was a twofold law given to Adam; the natural law, which was concreated with him, engraven on his heart in his creation, Gen. i. 27. *God created man in his own image*; compared with Eph. iv. 24.—*That ye put on the new man, which after God is created in righteousness, and true holiness.* This law was afterwards promulgated on mount Sinai, being much obliterated by sin. And there was the symbolical law, declared in the text, which, not being known by nature's light, was revealed to Adam, probably by an audible voice. By this God chose to try, and Adam was bound to exemplify, his obedience to the natural law written on his heart. And this being a thing in its own nature altogether indifferent, the binding of it upon him by the mere

will

will of the divine Lawgiver, did clearly import the more ſtrong tie of the natural law upon him in all the parts thereof. Thus perfect obedience was the condition of this covenant.

3. The ſanction, or penalty in caſe of the breach of the covenant: *In the day that thou eateſt thereof, thou ſhalt ſurely die.* Life was on the one hand, death on the other, and that in caſe of any the leaſt breach. For if death was entailed on doing of that which was only evil, becauſe it was forbidden; much more might Adam underſtand it to be entailed on his doing of any thing forbidden, becauſe evil, or contrary to the nature or will of God, the knowledge of which was impreſſed on his heart in his creation. The ſanction is plainly expreſſed, not the promiſe; becauſe the laſt was plainly enough ſignified to him in the tree of life, and he had ample diſcoveries of God's goodneſs and bounty, but none of his juſtice, at leaſt to himſelf. And it does not appear, that the angels were yet fallen; or if they were, that Adam knew of it.

4. Adam's going into the propoſal, and acceptance of theſe terms, is ſufficiently intimated to us by his objecting nothing againſt it. Thus the Spirit of God teaches us Jonah's repentance, and yielding at length to the Lord, after a long ſtruggle, chap. iv. *ult.*; as alſo Adam's own going into the covenant of grace, Gen. iii. 15. Beſides, his knowledge could not but repreſent to him, how beneficial a treaty this was; his upright will could not but comply with what a bountiful God laid on him; and he, by virtue of that treaty, claimed the privilege of eating of the other trees of the garden, among which was the tree of life, as appears from Eve's words unto the ſerpent, Gen. iii. 2. 3. *We may eat of the fruit of the trees of the garden: but of the fruit of the tree which is in the midſt of the garden, God hath ſaid, Ye ſhall not eat of it, neither ſhall ye touch it, leſt ye die.*

Now, it is true, we have not here the word *covenant;* yet we muſt not thence infer, that there is no covenant here, more than we may deny the doctrine of the Trinity and ſacraments, becauſe theſe words do not occur where theſe things are treated of in ſcripture, nay are not to be found in the ſcripture at all. But as in thoſe caſes, ſo here

here we have the thing; for the making over of a benefit to one, upon a condition, with a penalty, gone into by the party it is propofed to, is a covenant, a proper covenant, call it as you will.

The truth deducible from the words is this:

DOCT. *There was a covenant of works, a proper covenant, between God and Adam the father of mankind.*

In handling this important point, I fhall,

I. Confirm the great truth expreffed in the doctrine, and evince the being of fuch a covenant.

II. Explain the nature of this covenant.

III. Conclude with fome practical ufes.

The TRUTH *of the Covenant of Works confirmed.*

I. I fhall confirm this great truth, and evince the being of fuch a covenant. It is altogether denied by the Arminians, that there was any fuch covenant; and amongft ourfelves, by Profeffor Simfon *, that it was a proper covenant. The weight of this matter lies here, That if the covenant made with Adam was not a proper covenant, he could not be a proper federal head; and if he was not, then there cannot be a proper imputation of Adam's fin unto his pofterity. None could ever dream, but there muft be a manifold difference betwixt covenants between God and man, and thofe between men and men. There is no manner of equality betwixt God and man; God could require all duty of men without any covenant; yea, they have nothing but what is from him, and fo owe unto

---

* Mr John Simfon, Profeffor of Divinity in the college of Glafgow, was twice profecuted before the judicatories of the church, firft for Pelagian and Arminian errors, and laftly for Arianifm. Among his Arminian and Pelagian errors, vented in his anfwers to the libel exhibited againft him by the Rev. Mr James Webfter of Edinburgh, and in his letters to Mr Rowan, he held, in exprefs terms, " That there was no " proper covenant made with Adam for himfelf and his pofterity: " That Adam was not a federal head to his pofterity; and that if Adam " was made a federal head, it muft be by divine command, which is " not found in the Bible." Thefe dangerous errors were folidly and judicioufly refuted by the Rev. Meff. James Flint and John Maclaren, both minifters of Edinburgh.

him.

him. But these things do not hinder, that, upon God's condescending to enter into a covenant with man, there may be a proper covenant betwixt them. Though all similitudes here must halt; yet we may illustrate the matter thus: Suppose a father to propose to his son, that if he will obey his orders, and especially in one point give him punctual obedience, for instance, labour his vineyard, he will give him a certain sum of money; and the son having nothing to labour it with, the father furnisheth him with all things needful thereto: the son accepts of this proposal. Can any man say, that there is not a proper bargain or covenant in this case, betwixt that father and his son, although the son was tied by the bond of nature to obey his father's commands in all this, antecedently to the bargain, and though he has nothing to labour it with, but what he has from the father? Let him fulfil his father's orders now according to the covenant, and he can challenge the sum as a debt, which he could not do before. Thus was the covenant of works betwixt God and Adam, and that a proper covenant. For proof of this, consider,

1. Here is a concurrence of all that is necessary to constitute a true and proper covenant of works: The parties contracting, God and man; God requiring obedience as the condition of life; a penalty fixed in case of breaking; and man acquiescing in the proposal. Neither can the force of this be evaded, by comparing it with the consent of subjects to the laws of an absolute prince. For such a law proposed by a prince, promising a reward upon obedience to it, is indeed the proposing of a covenant, the which the subject consenting to for himself and his, and taking on him to obey, does indeed enter into a covenant with the prince, and having obeyed the law, may claim the reward by virtue of paction. And so the covenant of works is ordinarily in scripture called *the law*, being in its own nature a pactional law.

2. It is expresly called a *covenant* in scripture, Gal. iv. 24. *For these are the two covenants; the one from the mount Sinai*, &c. This covenant from mount Sinai was the covenant of works, as being opposed to the covenant of grace; namely, the law of the ten commandments, with promise and sanction, as before expressed. At Sinai
it

it was repeated indeed, but that was not its firſt appearance in the world. For there being but two ways of life to be found revealed in ſcripture, one by works, the other by grace; the latter hath no place, but where the former is rendered ineffectual: therefore the covenant of works was before the covenant of grace in the world; yet the covenant of grace was promulgated quickly after Adam's fall; therefore the covenant of works behoved to have been with him before. And how can one imagine a covenant of works ſet before poor impotent ſinners, if there had not been ſuch a covenant with man in his ſtate of integrity?

Hoſ. vi. 7. *But as for them; like Adam, they have tranſgreſſed the covenant.* Our tranſlators ſet the word *Adam* on the margin. But in Job xxxi. 33. they tranſlate the very ſame word, *as Adam*. This word occurs but three times in ſcripture, and ſtill in the ſame ſenſe. Job xxxi. 33. *If I covered my tranſgreſſions as Adam.* Pſal. lxxxii. 7. *But ye ſhall die like Adam.* (Compare ver. 6. *I have ſaid, Ye are gods; and all of you are children of the Moſt High;* with Luke iii. 38.—*Adam, which was the ſon of God.*) And here, Hoſ. vi. 7. While Adam's hiding his ſin, and his death, are made an example, how natural is it that his tranſgreſſion that led the way to all, be made ſo too? This is the proper and literal ſenſe of the words: it is ſo read by ſeveral, and is certainly the meaning of it.

3. We find a *law of works* oppoſed to *the law of faith,* Rom. iii. 27. *Where is boaſting then? It is excluded. By what law? of works? Nay; but by the law of faith.* This law of works is the covenant of works, requiring works or obedience as the condition pleadable for life; for otherwiſe the law as a rule of life requires works too. Again, it is a law that does not exclude boaſting, which is the very nature of the covenant of works, which makes the reward to be of debt. And further, the law of faith is the covenant of grace; therefore the law of works is the covenant of works. So Rom. vi. 14. *Ye are not under the law, but under grace.* And this was the way of life without queſtion, which was given to Adam at firſt.

4. There were ſacramental ſigns and ſeals of this tranſaction

action in paradise. As it has pleased the Lord still to deal with man in the way of a covenant, so it has pleased him to append seals to these covenants. God's covenant with Noah, that he would not destroy the earth again with water, had the rainbow as a sign of it to confirm it, Gen. ix. 12. 13. The covenant with Abraham had circumcision; that with the Israelites, circumcision and the passover; and the new covenant with the New-testament church, baptism and the Lord's supper. So to the covenant of works, God appended as seals, the two trees; the tree of life, Gen. iii. 22.—*And now left he put forth his hand, and take also of the tree of life, and eat, and live for ever;* and the tree of the knowledge of good and evil, mentioned in the words of the text. When we find then confirming seals of this transaction, we must own it to be a covenant.

5. *Lastly*, All mankind are by nature under the guilt of Adam's first sin, Rom. v. 12. *As by one man sin entered into the world, and death by sin; and so death passed upon all men, for that all have sinned:* and so are under the curse of the law, before they have committed actual sin; hence said to be *by nature the children of wrath*, Eph. ii. 3.; which they must needs owe to Adam's sin, as imputed to them. This must be owing to a particular relation betwixt them and him: which must either be, that he is their natural head simply, from whence they derive their natural being; but then the sins of our immediate parents, and all other mediate ones too, behoved to be imputed rather than Adam's, because our relation to them is nearer: or because he is our federal head also, representing us in the first covenant. And that is the truth, and evidences the covenant of works made with Adam, to have been a proper covenant.

Of the NATURE *of the Covenant of Works.*

II. I shall explain the *nature* of the covenant of works made with Adam. In order to this, I shall consider,
1. The *parties* contracting in this covenant;
2. The *parts* of the covenant; and,
3. The *seals* of it.

The

The PARTIES *in the covenant of works.*

FIRST, I shall consider the *parties* contracting in this covenant. These were two.

GOD *the first party in the covenant.*

FIRST, On the one hand, God himself, the Father, Son, and Holy Ghost: Gen. ii. 16. *And the Lord God commanded the man, saying,* &c. God, as Creator and sovereign Lord of man, condescended to enter into a covenant with man his own creature and subject, whom he might have governed by a simple law, without proposing to him the reward of life. Thus it was a covenant betwixt two very unequal parties. And here God shewed,

1. His supreme authority over the creature man, founded on man's natural dependence on him as his Creator: Rom. xi. 36. *For of him, and through him, and to him are all things.* He gave him a law which he was to obey, under the greatest penalty; not only the natural law, but that positive law depending on the mere will of the Lawgiver: Job xxv. 2. *Dominion and fear are with him.* And the truth is, it is a flower of the imperial crown of heaven, due to him only who is absolutely supreme, to stamp mere will into a law binding men.

2. His abundant goodness, in annexing such a great reward to man's service, which it could never merit; Heb. xi. 6.—*He is a rewarder of them that diligently seek him.* Here was a full fountain of goodness opened afresh, after he had let out signal goodness to man in his creation and settlement in the world: after all this bounty, appears a method how to make him eternally happy in another and better world.

3. His admirable condescension, in stooping to make a covenant with his own creature. It is true, he was a holy creature, yet he was but a creature. What God might have exacted of him by mere authority, he is pleased to require by compact, so making himself debtor to man upon man's obedience, which without a covenant he could not have been.

Adam,

Adam, as a public person, the other party in the covenant.

SECONDLY, On the other hand was Adam, the father of all mankind, Who muſt be conſidered here under a twofold notion.

Firſt, As a *righteous* man, morally perfect, endued with ſufficient power and abilities to believe and do whatſoever God ſhould reveal to or require of him, fully able to keep the law. That Adam was thus furniſhed, when the covenant was made with him, appears,

1. From plain ſcripture: Eccl. vii. 29. *God hath made man upright.* There was an agreeableneſs of the powers of his ſoul to the holy law of God, which is habitual righteouſneſs, here aſſerted. Likewiſe it is ſaid, Gen. i. 31. *God ſaw every thing that he had made, and behold, it was very good.* Not only were all things made *good*, but *very good.* Every thing had the goodneſs agreeable to its nature, that it was fit for the end God made it for: and ſo man being made to ſerve God, was fitted for that ſervice. So man was *very good* morally; for that is agreeable to his rational nature, without which he could not be reckoned *very good.*

2. Man was created in the image of God, Gen. i. 27. And ſo,

(1.) His mind was endued with knowledge; for that is a part of the image of God on man: Col. iii. 10. *And have put on the new man, which is renewed in knowledge, after the image of him that created him.* We have a moſt ample teſtimony of this, Gen. iii. 22. Heb. *Behold the man, that was as one of us, to know good and evil.* He was ſufficiently able to know good and evil; good, to follow it, and evil, to avoid it. He had a light of knowledge within him, which, rightly improved, might have directed his way, through all dangers, during the time of his trial.

(2.) His will was endued with righteouſneſs; Eph. iv. 24. *And that ye put on the new man, which after God is created in righteouſneſs.* It was, by its natural ſet received in his creation, ſtraight with the will of God. The holy law was not only written in his mind, by the knowledge of it; but in his heart, by the inclinations of his will to

Cov. I.   B   wards

wards it. No contrary bent was in him, nor propensity to evil: that was inconsistent with the image of God in perfection, and would have been sin in him.

(3.) His affections were holy: Eph. iv. 24. *And that ye put on the new man, which after God is created in—true holiness.* This speaks the purity and orderliness of them. He was not created without passions and affections, as love, joy, delight, &c. for these belong to man's nature; Acts xiv. 15. *We are men of like passions with you,* said Barnabas and Paul to the people at Lystra. The affections are like winds to the ship at sea: but there were no poisonous blasts to be found among them; and no violent and impetuous blasts neither, as there are now. But there was a pleasant, regular gale of them, whereby he might have made way through all dangers.

(4.) He had an executive power, whereby he was capable to do what he knew to be his duty, and inclined to do. He was made *very good,* Gen. i. 31.; which implies not only a power to do good, but a facility in doing it, free from all clogs and hinderances. Now the spirit may be willing, but the flesh is weak: but there was no such thing with Adam; there was no mixture of corruption in his soul, and nothing from the body to hinder his course of obedience.

3. and *lastly,* If man had not been so furnished, that covenant could not have been made with him. It was inconsistent with the justice and goodness of God, to have required that of his creature, for which he had not ability to perform given him by his Creator. Wherefore, before Adam could be obliged to perfect obedience, he behoved to have ability competent for it; otherwise that saying of the wicked and slothful servant had been true, Matth. xxv. 24.—*Lord, I knew thee that thou art an hard man, reaping where thou hast not sown, and gathering where thou hast not strawed.* The case now is not the same with us, Adam having received and lost that power for himself and us. For although one cannot demand payment of a debt, which he never lent or gave any manner of way; yet having once lent the sum, he may require it of the debtor and his heirs, though they be not able to pay.

Thus

Thus was man perfectly furnished and fitted to enter into this covenant.

USE. (1.) How low is man now brought, how unlike to what he was at his creation! Alas! man is now ruined, and sin is the cause of his ruin. (2.) What madness is it for men to look to that covenant for salvation, when they are nowise fit for the way of it, having lost all the furniture and ability required for their fulfilling it? (3.) See how ye stand with respect to this covenant; whether ye are discharged from it, by being brought within the bond of the new covenant in Christ, or not.

Secondly, Adam, in the covenant of works, is to be considered as the *first man*, 1 Cor. xv. 47. in whom all mankind was included. And he was,

1. The *natural root* of mankind, from which all generations of men on the face of the earth spring. This is evident from Acts xvii. 26. *God hath made of one blood, all nations of men, for to dwell on all the face of the earth;* which determines all men to be of one stock, one original, or common parentage. And this also appears from Gen. iii. 20. *Adam called his wife's name Eve, because she was the mother of all living;* which determines that to be only Adam's family. And of him was also Eve, who was not only formed for him, but *of* him, Gen. ii. 21. 22. 23. Thus Adam was the compend of the whole world.

2. The *moral root*, a public person, and representative of mankind: Eccl. vii. 29. *God made man upright.* And as such the covenant of works was made with him. As to this representation by Adam, we may note,

(1.) That the man Christ was not included in it; Adam did not represent him, as he stood covenanting with God. This is manifest, in that Christ is opposed to Adam, as the *last* and *second Adam* to the *first Adam*, 1 Cor. xv. 45. one representative to another, ver. 48. And if that covenant had been kept, Christ had not come, whose work it is to repair the loss by the breach of the first covenant, by establishing another covenant for that end. Besides, Christ was not born, as all others are, by virtue of that blessing of fruitfulness, given before the fall, under the covenant of works, while it yet remained unbroken; but by virtue of a special promise given after the fall, which promise was the erecting of another covenant, namely, the covenant of grace, whereof Christ was the head, Gen. iii. 15.

(2.) Whether Eve was included in this representation or not, is not so clear. I find she is excepted by some. It is plain, that Adam was the original whence she came, as he and she together are of all their posterity. He was her head, Eph. v. 23. *For the husband is the head of the wife.* The thread of the history, Gen. ii. gives us the making of the covenant of works with Adam, before the formation of Eve. The covenant itself runs in terms as delivered to one person, ver. 16. 17. *Of every tree of the garden* THOU *mayst freely eat: but of the tree of the knowledge of good and evil,* THOU *shalt not eat of it,* &c. From whence it seems to me she was included. It is true, she fell by her own transgression: and so might any of Adam's posterity have fallen to themselves, as she did to herself, during the time of probation in this covenant; but the ruin of mankind was not completed till he did eat. And therefore Adam is first convicted, though Eve was first in the transgression, Gen. iii. 9.

(3.) Without question, all Adam's posterity by ordinary generation were included in it. He stood for them all in the covenant, and was their federal head, that covenant being made with him as a public person representing them all. For,

[1.] The relation which the scripture teaches betwixt Adam and Christ, evinceth this. The one is called the *first Adam*, the other the *last Adam*, 1 Cor. xv. 45.; the one the *first man*, the other the *second man*, ver. 47. But Christ is not the second man, but as he is a public person representing all his elect seed in the covenant of grace, being their federal head: therefore Adam was a public person representing all his natural seed in the covenant of works, being their federal head; for if there be a second man, there must be a first man; if a second representative, there must be a first. Again, Christ is not the last Adam, but as the federal head of the elect, bringing salvation to them by his covenant-keeping: therefore the first Adam was the federal head of those whom he brought

death

death upon, by his covenant-breaking; and these are *all*, ver. 22. *For as in Adam all die, even so in Christ shall all be made alive.* And therefore the apostle, Rom. v. 14. calls Adam a *figure* or type of Christ. Accordingly, each of these representatives are held forth, with their respective parties represented by them, being made like unto them, 1 Cor. xv. 48. *As is the earthy, such are they also that are earthy: and as is the heavenly, such are they also that are heavenly.*

[2.] Adam's breaking of the covenant is in law their breaking of it: it is imputed to them by a holy God, whose judgement is according to truth, and therefore can never impute to men the sin which they are not guilty of: Rom. v. 12. *As by one man sin entered into the world, and death by sin; and so death passed upon all men, for that* ALL HAVE SINNED. Now, if we inquire what is the particular sin here meant; the apostle makes it evident, that it is Adam's *first* sin, ver. 15. 19.—*If through the offence of one, many be dead.—By one man's disobedience many were made sinners.* And that sin was his breaking of the covenant. Now, we could never be reckoned breakers of the covenant in him, if we were not reckoned first makers of it in him; that is, that Adam was our federal head in that covenant, so that it was made with us in him.

[3.] The ruins by the breach of that covenant fall on all mankind, not excepting those who are not guilty of actual sin. Hence believers are said to have been *by nature the children of wrath, even as others*, Eph. ii. 3. and *death* is said to have *reigned, even over them that had not sinned after the similitude of Adam's transgression*, Rom. v. 14. All were excluded from paradise, and from the tree of life, in the loins of Adam; the ground was cursed to them, as well as to him. Yea, *all die* spiritually, and that in him, 1 Cor. xv. 22.; yet it is only *the soul that sinneth, shall die*, Ezek. xviii. 4. They thus die, who are not chargeable with personal sins, Rom. v. 14. It must be by virtue of that original threatening then, Gen. ii. 17. *In the day that thou eatest thereof, thou shalt surely die.* And if they die by virtue of that threatening, they were under that law to which it was annexed: but they
could

could no other way be under it, than as in Adam their federal head and reprefentative.

[4.] *Laftly*, The fin and death we come under by Adam, is ftill reftrained unto that fin of his by which he brake the covenant of works: Rom. v. 15.—19.—*Through the offence of one, many be dead.—The judgement was by one to condemnation.—By one man's offence, death reigned by one.—By the offence of one judgement came upon all men to condemnation.—By one man's difobedience many were made finners.* As for Adam's after-fins, the fcripture takes no notice of them that way. If our communion with him in fin and death, did depend merely on his natural relation to us, the conveyance of guilt from him unto us, could not have ceafed, till his whole guilt contracted all his life over had difburdened itfelf upon us: becaufe the natural relation ceafed not, but was ftill the fame. It depended then upon fome fupervenient relation, the which could be no other but that he was conftituted a public perfon, reprefenting us in the firft covenant: the which ceafed, when he went in for himfelf into the fecond covenant. The fhip whereof he was made fteerfman, being fplit, the covenant of grace, as another fhip, came up, of which Chrift was the fteerfman; and this covenant was let out as a rope to hale the paffengers to land. This Adam laid hold on, and fo quitted his firft poft, that his after mifmanagement could no more harm his pofterity as formerly.

The EQUITY *of this reprefentation.*

This reprefentation was *juft* and *equal*, though we did not make choice of Adam for that effect. The juftice and equity of it appears, in that,

1. God made the choice; he pitched on Adam as a fit perfon to reprefent all mankind; and there is no mending of God's work, which is perfect, Eccl. iii. 14. There was infinite wifdom at the making of it; and fovereign authority to eftablifh it. The covenant propofed to Adam, could not but in duty be confented to by him; and there is the fame obligation on his pofterity. If judges on earth may name and give tutors to minors, might not the Judge of all the earth do the fame to his own creatures?

2. Adam

2. Adam was undoubtedly the moſt fit choice. He was the common father of us all: ſo being our natural head, he was fitteſt to be our federal head. He was in caſe for managing the bargain to the common advantage, Eccl. vii. 29. being *made upright*, and furniſhed with ſufficient abilities. And his own intereſt was on the ſame bottom with that of his poſterity. Thus his abilities, and natural affection, concurring with his own intereſt, ſpoke him to be a fit perſon for that office.

3. *Laſtly*, The choice was of apiece with the covenant. The covenant, in its own nature moſt advantageous for man, though it could not be profitable to God, Job xxxv. 7. was a free benefit and gift on God's part; foraſmuch as man had not a claim to the life promiſed, but by the covenant. So that as the covenant owed its being, not to nature, but a poſitive conſtitution of God; ſo did the choice owe its being to the ſame reaſon. God joined the covenant and repreſentation together; and ſo the conſent of Adam or his poſterity, to the one, was and is a conſenting to the other.

The PARTS *of the covenant of works.*

SECONDLY, I come now to diſcourſe of the *parts* of the covenant. Theſe are the things agreed upon betwixt God and man in this tranſaction; the which God propoſed, and man aſſented to, which made it properly God's covenant. It was himſelf who ſettled and drew all the articles of it, by himſelf alone, Rom. xi. 34. *For who hath known the mind of the Lord*, (ſays the apoſtle), *or who hath been his counſellor?* Nothing was left to man, but to receive, acquieſce in, and conſent to it, as is manifeſt from the text. This was becoming the inequality of the parties; ſuitable to God's ſovereign authority over man, whoſe propoſals to his creature are in effect laws; and ſuitable to the meanneſs of man in his beſt eſtate, who hath nothing but what he receives, and can never profit his Maker. And hence may be inferred,

1. That for a man's entering into the covenant of grace, there is no more required but the ſoul's hearty aſſent to the propoſal of the covenant made to him in the goſpel. For ſurely there is no more required of a ſinner to inſtate him

him in the second covenant, a covenant of grace, than was required of Adam in innocence, to initate him in the covenant of works: If. lv. 3. *Incline your ear*, (says the Lord), *and come unto me; hear, and your soul shall live, and I will make an everlasting covenant with you, even the sure mercies of David.* Herein the two covenants are at least equal. What casts the balance on the side of the covenant of grace is, that it is an everlasting one, and a soul once in it can never fall out again, Cant. iii. 10.

2. That surely God has made the second covenant himself; proposeth it to us, and requires us to embrace it; and has not left it to us, to frame and mould it according to our mind, and then call on him to consent to the covenant we have framed. If he drew the whole of the first covenant to innocent man, much more has he drawn the whole of the second covenant for sinners. Let them know then, that it is their duty to study what God has proposed in his gospel, to examine themselves as to their liking of that way of salvation; and if their souls be content with it as it is laid down, let them embrace it.

3. Forasmuch as faith is the soul's assent to the covenant of grace, it cannot be the condition of that covenant properly so called. For consenting to a covenant, is a consenting to the condition of it, and all the rest of the parts thereof; as we see in the first covenant, and may perceive in the second also in respect of Christ, where his doing and dying were the only proper conditions which he assented to; Psal. xl. 7. *Then said I, Lo, I come: in the volume of the book it is written of me.* But assenting to the condition of a covenant, cannot be the condition itself properly speaking; otherwise we own faith to be the condition on our part, that is, the mean by which we are interested in Christ and the covenant: even as the woman's taking of the man may be called the condition of the marriage-covenant; which any may see is not the proper condition of it, but marriage faithfulness.

Now, the parts of the covenant of works agreed upon by God and man were three: the *condition* to be performed by man; the *promise* to be accomplished to man, upon his performance of the condition; and the *penalty*, in case of man's breaking the covenant, not fulfilling the condition.

I. *The*

I. The CONDITION *of the covenant of works.*

The *first* part of the covenant is the *condition* to be performed by man. This was obedience to the law, fulfilling the commands God gave him, by doing what they required, Rom. x. 5.; upon the doing of which, he might claim the promised life, in virtue of the compact. So was this covenant, a covenant properly conditional. For understanding of this, we must consider,

1. What *law* he was by this covenant obliged to yield obedience to. And,
2. What *kind* of *obedience* to the law he was by this covenant obliged to yield, as the condition of it.

FIRST, Let us consider what *law* he was by this covenant obliged to yield obedience to.

Man under a twofold law, NATURAL *and* SYMBOLICAL.

First, The *natural* law, the law of the ten commandments, as the New Testament explains it, Gal. iii. 10.— *Cursed is every one that continueth not in all things, which are written in the book of the law to do them.* The sum of this law is comprehended in what our Lord says, Matth. xxii. 37. 38. 39. *Thou shalt love the Lord thy God with all thy heart, and with all thy soul, and with all thy mind. This is the first and great commandment. And the second is like unto it, Thou shalt love thy neighbour as thyself.* That this law was given to Adam, is manifest, if it is considered, that he was created righteous and holy, Gen. i. 27. compared with Eph. iv. 24. And all created righteousness and holiness is a conformity to the moral law, the perpetual rule of righteousness. And that he knew that law, is evident, in that the knowledge of it is an essential part of righteousness and holiness, or the image of God, Col. iii. 10. Moreover, the remains of this law with the very Heathens, Rom. ii. 15. are an evidence of its being given to Adam in perfection; as the remains of a fallen house, shew that sometime a house stood there.

If it be inquired, How that law was given him? It was written on his mind and heart, Rom. ii. 15. and that in

Cov. I.   C   his

his creation, Eccl. vii. 29. Therefore it is called the *natural* law. He was no sooner a man, than he was a righteous man, knowing the natural law he was under, and being conformed to it in the powers and faculties of his foul. That fame law which God gave from Sinai with thunder and lightening, in all the precepts of it, was breathed into Adam's foul, when God breathed into him the breath of life, and he became a living foul.

This law was afterwards incorporated into the covenant of works, and was the chief matter of it. I fay, afterwards; for the covenant of works is not fo ancient as the natural law. The natural law was in being when there was no covenant of works; for the former was given to man in his creation, without paradife; the latter was made with him, after he was brought into paradife, Gen. ii. 7. 8. 15. 16. 17. The natural law had no promife of eternal life, for God might have annihilated his creature though he had not finned, till once the covenant of works was made. But then God annexed to the natural law, a promife of eternal life, and a threatening of eternal death; and fo it became a covenant of works.

How then can men make fuch ado againft believers being delivered from the law as it is the covenant of works, as if the law could no more be a rule of life to believers if that be fo? It was a rule of life to Adam before the covenant of works; and it may, yea and muft be a rule of life to believers, after the covenant of works is gone as to them. God made it once the matter of the covenant of works, and in that covenant a rule of life to Adam and all his natural feed: and why may it not be made the matter of the law of Chrift, and therein be a rule of life to them that are his?

Ufe. See your deep concern in this covenant; and confider that your help is not therein, but in laying hold on Chrift, the head of the fecond covenant.

Secondly, Adam was obliged, by the covenant of works, to yield obedience to the *pofitive fymbolical* law, forbidding him to eat of the tree of the knowledge of good and evil, recorded in the text. This law Adam had not, nor could have, but by revelation: for it was no part of the law of nature, being in its own nature indifferent, and altogether

together depending on the will of the Lawgiver, who, in a confiftency with his own and man's nature too, might have appointed otherwife concerning it. But this law being once given, the natural law obliged him to the obfervance of it, inafmuch as it ftrictly bound him to obey his God and Creator in all things, binding him to love the Lord with all his heart, foul, mind, and ftrength. Hence it follows,

1. That in as far as this law was obeyed, the natural law was obeyed; and the breaking of the former, was the breaking of the latter alfo. They were but feveral links of one chain, conftitutions of the Supreme Lawgiver, which in point of obedience ftood and fell together.

2. That whatfoever is revealed by the Lord, to be believed, or to be done, the natural law of the ten commandments obligeth to the believing or doing of it, Pfal. xix. 7. *The law of the Lord is perfect.* Hence faith is reckoned a duty of the firft command. The gofpel reveals the object of faith, and the natural law lays on the obligation to the duty of believing.

This law was not given, becaufe of any evil that was in the fruit itfelf of that tree: for *God faw every thing that he had made, and behold, it was very good,* Gen. i. 31. It was not forbidden becaufe it was evil, but evil, becaufe forbidden. Yet was the giving of that law, an action becoming the divine perfections, however fmall the matter feems to be in itfelf. In the moft minute things, God appears greateft.

(1.) Herein man's obedience was to turn upon the precife point of refpect to the will of God, which was a trial of his obedience exactly fuited to the ftate he was then in, and by which the moft glaring evidence of true obedience would have been given. So this was a moft fit probatory command. To love God, and one's neighbour, nature itfelf taught Adam. Not to have another God, worfhip images, take God's name in vain; to keep the fabbath, returning once a-week only; thefe could not have given fuch a demonftration of man's obedience to his Creator, having fuch affinity with the nature of God, in themfelves, and with his own pure nature too. As little could the commands of the fecond table have been fo, he having no neighbour

neighbour then in the world with him, and Eve only his own flesh, for a confiderable time after.

(2.) Thus his obedience or difobedience behoved to be moft clear, confpicuous, and undeniable, not only to himfelf, but to other creatures capable of obfervation: forafmuch as this law refpected an external thing obvious to fenfe, and the difcerning of any, who yet could not judge of internal acts of obedience or difobedience. So that God might be *clear in judging*, Pfal. li. 4. in the eyes of angels good and bad, and of man himfelf.

(3.) It was moft proper for afferting God's dominion over man, being a vifible badge of man's fubjection to God. God had made man lord of the inferior world, fet him down in paradife, a place furnifhed with all things for neceffity and delight: fo it was becoming the divine wifdom and fovereign dominion, to difcharge him from meddling with one tree in the garden, as a teftimony of his holding all of him as his great Landlord.

(4.) It was a moft proper moral inftrument, and fuitable means, to retain man in his integrity, who though a happy creature, was yet a changeable one. So far was it from being a bar in his way to further happinefs, as Satan alledged, Gen. iii. 5. The tree of knowledge, as it ftood under that prohibition, was a continual monitor to him to take heed to himfelf, a watchword to beware of the enemy, a plain lecture of his mutable ftate, wherein he might learn that he was yet but in favour on his good behaviour. Befides, it was a fign of emptinefs hung at the door of the creation, with that infcription, " Here is not your reft:" fo pointing him to God, as the alone fountain of happinefs, forafmuch as there was a want even in paradife.

(5.) It was a compend of the law of nature. Love to God and one's neighbour was wrapt up in it; and all the ten commands were fummarily comprehended therein. For in not eating thereof, he would have teftified his fupreme love to God, and his due love to his pofterity: and in eating thereof, he caft off both, and fo broke all the ten commandments.

The NATURE *of the* OBEDIENCE *due by man to the law.*

SECONDLY, Let us confider what *kind* of *obedience* to the law, Adam was, by this covenant, obliged to yield, as
the

the condition of it. To this twofold law, natural and symbolical, he was to yield,

First, *Perfect* obedience. Imperfect obedience could not have been accepted under this covenant; neither for justification, for it would have condemned man, Gal. iii. 10; nor, under the covenant of grace, could it be accepted for that end neither, and therefore *it became* the second Adam *to fulfil all righteousness*, Matth. iii. 15.: nor yet could it be accepted in point of sanctification under that covenant, though under the covenant of grace it is. The reason is, because under the first covenant, the work must first be accepted for its conformity to the law, and then the person for the work's sake: but imperfect obedience could never be accepted of God for its own sake; for God is *of purer eyes than to behold evil, and cannot look on iniquity*, Hab. i. 13. But under the second covenant, the persons of believers are first accepted for Christ's sake, Eph. i. 6. and then their works for the same Christ's sake, Heb. xi. 4. So then the condition of this covenant was perfect obedience, and that,

1. Perfect in respect of the *principle* of it. His nature, soul, and heart, behoved always to be kept pure and untainted, as the principle of action. So the law is explained, Luke x. 25.—28. *And behold, a certain lawyer stood up, and tempted him, saying, Master, what shall I do to inherit eternal life? He said unto him, What is written in the law? how readest thou? And he answering said, Thou shalt love the Lord thy God with all thy heart, and with all thy soul, and with all thy strength, and with all thy mind; and thy neighbour as thyself. And he said unto him, Thou hast answered right: this do, and thou shalt live.* Where the least blemish is in the soul, mind, will, or affections, it must needs make the actions sinful: *Who can bring a clean thing out of an unclean? not one*, Job xiv. 4. *A corrupt tree cannot bring forth good fruit*, Matth. vii. 18. Where there is any indisposition for, or reluctancy to duty, there is a blemish in the frame of the soul. Therefore of necessity man behoved to retain a perfect purity in his soul, as the condition of that covenant. God gave man a heart perfectly pure, and commanded him to keep it from being in the least tainted; he put on him a

fair

fair white garment of habitual inherent righteousness, and commanded it to be kept free from the least spot, under the pain of death.

2. Perfect in *parts*, nowise defective or lame, wanting any part necessary to its integrity, James i. 4. And it behoved to be thus perfect, (1.) In respect of the parts of the law, Gal. iii. 10. His obedience behoved to be as broad as the whole law natural and positive; extending to all the commands thereof laid on him: nothing committed that the law forbade, nothing omitted that the law required. One link of this chain being broken, all was broke together; *for whosoever shall keep the whole law, and yet offend in one point, he is guilty of all*, James ii. 10. (2.) In respect of the parts of the man, Luke x. 27. 28. forecited. His mind, will, and affections, his soul, and his body, all of them behoved to be employed in obedience to the law: it behoved to be the obedience, as of the whole law, so of the whole man. Thus was he bound to internal and external obedience, in the whole compass of both, according to the law. (3.) In respect of the parts of every human action, Gal. iii. 10. The law requires in every such action, a goodness of the matter, manner, and end: a failure in any of these, in any one action, broke this covenant. So in every action, what he did behoved to be good; that good thing, to be well done; and all to the glory of God, as the chief end. The least mismanagement in any of these respects, the least squint look, would have marred all.

3. Perfect in *degrees*, Luke x. 27. 28. above cited. His obedience, as the condition of this covenant, was to be not only of equal breadth with the law, but of equal height with it, in every point. Every part of every action, behoved to be screwed up to that pitch determined by the law: all that was lower than it, was to be rejected as sinful.

Secondly, Adam was, by this covenant, obliged to yield *perpetual* obedience, Gal. iii. 10. Not that he was for ever to have been upon his trial; for that would have rendered the promise of life vain and fruitless, since he could never at that rate have attained the reward of his obedience. But it behoved to be perpetual, as a condition of the

the covenant, during the time set by God himself for the trial; which time God has not discovered in his word. The time of this life is now the time of trial. Our Lord Jesus Christ, in the room of the elect, obeyed the law about the space of thirty-three years; for so long he lived. Whatever was the time appointed for man's trial, according to that covenant; his obedience behoved to be perpetual during that time, without interruption of the course of it, without defection and apostacy from it. Till that time had expired in a course of continued obedience, he could not have claimed the final reward of his work. But that time being so expired, he would have been confirmed in goodness, so that he could no more fall away, as a part of the life promised. And the covenant of works would have for ever remained as man's eternal security for, and ground of, his eternal life; but no longer as a rule of his obedience, for that would have been to reduce him to the state of trial he was in before, and to have set him anew to work for a title to what he already possessed, by virtue of his supposed keeping of that covenant. Yet man could be in no state, wherein he should not owe obedience to his Creator, no not in the state of glory: And if he owed obedience still, he behoved still to have a rule; and for that effect, the law of nature, which is perpetual, would have returned to its primitive constitution, the form of the covenant of works being done away from it; and so have been man's rule in the state of confirmation. Hence it follows,

1. That forasmuch as the Lord Jesus Christ has mended and perfected that work, which Adam marred; believers being united to him, are so confirmed in a state of grace, that they cannot but persevere, and that for ever. Hence it is observable, that the just by faith are declared to be entitled to that very benefit which Adam was by his obedience to have been entitled to, Hab. ii. 4. *The just shall live by his faith*; namely, a life which shall persevere and endure for ever. And therefore the apostle useth that scripture to prove the perseverance of believers, and the certainty of their eternal salvation, Heb. x. 38. 39. *Now the just shall live by faith: but if any man draw back, my soul shall have no pleasure in him.* But we are not of them

who draw back unto perdition; but of them that believe, to the saving of the soul. And believers are declared actually to have eternal life, though that life is not yet come unto its full vigour, which is reserved for heaven: John xvii. 3. *This is life eternal, that they might know thee the only true God, and Jesus Christ whom thou hast sent.* 1 John v. 13. *These things have I written unto you that believe on the name of the Son of God; that ye may know that ye have eternal life.*

2. As it is in vain for Christless sinners, utterly impotent for any good, to pretend to work that they may procure themselves life; so believers ought not to work for life, or that they may, by their holiness and obedience, gain life. For believers in Christ have life already in him, by virtue of his working perfectly and perpetually in their room and stead; and for them to pretend so to work for it, is to cast dishonour on Christ's perfect and perpetual obedience. The truth is, holiness is a main part of that life and salvation we have by Jesus Christ: 1 Cor. i. 30. *Of him* [i. e. God] *are ye in Christ Jesus, who of God is made unto us—sanctification.* Tit. iii. 5. *Not by works of righteousness, which we have done, but according to his mercy he saved us by the washing of regeneration, and renewing of the Holy Ghost.* Chap. ii. 14. *Who gave himself for us, that he might redeem us from all iniquity, and purify unto himself a peculiar people, zealous of good works.* And were there more pressing of faith to obtain holiness, and less dividing of holiness from life and salvation, making the former the means to procure to ourselves the latter, there would be more true holiness in these dregs of time.

3. They that are not holy, have no saving interest in Jesus Christ; and while they continue so, shall never see the face of God in peace: Heb. xii. 14. *Without holiness no man shall see the Lord.* Where is the man that pretends to be in Christ, and to have faith, and yet makes no conscience of a holy life, of the duties of piety towards God, and righteousness and mercy towards his neighbour; but tramples on any of the ten commandments? I say to him with confidence, as the apostle Peter said to Simon Magus, Acts viii. 21. *Thou hast neither part nor lot in this matter: for thy heart is not right in the sight of God.*

Has

Has Christ fulfilled the covenant, that Adam broke; and are not all that are united to him, made thereupon partakers of life? How can it be otherwise according to the faithfulness of God? Surely then, thou who art living in sin, and so art dead while thou livest, hast no saving interest in him.

4. Though the believer is under the law of the ten commandments as a rule of life, he is not under the law as a covenant of works in any sense: neither does the law he is under adjudge him to eternal life upon his obedience, nor lay him under the curse, and adjudge him to eternal death, for his sins. But the law as to him is stript of its promise of eternal life to obedience, and of its threatening of eternal death to his sins. This is the apostle Paul's doctrine, Rom. vii. 4. *Wherefore, my brethren, ye also are become dead to the law by the body of Christ; that ye should be married to another.* Chap. vi. 14.—*Ye are not under the law, but under grace.* Chap. viii. 1. *There is no condemnation to them which are in Christ Jesus.* Gal. iii. 11. 12. 13. *That no man is justified by the law in the sight of God, it is evident: for, The just shall live by faith. And the law is not of faith: but, The man that doth them, shall live in them. Christ hath redeemed us from the curse of the law, being made a curse for us.* And how can it be otherwise, unless one will say, that Christ, by his perfect and perpetual obedience, has not set his people beyond the reach of the curse, nor secured their life?

Lastly, Adam was, by this covenant, obliged to yield *personal* obedience. Hence says the Lord, Lev. xviii. 5. *Ye shall keep my statutes and my judgements: which if a man do, he shall live in them.* Which words the apostle Paul quotes, Rom. x. 5. *Moses describeth the righteousness which is of the law, That the man which doth those things, shall live by them.* It behoved to be personal obedience. Not that every person of Adam's race, according to the original constitution, behoved to yield this obedience for himself, in order to obtain the life promised. It is true indeed, that all Adam's children, who should have been born and grown up, before the time of his trial was expired, would have been obliged (it would seem) to that obedience for that end,

end, in their own perfons : and if they had failed in it, the lofs would have been to themfelves, and to themfelves only. This may be learned from the cafe of Eve, noticed before. But that, in cafe Adam had ftood out the whole time of his trial, every one of his pofterity after that fhould yet have been obliged to yield obedience for life in their own perfons, is what I cannot comprehend. For then, to what purpofe was the reprefentation of mankind by Adam? For what end was he conftituted their federal head? It is plain, that, by Adam's breaking of the covenant, death has come on them, who had no being in the world in Adam's time: and how this can be confiftent with the goodnefs of God, and the equity of his proceedings, unlefs they were to have had the promifed life upon his running the fet courfe of his obedience, I fee not: and therefore muft conclude, that after Adam's ftanding out the fet time, all mankind then ftanding with him, would have been confirmed; and thofe who fhould afterwards have come into the world, would not only have had original righteoufnefs conveyed to them from him, but have been confirmed too in holinefs and happinefs, fo that they could not have fallen.

It is true, the covenant of works now propofes the fame condition to every man under it, that it did to Adam, to be performed in his own perfon for himfelf, if he will have life by it. The reafon is plain, Adam finning was no more the reprefentative in that covenant, to act for them; fo they muft take the fame way every one for themfelves, that he was to have taken for himfelf and all his pofterity. While the pilot manages the fhip carefully and fkilfully, fo as fhe makes her way towards the port, the paffengers have nothing to do for their own fafety, all is fafe by his management: but if he run the fhip on a rock, and fplit it, and make his efcape, every one of the paffengers muft be pilot for himfelf, and work for his own life and fafety.

But this obedience behoved to be perfonal obedience in the following refpects. It behoved to be performed,

1. By man himfelf, and not another for him, Lev. xviii. 5. forecited. The covenant of works knew nothing of a furety, or mediator. *In the day thou eateft, thou fhalt die,*

die, plainly imports, that man the moment he finned, broke the covenant, and was a dead man in law. If he could have provided a furety who should have obeyed, when he difobeyed, that would not have fulfilled that covenant, or kept it. If a furety was to have place, it behoved to be by a new bargain, wherein a new reprefentation was fettled.

2. By one perfon, and not by more: that is, the righteoufnefs of this covenant behoved to be of one piece, and not one part wrought by one, and another part wrought by another. The finning foul behoved to die; and imperfect righteoufnefs could not be accepted in part, more than it could be in whole, becaufe fuch righteoufnefs is not righteoufnefs indeed, but finful want of conformity to the law. Hence it follows,

(1.) That God's accepting of a furety, as well as his providing one, for loft finners in the fecond covenant, was purely of free grace. For *in him*, says the apoftle, *we have redemption through his blood, the forgivenefs of fins, according to the riches of his grace*, Eph. i. 7. He might have held man to the firft bargain, and made all mankind utterly miferable without remedy, having once broke the firft covenant. But the riches of fovereign free love and grace brought forth a new bargain, wherein a furety was admitted, when that benefit to us might have been refufed; yea and was provided by him too, when we could never have procured one to take that burden on him for us.

(2.) That the purchafe of our falvation by the precious blood of Chrift, which was a full price for it, is fo far from lowering the riches of free grace in it, that it exceedingly heightens the fame. When you hear of free pardon and falvation to finners, through the fatisfaction of Chrift, beware of imagining, that the fatisfaction fpoils the freedom of it: but remember, that God the Father, Son, and Holy Ghoft, might have in juftice infifted on our own perfonal perfect fatisfying of the demands of the covenant of works; and yet fuch was their love and grace to poor finners, that the Father parts with his Son to die for us, the Son lays down his life in our ftead, and the Holy Spirit freely applies his purchafe to finners. So that all is of free grace to us. If it had been confiftent with the nature of God, to have forgiven sin without satisfaction, such remission would have been of free grace: but when there behoved to be a satisfaction made, and God admitted a surety, and provided the same himself, this speaks unspeakable riches of grace: as if a king should give his own son to satisfy the law for a traitor: John iii. 16. *For God so loved the world, that he gave his only begotten Son, that whosoever believeth in him, should not perish, but have everlasting life.*

(3.) That there can be no mixing of our own righteousness, in greater or lesser measure, with the righteousness of Christ, in our justification, by the second covenant, Gal. iii. 12. For *the law is not of faith: but, The man that doth them shall live in them.* We must betake ourselves wholly to the one or to the other. For the demands of the first covenant must be answered, by that righteousness on which we can be justified; and unless we have of our own a perfect righteousness to produce for that end, nothing we have can be accepted in that point, since there is no admitting of a pieced righteousness. And evident it is, that we cannot pretend to a perfect righteousness of our own, and therefore must go wholly to Christ for one.

II. *The* PROMISE *of the covenant of works.*

The *second* part of this covenant is the *promise* to be accomplished to man, upon his performance of the condition. That was a promise of life, Rom. x. 5. forecited, which was implied in the threatening of death in case of sinning. For understanding of this promised life, we must consider the condition to be performed, two ways; 1. In the *course* of its performance; 2. As *actually* performed, and *completely* fulfilled.

FIRST, In the *course* of its performance, while man should have been in the way running the race of his obedience to obtain the crown; while he should have been on his trials for the subsequent reward, holding the way of God's commandments, and walking in the path chalked out to him by the divine law, during the time of his probation, without going off the way in the least. In this case the promise would have held pace with his continuance

ance in the courfe of obedience: and, by virtue of the covenant, he would have enjoyed a concomitant reward of life. For *in keeping of God's commands*, fays the pfalmift, *there is great reward*, Pfal. xix. 11. This is evident from the terms of the covenant in the text, which manifeftly imply this, namely, "While thou doft not eat thereof thou fhalt furely live." Now, this promifed life was twofold, natural and fpiritual, each of them perfectly profperous: for in fcripture-language, *to live*, is to live profperoufly, or in profperity, 1 Sam. xxv. 6. And man's profperity in the ftate of integrity, could not be a mixed profperity, as now in this finful ftate, but truly perfect, without mixture of any thing that might mar it. And as for the life itfelf, natural and fpiritual, they were both given him in his creation. So then the life promifed, and to be accomplifhed in the courfe of his performance of the condition of the covenant, was a profperous natural life, and a profperous fpiritual life.

A profperous natural life promifed.

Firft, A profperous natural life, perfectly profperous. The natural life was given to man by God's breathing in him the breath of life, Gen. ii. 7. knitting a rational foul unto his body, and fo animating it, which was prefently difcovered by man's breathing at his noftrils. While that union betwixt the foul and body remains, man lives a natural life. And thus man fhould have lived profperoufly, while performing the condition of the covenant. This implied a threefold benefit.

1. The continuation of natural life, Rom. vi. 23. Man's body was indeed made of duft; but by virtue of the covenant-promife, it would have been fecured from returning to the duft again. As it was created without any principle of death within it, fo the covenant barred all hazard of death from without it, from any other hand, as long as that covenant fhould be kept. Till the bond of the covenant was treacheroufly loofed by man himfelf, there was no loofing of the filver-cord that knits foul and body together.

2. The vigour of natural life. The keeping of the covenant was a perfect fence againft all decay and languifh-

ing

ing of natural life, which tends unto death. Since man even in that state was to eat, drink, and sleep, no doubt his body was to be supported by these means: but the fruits of the untainted earth were fitted for the preservation of such a life; and while his soul continued pure, he could not but make a regular use of them, according to the appointment of the Creator.

3. The comfort of natural life, pure and unmixed with the sorrows of it, the which are now felt, but not till sin entered. All men know, that life is one thing, and the comfort of life another: but these could not be divided, till the wedge of sin was driven to separate them. This lay in these two things.

(1.) Freedom from all evils and inconveniencies of life, which might embitter it to him. What these are, we all know from experience; a flood of them being let out on the world by the first sin, not to be dried up till the world end, and death and hell be cast into the lake of fire: Gen. iii. 17. 18. 19. *And unto Adam he said, Because thou hast hearkened unto the voice of thy wife, and hast eaten of the tree of which I commanded thee, saying, Thou shalt not eat of it: cursed is the ground for thy sake; in sorrow shalt thou eat of it all the days of thy life. Thorns also and thistles shall it bring forth to thee: and thou shalt eat the herb of the field. In the sweat of thy face shalt thou eat bread, till thou return unto the ground; for out of it wast thou taken: for dust thou art, and unto dust shalt thou return.* Hence in man's primitive state, labour was to be without toil, strength without mixture of weakness and uneasiness, health without pain, or sickness, or indisposition of body.

(2.) The comfortable enjoyment of life with the conveniencies of it, Gen. ii. 16. *Of every tree of the garden thou mayst freely eat.* Life itself sometimes is burdensome now, and the good things of it are beset as with thorns and briers: but innocent Adam could have had none of these things to complain of. He was lord of the inferior creatures, and they were at his disposal: what sweet and comfort the creatures could yield to him, he was master of, and could not but have a more exquisite taste of, than any man since. He was clothed with the greatest honour, and

and had it with the profits and refined pleasures of life, to enjoy with God's favour.

We know then where to lay the blame of all miseries of this life, and death itself. The breaking of that covenant opened the sluice to that flood of them which now overflows the world.

A prosperous spiritual life promised.

Secondly, A prosperous spiritual life, perfectly prosperous. The soul of man was and is in its own nature immortal, not liable to the dissolution which the body is liable to. But besides, it was endued with spiritual life, whereby it lived to God in union and communion with him, as bearing the image of God, a lively image of his righteousness and holiness, Gen. i. 27. Eccl. vii. 29. And thus man would have lived prosperously, performing the condition of the covenant. And this implied a fourfold benefit.

1. The continuation of the image of God in him, the uprightness of his nature in which he was created. Nothing could have marred that, while the covenant was kept. The knowledge of his mind would have remained with him, the righteousness of his will, and holiness of his affections. That glorious likeness to God in which he was created, was a beauty which nothing but sin could mar.

2. The continuance of the love and favour of God. He was the friend of God, the favourite of heaven; and as long as he kept the covenant, nothing could dissolve the friendship. Life lies in God's favour, and upon his good behaviour he was surely to enjoy it still. It could never have left him, as long as he kept God's way. For God cannot but love, favour, and delight in his own image, in whomsoever it is preserved entire.

3. Ready access to God, and fellowship with him. The covenant was a covenant of friendship; and while sin was held out, there was nothing to mar his intercourse with God. He would still have had immediate communion with God: for there was no need of a mediator, where there was no breach, Gal. iii. 20. The means of communion with God, prayers, praises, &c. would at no time

time have been dry wells of falvation to him: no defertions, nor hidings of God's face, could have place.

4. *Laftly*, The daily comfort of his perfeverance. He would ftill have had the pleafure there is in the very keeping of God's commands, and the comfortable feaft of the teftimony of a good confcience, upon every piece of obedience performed by him. And the greater this would have been, the longer he had continued, and the nearer he had come to the end of his race, where was the crown to be received.

Thus may we fee God's bounty, and man's ingratitude. He had wages in hand allowed him, a prefent reward of his work, according to that, *Thou fhalt not muzzle the mouth of the ox that treadeth out the corn.* Yet would he needs better his condition before the time, and fo quite marred it.

Eternal life in heaven promifed.

SECONDLY, For underftanding of this promifed life, we muft confider the condition to be performed, as *actually* performed, and *completely* fulfilled. God had appointed to man a time of trial and probation, during which he was carefully to take heed to himfelf, that he obeyed perfectly and perpetually, as being liable to fin; and fo to give proof of himfelf, of his awful refpect to his Creator's will, and his right management of the talents given him by his great Lord to trade with. In this cafe, *viz.* upon man's ftanding in his innocence till that time was expired, eternal life was by the promife fecured to him as the reward of his work, Matth. xix. 17. And in it thefe four benefits were implied.

1. The confirmation of his foul in innocence, righteoufnefs and holinefs, that he fhould be fet beyond hazard of finning, and that for evermore; as the confirmed angels are. Being juftified upon his perfonal, perfect, and perpetual obedience, this would have followed of courfe, acording to the tenor of the covenant; otherwife he would have been for ever upon trial, which is inconfiftent with the nature of the covenant. Mutability is woven into the very nature of the creature, and fo Adam was created mutable: but he would have been, upon his obedience,

fecured

secured from actual liableness to change for evermore. The need of watching would have been over with him in that case, as it is with the saints in heaven.

2. The setting of his body absolutely and for ever out of all hazard of death, even remote hazard. While he was in the state of trial, there was a possibility of death's making an approach to it, *viz.* on supposition of sin. But had the condition of the covenant once been fully performed, there had been no more any possibility of his dying, Rom. vi. 23. because no more possibility of sinning.

3. The settling of the love and favour of God upon him for ever, without any hazard of his falling out of it. This also necessarily would have followed on his confirmation in righteousness. The sun of favour from God, from that time, should have shone so upon him, as it could never more have gone down. The friendship would have been so confirmed, that there should have been no more a possibility of a breach, for ever.

4. *Lastly*, The transporting of him soul and body to heaven, there to enjoy the perfection of blessedness through eternity. He should not always have lived in the earthly paradise, where he was to eat, drink, sleep, &c. but, in God's own time, been carried to the heavenly paradise, to live there as the angels of God. He was happy while he was in the course of obedience, and had communion with God. But there he should have been perfectly happy, and had more near and full communion with God, Psal. xvi. *ult.* for ever.

I am not here to launch forth into the subject of heaven's happiness, which man should have enjoyed by this covenant, had he kept it. Only in a word, for the substance of it, it would have been the same, that the saints shall enjoy for ever: for it was the life which Adam lost for himself and his posterity, that Christ purchased by his obedience and death for his spiritual seed, Rom. x. 5. compared with Hab. ii. 4. both forecited. And that was eternal life in heaven without controversy. Our Lord Jesus Christ himself proposing the covenant of works to a legalist, holds forth eternal life as the promise of it, to be had on performance of the condition, Luke x. 25.—28. *And behold, a certain lawyer stood up, and tempted him, saying, Master, what shall I do to inherit eternal life? He said unto him, What is written in the law? how readest thou?* *And he answering, said, Thou shalt love the Lord thy God with all thy heart, and with all thy soul, and with all thy strength, and with all thy mind; and thy neighbour as thyself And he said unto him, Thou hast answered right: this do, and thou shalt live.* And the weakness of the law to give eternal life now, proceeds only from our inability to fulfil the condition of it, Rom. viii. 3. For which cause Christ put himself in the room of the elect, to fulfil that obedience which they were unable to give, Gal. iv. 4. 5. and so consequently gained that life to them, which they should otherwise have had, if man had not sinned. Besides, it is evident, that, by the breach of this covenant, man now falls under eternal death in hell: therefore on the grounds of the goodness of God, and the equity of his proceedings, one may conclude, that eternal life in heaven was promised.

The difference between innocent Adam's and the saints heaven.

Yet there would have been considerable difference betwixt innocent Adam's heaven, and the Mediator's heaven, which the saints shall be possessed of: but the advantage lies to the side of the latter. There are four things that would have been wanting (if I may so speak) in innocent Adam's heaven, that will be found in the saints heaven.

(1.) The additional sweetness of the enjoyment, that arises from the experience of want and misery. Two men are set down at a feast; the one never knew what hunger and want meant; the other never got a full meal all his days, but want and hunger were his daily companions. Which of the two would the feast be sweetest to? The case is plain. Sin is the worst of things, there is no good in it; the effects of sin, sorrow, misery, and trouble, are bitter: but God permitted the one, and has brought the other on, in depth of wisdom; for out of these is a sauce drawn, that will give an additional sweetness to the supper of the Lamb in the upper house. While the saints walk in their white robes, and remember the filthy, ragged, black garments

they

they went in some time a-day; it will raise their praises a note higher, than innocent Adam's, while he should have looked on his, which there was never a spot upon. When after many tossings on the sea of this world, and the floods of difficulties and dangers from sin and Satan which have encompassed them, the saints happily arrive on the shore of the heavenly Canaan, their relish of the pleasures to be enjoyed there will be the more exquisite and delightful.

(2.) The fairest flower in heaven to be seen by bodily eyes, would have been wanting in innocent Adam's heaven, namely, the man Christ. It is a groundless antiscriptural notion, that the Son of God would have been incarnate, though man had never sinned, John iii 16. 1 Tim. i. 15. It was for sinners the Saviour was sent. The ruin of man's nature in the first Adam, was the occasion sovereign love took to raise it up to the highest possible pitch of glory and dignity, in the person of the Son of God. There our nature is personally united to the divine nature, even in the person of the Son: and the man Christ is in heaven more glorious than a thousand suns. It is true, Adam would have had the sight and enjoyment of God, Father, Son, and Holy Ghost; but he could not have said, as they, "Behold God in our nature, our elder Brother," &c.

(3.) The charter, written with blood, securing the enjoyment of heaven's happiness. Adam would have had good security indeed for it, by the fulfilled covenant of works: but behold a more glorious charter, the covenant of grace, written with the blood of the Son of God, Heb. xiii. 20. Every draught of the well of the water of life that innocent Adam would have had in his heaven, he might have cried out with wonder concerning it, "O the gracious reward of my obedience!" But the saints shall say of theirs, "O the glorious purchase of my Redeemer's blood; this is the purchase of the blood of the Son of God:" Rev. vii. 9. 10. *After this I beheld, and lo, a great multitude, which no man could number, of all nations, and kindreds, and people, and tongues, stood before the throne, and before the Lamb, clothed with white robes, and palms in their hands; and cried with a loud voice, saying, Salvation to our God which sitteth upon the throne, and unto the Lamb.*

(4.) Lastly,

(4.) *Lastly*, The manner of living, as members of the myſtical body of Chriſt. Innocent Adam would have lived for ever in heaven as the friend of God: but the ſaints ſhall live for ever there as members of Chriſt, John vi. 57. & xiv. 19. They ſhall be more nearly related to the Son of God, than Adam could have been, Eph. v. 30. He will be their Huſband, in an everlaſting marriage-covenant, their elder Brother, their Head, of which they are members; and through whom they will derive their glory, as they do their grace, from the Godhead, as united to Chriſt, the prime receptacle of grace and glory: Rev. vii. *ult. For the Lamb which is in the midſt of the throne, ſhall feed them, and ſhall lead them unto living fountains of waters: and God ſhall wipe away all tears from their eyes.* Rev. xxi. 23. *And the city had no need of the ſun, neither of the moon to ſhine in it: for the glory of God did lighten it, and the Lamb is the light thereof.*

Thus have I ſhewn you the nature of the promiſe of the covenant of works, and the life therein made over conditionally to man. If we conſider the life Adam could have expected from God, in a courſe of obedience, though there had been no covenant, we ſay, Adam performing obedience, according to the natural law written in his heart, would have had a proſperous life and being, while he had a being: this Adam might conclude from the good and bountiful nature of God. But ſtill it would have been conſiſtent with the nature of God, to have withdrawn his ſupporting hand from man, ſo as he might have ceaſed to be any more. And this would have been, but taking away freely, what he gave freely, being under no obligation to continue it; for even Adam's innocent works could not have properly merited at God's hand; Rom. xi. 35. *Who hath firſt given to him, and it ſhall be recompenſed unto him again?* They could have only merited improperly, by virtue of compact, not by the intrinſic worth of the thing. Hence,

1. The continuation of life to Adam, even while he continued obedient, was entirely due to the covenant God was pleaſed to make with him. And here was grace even in the covenant of works, that God was pleaſed by promiſe

mise to secure the continuance of man's being, while he continued obedient.

2. The right that Adam could have pled, to eternal life in heaven, by virtue of his obedience, was entirely founded on the covenant. If God had not revealed to him the promise of it, he could not have known that he should have it, nor could he have demanded it. The natural law had no such promise. And here was more grace in the covenant of works. And therefore it is no wonder, that though men overturn the gospel-doctrine of free grace, yet they will not take with it. The Pharisees of old, Luke xviii. 11. and the Papists to this day, own free grace in their profession; and what wonder, since innocent Adam, pleading life upon his works, could not have denied but he was debtor to free grace? But here lies the matter: they put in their own works, their repentance, holiness, and obedience, (turning faith into a work, that it may go in with the rest), between free grace and them, making themselves but debtors to it at the second hand, for life and salvation. And if one shall tell sinners, Here you are to do or work nothing, for life and salvation, but only receive the free-grace gift of life and salvation from Christ by faith, and be grace's debtors at first hand; though withal we tell them, that repentance, holiness, obedience, and good works, are the inseparable attendants of faith; they cry out, " Error, Antinomianism, Licentious doctrine!" Yet it is the doctrine of the gospel, that *not by works of righteousness, which we have done, but according to his mercy he saved us,* Tit. iii. 5.; and as the apostle says to the Ephesians, chap. ii. 8. *By grace are ye saved, through faith; and that not of yourselves: it is the gift of God.* And it is not the doctrine of the gospel, nor does the apostle say, *By grace ye are saved, through works;* for so would Adam have been saved according to the covenant of works, being debtor to free grace at the second hand, which the proud Pharisee was content to be. It is true, Adam's obedience was perfect, ours is not: but buying is buying still, though one buy ten times below the worth, as well as when he buys at the full value.

III. *The*

III. The PENALTY *of the covenant of works.*

We come now to confider the *penalty*, in cafe of man's breaking the covenant, not fulfilling the condition. This was death, death in its full latitude and extent, as oppofed unto life and profperity. This death was twofold. And we may fpeak of *it* as a thing that has fallen out.

Legal death.

FIRST, Legal death, whereby man finning became dead in law, being a condemned man, laid under the curfe, or fentence of the law binding him over to the wrath of God, and to revenging juftice: *For as many as are of the works of the law, are under the curfe: for it is written, Curfed is every one that continueth not in all things which are written in the book of the law to do them,* Gal iii. 10. Thus was man to die in the day he fhould break the covenant; and thus he died that very moment he finned, becaufe by his fin he broke the holy, juft, and good law of God; fet himfelf in oppofition to the holy nature of God; and caft off the yoke of fubjection to his Creator. This was an actual liablenefs to all miferies for fatisfying offended juftice. Thus the clouds gathered over his head, to fhower down upon him; and thus was he girded with the cords of death, which neither himfelf nor any other creature could loofe.

Real death.

SECONDLY, Real death, which is the execution of the fentence, Deut. xxix. 19. 20.; the threatened evils, and punifhments contained in the curfe of the law, coming upon him. And of this there are feveral parts, all which man became liable to, or fell upon him, when he finned. We take them up in thefe three; fpiritual, natural, and eternal death.

Spiritual death.

Firft, Spiritual death, which is the death of the foul and fpirit of man, Eph. ii. 1. being *dead in trefpaffes and fins.* This flows or refults from the feparation of the foul from God,

God, by the breaking of the silver-cord of this covenant, which knit innocent man to God, causing him to live and live prosperously, as long as it was unbroken; but being broken, that union and communion was dissolved, and they parted, If lix. 2. Thus man was separated from the fountain of life, upon which that death necessarily ensued. This death may be considered,

1. As immediately seizing him, upon the breaking of the covenant. And thus a twofold spiritual death seized him, as the penalty of the covenant; a *moral*, and a *relative* death.

(1.) A *moral* death of the soul, by which it was divested of the image of God, viz. saving knowledge, righteousness, and holiness; and the whole nature was corrupted, Eph. ii. 1.; and so left destitute of a principle of vital spiritual actions, that it can no more think, will, or do any thing truly good, than a dead man can perform the functions of life: *As it is written, There is none righteous, no not one: there is none that understandeth, there is none that seeketh after God. They are all gone out of the way, they are together become unprofitable, there is none that doth good, no not one*, Rom. iii. 10. 11. 12. The soul of man was a curious piece of workmanship, made by the finger of God; it was set up, and set a-going for its Master's use, like a watch: but sin broke the chain and spring; so all the wheels of a sudden stood moveless, and could go no more.

(2.) A *relative* death of the soul, by which the blessed relation man stood in to God was extinguished. He was no more the friend of God, the favourite of his Maker. This was a death indeed, Psal. xxx. 5. He enjoyed the friendship, favour, and fellowship of God, upon his good behaviour: he sinned, and so he behoved to lose them. Thus God became his enemy as Rector and Judge of the world, and he was set up as a mark for the arrows of wrath.

2. As preying upon the soul of man, through the course of his natural life in the world. Sin laid the soul as it were in the grave, the house of death; and there being dead while the man liveth, devouring death works and preys in and upon it, two ways.

(1.) In

(1.) In the progress of sin and corruption in the soul, as the body in the grave rots more and more, Psal. xiv. 3. The soul being spiritually dead, the longer it lies in that case, the more loathsome and abominable it becomes. Swarms of reigning lusts breed in it, and are active therein: the remains of the image of God are defaced more and more in it; and the soul still set farther off from God. All actual sins are the workings of this death, the motions of the verminating life of the soul in the grave of sin, Eph. ii. 1. 2. So that they are not only sins in themselves, but punishments of the first sin, which cannot cease to follow on God's departing from the soul; which may persuade us of the absurdity of that principle, That there is no sin in hell.

(2.) In strokes of wrath on the soul. Where the carcase is, there these like so many eagles gather together. The sinning soul becomes the centre, wherein all manner of spiritual plagues meet together; as worms do in bodies interred, to feed there, Job xx. 26. These are manifold: some of them felt, as sorrows, terrors, anxieties, crosses, and troubles crossing the man's will, and so vexing, fretting, and disquieting him: these are indeed a death to the soul, having a curse in them, like so many invenomed arrows shot into man: Some of them not felt, so as to make the man groan under them, as blindness of mind, hardness of heart, strong delusions: but they are the more dangerous, as wounds bleeding inwardly.

Natural death.

Secondly, Natural death, which is the death of the body. This results from the separation of the soul from the body. It is twofold; stinged, and unstinged death. Unstinged death parts the soul and body indeed, but not by virtue of the curse for sin. This is the lot of the people of God, 1 Cor. xv. 55. and is not the penalty of the covenant of works: for that is death with the sting of the curse, Gal. iii. 10. which death Christ died, which penalty he paid, and so freed believers from it, Gal. iii. 13. So that there is a specifical difference betwixt the death of believers, and that death threatened in the covenant of works; they are not of the same kind; no more than they die the death that Christ died.

The natural death, the penalty of the covenant of works, then, is not simply the death of the body, but the stinged death of the body, the separation of soul and body by virtue of the curse; that as they joined in sin against God, they might be separated for the punishment of it, for a time; though afterwards to be reunited at the resurrection, with a change of their constitution. For that there will be a change on the bodies of the wicked, as well as on the bodies of the godly, is evident, in that they shall continue united to their souls in hell, without food, and under torments; either of which, according to their present constitution, would dissolve their frame, and issue in death. Now, this natural death may be considered two ways, as the penalty of the covenant of works; inwardly, and outwardly.

1. Inwardly, in the body of man. There death got its seat in the day that he sinned; there it spread itself from the soul, where it began, that fatal moment of yielding to the tempter. And thus it may be considered three ways; in its beginning, progress, and consummation.

(1.) In the beginning of it. That day that man sinned he became mortal, Gen. iii. 19. The crown of immortality, which he held of his Creator, by virtue of the covenant of works, fell from off his head, and he became a subject of the king of terrors. That day he got his death's wounds, of which he died afterwards. The mutiny then began among the constituent parts of the body, (witness the terror, anxiety, and shame, causing a motion of the blood and spirits, which before their sinning they were unacquainted with); and the end of that was the destruction and dissolution of the whole frame.

(2.) In the progress of it, in maladies and diseases, whereby death carries on its subjects towards the house appointed for all living, Eccl. iii. 20. Every pain, gripe, or stitch, is death's working like a mole in the body of man. Every sickness and disease is a forerunner of death, coming before to give warning of its approach. The sweat, toil, and weariness that man is liable to, are foretokens of the body's falling down at length into the dust,

Gen. iii. 19. Man has now his morning, mid-day, and afternoon; and then comes the night. He has his spring, summer, and autumn, and then winter. Like a flower he has his bud, blossom, fading, and then his falling off. But innocent man would have had a lasting mid-day, summer, and blossom. What follows these respectively, is owing to the breach of the covenant.

(3.) In the consummation of it, by the separation of the soul from the body, Heb. ix. 27. The pins of the tabernacle being loosed, it lies along upon the earth at length. The body of man, like an old house, falls all down together, while the soul, the inhabitant, makes its escape, and leaves it. They joined in breaking of the covenant, and are punished with separation; the body going to the dust, and the soul to God who gave it, to receive its sentence.

2. Outwardly, upon the creatures, on which the body of man has a dependence as to its life and welfare. What dependence we have on the creatures as to these, every one knows by experience. Without the air we cannot breathe; and as the temperature of it is, it is well or ill with our bodies. On the product of the earth we live; the fruits thereof are the support of our natural life, with the beasts that feed on them. The earth depends on the heavens; and according to their influence upon it, so is it serviceable to us. See the chain of dependence among the creatures, Hof. ii. 21. 22. *And it shall come to pass in that day, I will hear, saith the Lord, I will hear the heavens, and they shall hear the earth, and the earth shall hear the corn, and the wine, and the oil, and they shall hear Jezreel.* Now, man's natural life being so much bound up in these, the life promised him in the covenant could not but comprehend the continuing of these in their original constitution, Gen. i. *ult.* and fitness for the support of man's natural life and vigour, as means for that end. And so death, the penalty of the covenant, must needs spread itself even to them; and that upon the same score. Thus also it may be considered three ways; in its beginning, progress, and consummation.

(1.) In the beginning of it. And that was the curse laid upon the creature for the sake of the sinner man:

Gen.

Gen iii. 17. *Cursed is the ground for thy sake*, said the Lord unto Adam. Man became vanity by his sin, and the creatures were made subject to vanity on his account; so that they could not reach the end of their primitive constitution, but fainted as it were in the way: for, says the apostle, Rom. viii. 20. *the creature was made subject to vanity, not willingly.* Nay, such a burden lies on the creation, as makes the whole to *groan, and travail in pain,* ver. 22. Where can we turn our eyes now, but we may see death riding in triumph? The earth's barrenness often paints death on the faces of the inhabitants, by scarcity and famine; the air is sometimes impoisoned with pestilential vapours, that kill and sweep away multitudes; the fire often burns and torments men; the waters swallow them up; beasts wound, bruise, and kill them; nay, we are not secure from the very stones of the field. The very sun in the heavens, approaching to us, scorches and causes languishing; and removing from us, causes us shiver with cold; and hiding itself under clouds, damps mens spirits. For death has spread itself over all.

(2.) In the progress of it, Psal. cii. 26. Man's declining in the several ages is manifest. Men are of lesser stature, lesser bones and strength, than sometime they were. And why, but because our mother earth is past her prime, and entered into her old age, and her breasts afford not such nourishment as in her youth. Hence man's days are very few now, in comparison of what they were before the flood, when the curse had not sunk so deep into the earth, as it has done from that time, when it had well nigh extinguished her vigour. And whence is this weakness in the earth, but from this, that the heavens also faint, are waxed old, and afford not such influences as before? And whence is that, but from the sin of man in breaking the covenant of friendship with God, pursued by death, which extends itself to all things that have any hand in preserving that life, which it has a commission to take away?

(3.) In the consummation of it, in the destruction by fire that is awaiting the world. For *in the day of the Lord, the heavens shall pass away with a great noise, and the elements shall melt with fervent heat, the earth also and the* works that are therein shall be burnt up, 2 Pet. iii. 10. The visible heavens and the earth are now like an old worn garment; then shall the old garment be rent in pieces, and cast into the fire. Man's old house the earth, that has often been made to shake with earthquakes, shall then fall all down to ashes together: and the whole furniture of it, God's works and mens works in it, shall be burnt up. The roaring seas shall be silent at length, and be no more. Yea, the sun who now runs his race like a strong man, shall fall as breathless. And the whole world, this beautiful fabric of heaven and earth, shall have a dying day. The death threatened in the covenant of works, shall pull all down together. And then death itself, with all the appurtenances thereof, shall be penned up in hell for ever, Rev. xx. 14. by the power of the glorious Mediator, If. xxv. 8.

Eternal death.

Thirdly, Eternal death, which issues from the eternal separation of both soul and body from God, in hell, Matth. xxv. 41. This is the full accomplishment of the curse of the covenant of works; and presupposeth the reunion of the soul and body, in a dreadful resurrection to damnation; the criminal soul and body being brought forth from their separate prisons, and joined together again, that death may exercise its full force upon them for ever and ever. That this was the penalty of the covenant of works, is manifest from the event, testified by the holy scriptures; this being the lot of all those, who, not embracing the covenant of grace, live and die under the covenant of works. For, says the apostle, 2 Thess. i. 7. 8. 9. *The Lord Jesus shall be revealed from heaven, with his mighty angels, in flaming fire, taking vengeance on them that know not God, and that obey not the gospel of our Lord Jesus Christ: who shall be punished with everlasting destruction from the presence of the Lord, and from the glory of his power.* And this death may be considered two ways; (1.) as it flows from the sanction of the covenant of works; and, (2.) as it flows from the nature of the creature fallen under that sanction.

1. As it flows from the sanction of the covenant of works,

works, requiring satisfaction to offended justice, and all the wronged attributes of God. And thus it is a punishment inflicted to satisfy for the offence, and repair the honour of God impaired by man's sin. And that punishment is twofold; the punishment of loss, and the punishment of sense.

(1.) The punishment of loss: Matth. xxv. 41. *Depart from me, ye cursed.* Man having sinned, and this death once seizing him, he is deprived of God's favour, and all comfortable communion with him of any sort is blocked up. The sun sets upon him, and the midnight darkness of God's forsaking of his creature falls on. Justice suffers not one grain of comfort to be put into the sinner's cup. All the least chinks, by which the least beam of the Lord's countenance might shine into the soul, are stopt; and the creature is left absolutely comfortless. Thus it is with the damned in hell: and thus Christ, as man's surety, had the sun of his Father's countenance eclipsed, when on the cross he cried with a loud voice, *My God, my God, why hast thou forsaken me?* Matth. xxvii 46.

(2.) The punishment of sense, in most grievous torments of soul and body: Matth. xxv. 41. *Depart from me, ye cursed, into everlasting fire.* When death has proceeded thus far with the sinner, the waves of God's wrath go quite over his head, arrows of vengeance dipt in the poison of the curse fly at him continually: *Who knows the power of* them? Psal. xc. 11. The damned are inexpressibly miserable under them for ever and ever. By them was *the heart* of our glorious Redeemer *melted like wax in the midst of his bowels*, Psal. xxii. 14.

All this is requisite to shew just indignation against sin, and to wipe off the stain left by it on the honour of God.

2. As it flows from the nature of the creature fallen under the sanction of the covenant. And thus in this death, these dreadful circumstances do concur.

(1.) An irrecoverable loss of God's friendship, favour, and image, Matth. xxv. 41. No more communication for ever can be between God and the creature brought to this dreadful pass. All passage of sanctifying influences is stopt: the curse lies on the creature, which bars all emanations

nations of love and favour from heaven, and leaves it under unalterable barrenness. The holy frame of the soul marred by sin, must remain so, never to be mended.

(2.) Perpetual bitter despair, Mark ix. 44. The creature once sunk into this sea of wrath, can never get up its head, nor see the shore; and knows it never shall. Hence absolute despair seizeth them, and all hope is plucked up by the roots. This lies as a talent of lead upon them, and must continually cut them to the heart. When the man Christ was forsaken of his Father, he knew he was able to get through the floods of wrath, and that he would at length joyfully set his foot on the shore: but that was because he was God as well as man. But weak man can never get through.

(3.) Continual sinning. Think and act they must; and how can they but sin, when their corrupt nature remains with them in hell? Submission to just punishment is their duty: but how can they do that, in whose hearts is not the least measure of God's grace? Nay, they will gnash their teeth, in rage against God.

(4.) The eternity of the whole. Because they cannot pay out the debt to the full, therefore must they ever lie in the prison. The wrong done by sin to the honour of God is an infinite one, because done against an infinite God: and therefore the satisfaction can never be completed by a finite sufferer. So the yoke of punishment is wreathed about the neck of the sinner, for ever and ever, never to be taken off.

This was the penalty of the covenant of works. And thus much of the *parts* of the covenant.

The SEALS *of the covenant of works.*

THIRDLY, It remains now to consider the *seals* of the covenant of works, whereby it was confirmed to Adam. It has pleased God to append seals to his covenants with men in all ages, for the confirmation of their faith of the respective covenants: and this covenant seems not to have wanted some seals appended thereto for the same effect. Though innocent Adam was not called to faith in a Redeemer, no such object of faith being revealed or competent in that

state;

state; yet was faith in God always a duty of the first command, and innocent Adam under this covenant was required to have and exercise a faith agreeable to the nature of the covenant he was under. That was, a firm persuasion, that he should have life upon his performing of perfect obedience, but should die upon the least disobedience to his Creator. And according as he maintained this faith, so was his obedience. Therefore Satan set himself first of all to attack the faith of our first parents, Gen. iii. 4.; and when he had got it knockt on the head, then he carried his ruining project, according to his wish. No wonder than he still set himself in a peculiar manner against that grace. Now, for confirming of this his faith, there were two sacramental seals appended to the covenant; the tree of the knowledge of good and evil, and the tree of life.

1. The tree of the knowledge of good and evil, Gen. ii. 17. What sort of a tree it was, the scripture doth not determine, nor do the Jews pretend to define. Some gather from Cant. viii. 5. *I raised thee up under the apple-tree*, that it was an apple-tree. But it is plain from the original text, that these are not the words of Christ, but of the spouse to Christ; and the book being allegorical, it is too slender a ground at best to build such a fact upon. Whatever it was, it was not so called, as having a power really to make men wise. So the tempter pretended, Gen. iii. 5. but he was a liar from the beginning, John viii. 44. But it was a sign both of good and evil; sealing to him all good, while he should abstain from it, and evil, if he should eat of it; and so confirming his faith in both parts of the persuasion of it. And eventually, by eating of it, he knew good by the loss of it, and evil by the feeling of it. Though it was not to be touched, it might be seen, even as the rainbow, the seal of the covenant with Noah.

2. The tree of life, Gen. ii. 9. The which, though it might be an excellent means of preserving the vigour of natural life, as other trees of paradise also, yet it could not have a virtue in itself of making man every way immortal. But it was a notable sacramental sign of life and eternal happiness, according to the nature of that covenant.

nant. The which is intimated by the eternal quickening virtue of our Lord Jesus Christ, to the perfect happiness of the saints, coming under that name in the New Testament, Rev. xxii. 2.; he being that in reality, which the tree of life did signify. And thus the eating of it served to confirm Adam's faith, according to that covenant, namely, his persuasion of life upon his performing of perfect obedience. The which is clearly intimated, Gen. iii. 22. But man having lost his right to the life signified, by his sin, could no more be admitted to the partaking of the sacramental sign of it.

The doctrine of the covenant of works applied.

USE. What is said upon this subject, serves for *instruction*, *refutation*, and *exhortation*.

USE I. for *instruction*. Here as in a glass ye may see several things, concerning God, concerning man in his best estate, concerning Christ, and concerning man in his present fallen state.

First, Concerning God, look into this covenant, and behold,

1. The wonderful condescension of God, and his goodness and grace toward his creature man. He stoopt so low as to enter into a covenant with his own creature, a covenant wherein he shewed himself a most bountiful and gracious God towards man. Man was not at his own, but God's disposal. Death was the natural wages of sin; but the life promised could not have been pleaded, but upon the foot of a covenant. Before that covenant man was bound to all obedience: but God was free to have disposed of him after all, as he should see meet. But he made himself debtor to man for eternal life, upon his performing of perfect obedience; yet in the mean time his strength to obey was all from God, and there was no proportion betwixt man's work and the reward.

2. The spotless holiness and exact justice of God against sin. When we look to the condition, and the penalty of this covenant, we must needs cry out, *Who is like unto thee, O Lord, glorious in holiness?* Exod. xv. 11. and, *Thou art of purer eyes than to behold evil, and canst not look on iniquity,*

The Doctrine applied.

iniquity, Hab. i. 13. See here, sinners, how God looks on the least sin. Is it not the abominable thing which he hates, with a perfect hatred? Such an evil it is, as is enough to ruin a world of creatures among whom it spreads its baleful influence, and to dissolve the whole fabric of heaven and earth.

Secondly, Concerning man in his state of primitive integrity.

1. Man was a holy and happy creature in his first estate. He was a spotless creature, meet to transact with God, and to entertain communion with him, immediately by himself, without a mediator. He was then able to obey perfectly all the ten commandments. He was happy in God's favour and covenant-friendship. Ah! how is he now fallen like a star from heaven!

2. Man at his best estate, standing on his own legs, is a fickle creature, liable to change. The penalty set him in the covenant, spoke him to be mutable, capable of forgetting his duty to his Maker, and his own interest: and the doleful event confirmed it. Why should men put their trust in men, and make flesh their arm? The most accomplished mere man that ever was on earth, was capable of being unfaithful to his trust, and actually was so. No wonder now that every man be a liar.

Thirdly, Concerning Christ the Saviour of sinners, behold here,

1. The absolute necessity of a Surety in the event of a breach of this covenant. The condition was so high, and the penalty so dreadful, in this covenant, that it being once broken, it was beyond the power of man to retrieve the matter. He must bear the heavy penalty, and that he could never discharge. He must begin again, and fulfil the condition; and that was beyond his power. Therefore there behoved to be a Surety, to act and suffer for man, or he was ruined without hope of relief. Hence said our blessed Lord himself, *Ought not Christ to have suffered these things?* Luke xxiv. 26. And no creature was able to have undertaken this important office; it was a burden too heavy for angels.

2. The love of Christ to poor sinners, in becoming surety for the broken men: John xv. 13. *Greater love*

hath no man than this, that a man lay down his life for his friends. Rom. v. 8. *God commendeth his love towards us, in that while we were yet sinners, Christ died for us.* None less than God-man was able to answer the demands of this covenant, when once broken: therefore the Son of God was pitched upon to be the second Adam, to repair the breach made by the first: Psal. lxxxix. 19. *I have laid help upon one that is mighty: I have exalted one chosen out of the people.* And when there was no helper, he offered himself to undergo the burden: Psal. xl. 6. 7. *Sacrifice and offering thou didst not desire, mine ears hast thou opened: burnt-offering and sin-offering hast thou not required. Then said I, Lo, I come.* If ever you would see what Christ has done for sinners, so as to be ravished with admiration of his matchless performance, study the covenant of works, which he fulfilled as the second Adam, after it was broken by the first.

Fourthly, Concerning man in his present fallen state.

1. It is no wonder, that however scarce good works are in the world, yet working to win heaven is so very rife. Legal principles and practices are natural to men; the covenant of works being that covenant that was made with Adam, and in him with all mankind, and so after a sort engrained in man's nature. And nothing less than the power of grace is able to bring man from off that way, to the way of salvation by Jesus Christ: 1 Cor. i. 23. 24. *Christ crucified is unto the Jews a stumbling-block, and unto the Greeks foolishness: but unto them which are called, both Jews and Greeks, he is the power of God, and the wisdom of God.* We are like those who being bred merchants, though their stock is gone, must still be trafficking with small wares.

2. Salvation by works of our own is quite impossible; there is no life nor salvation to be had by the law: Gal. iii. 10. *For as many as are of the works of the law, are under the curse.* Will ye bring your good meanings and desires, your repentance, your obedience, such as it is, and think to get life and salvation, and acceptance with God, thereby? Remember, if ye will be for doing to live, your obedience must be perfect and perpetual; and that if you fail, you are under the curse. That is the tenor of
the

the covenant of works, and it will abate nothing. And therefore ye muſt quit the way of that covenant, or periſh for ever; for ye are abſolutely incapable to anſwer its demands.

USE II. for *refutation.* With what is ſaid, theſe three things following are inconſiſtent.

1. That there was no proper covenant of works between God and Adam. The contrary has been already proved from the holy ſcripture, and the nature of the thing. If we yield that point, the imputation of Adam's ſin will have ſlender grounds to ſtand on; and if that fail, the doctrine of the imputation of Chriſt's righteouſneſs will be in hazard.

2. That believers are not wholly and altogether ſet free from the law as a covenant of works; from the commanding power of it, as well as the condemning power of it. If that be ſo, believers in Chriſt are yet in a miſerable caſe; for the commands of the covenant of works, are no leſs than commands of perfect and perpetual obedience, under the pain of the curſe: Rom. iii. 19. *Now we know that what things ſoever the law ſaith, it ſaith to them who are under the law; that every mouth may be ſtopped, and all the world may become guilty before God.* Compared with Gal. iii. 10. *For as many as are of the works of the law, are under the curſe.* But believers are ſet beyond the reach of the curſe, ver. 13. *Chriſt hath redeemed us from the curſe of the law, being made a curſe for us.* Rom. viii. 1. *There is no condemnation to them which are in Chriſt Jeſus.* They are dead to the law as it is a covenant of works; Rom. vii. 4. *Ye are,* ſays the apoſtle, *become dead to the law by the body of Chriſt;* and death ſets one altogether free. They are under the covenant of grace, and they cannot be under both at once; Rom. vi. 14.—*Ye are not under the law, but under grace.*

3. That believers muſt do good works to anſwer the demands of the law as a covenant of works, if they will obtain ſalvation. Truly our good works will never be able to anſwer theſe demands; and if we pretend to do them for that end, as the covenant of works will never accept them, ſo we caſt diſhonour on Chriſt, who has anſwered all theſe demands already for believers, by his per-

fect and perpetual obedience. When God fet Adam to feek falvation by his works, he was able for works; it was a thoufand times eafier to him to give perfect obedience, than for us to give fincere obedience. So we may be fure, that God bringing in a fecond covenant for the help of loft finners, would never put them again on feeking falvation by works, after their ftrength for them was gone.

Use III. of *exhortation.* Confider ferioufly of this covenant, with application to the particular ftate and cafe of your own fouls. Here was a folemn bargain made with our firft father, of the utmoft importance to him and all his pofterity: Will ye not lay to heart your own cafe with refpect to it? Confider,

1. That this covenant was made with Adam in your name, for you in particular, as well as the reft of his pofterity. So that you were all once under it, as really as if you had in your own perfons confented to the terms of it.

2. Whether ye be delivered from it or not. If ye be, happy are ye: if ye be not, there is a weight lying above your head, that will fink you for ever in the bottomlefs gulf of perdition, if ye get not loofe of that covenant, Gal. iii. 10. *For as many as are of the works of the law, are under the curfe: for it is written, Curfed is every one that continueth not in all things which are written in the book of the law to do them.*

3. None are delivered from it, but thofe whom God himfelf, man's covenant-party, has difcharged. The breaking of a bargain can never deliver the breaker from it, but lays him under the penalty. Nothing can deliver him, but a difcharge from the party he bargained with.

4. God difcharges none from it, but upon full fatisfaction made to all its demands on them: *Till heaven and earth pafs, one jot or one tittle fhall in no wife pafs from the law, till all be fulfilled,* Matth. v. 18. The finner fhall be obliged to give the law fair count and reckoning, and payment too, elfe he cannot have his difcharge. Confider if ye know any thing of this being done in your cafe.

5. *Laftly,* The only way to fatisfy this covenant, is by faith to lay hold upon Jefus Chrift the Surety, and to plead his obedience and death. The believer counts up to the law, all that Chrift has done and fuffered, as done

for him: so the accounts are cleared, and the believer is discharged, the discharge being written in the blood of his Surety. And so he is set free from it for ever.

Thus far of the *nature* of the covenant of works.

HEAD II.

Of the BREACH *of the Covenant of Works.*

HOSEA vi. 7.

But they like men have transgressed the covenant.

IN the beginning of this chapter, we have the Jews brought in repenting and turning to the Lord; which looks to that conversion of theirs that is yet to come, but hereby is ensured, and that by virtue of the resurrection of Christ. Meanwhile, they were to be laid under heavy strokes, and after a sort rejected. They were to be under a long eclipse of God's favour, the valley of vision being turned into a land of darkness. This looks to the Assyrian and Babylonish captivity, and further to the ruin of the whole nation by the Romans, and their long rejection, which they are under to this day.

The causes of this are condescended on, to justify God's proceedings against them. (1.) Their inconstancy in that which is good, ver. 4.—*Your goodness is as a morning-cloud, and as the early dew it goeth away.* Sometimes they seemed to promise fair for reformation, but all their fair blossoms quickly fell off. Such was the promising appearance Israel made when Jehu came to the kingdom, and such was that made by Judah in the days of Hezekiah and Josiah. Such too were the *Hosanna's to the son of David*, in Christ's time, which were soon after changed into *Crucify him, crucify him.* Therefore did the prophets and apostles testify against them, and denounce the judgements of God against them; and thereby ministerially hew and slay them, ver. 5. *Therefore have*

I hewed them by the prophets; I have slain them by the words of my mouth. (2.) Their breach of covenant with God, quite slighting and perverting, instead of pursuing, the ends of the covenant, ver. 6. 7. *For I desired mercy, and not sacrifice; and the knowledge of God, more than burnt-offerings. But they like men have transgressed the covenant: there have they dealt treacherously against me.* Breach of covenant is a land-ruining sin, and the sin of these nations at this day. (3.) An universal deluge of sin and defection from God, that had spread itself over all ranks. Israel and Judah both were carried away with it. Israel was *defiled,* ver. 10.; and Judah was ripe for destruction, ver. 11. *Also, O Judah, he hath set an harvest for thee,* &c. Priests and people were quite wrong, ver. 9. 10. magistrates and ministers, church and state; Ramoth-Gilead, a city of refuge, protecting wilful murderers, or delivering up those they ought to have protected; the priests profane, no better than robbers and murderers, ver. 8. 9. General defection is a cause and presage of a sweeping stroke.

It is the second of these that concerns our purpose: *They like men have transgressed the covenant.* Wherein two things may be considered.

1. The crime charged on them, *transgressing the covenant,* covenant-breaking. This is a crime of a high nature; it strikes at the root of society among men, and therefore is scandalous and punishable, though it be but a man's covenant. How much more atrocious is the crime, where God is the one party? God took the Israelites into covenant with himself, when he brought them out of Egypt; it was entered into with awful solemnity, Exod. xxiv. The design and ends of it were to lead them to Christ, and so to real holiness in the practice of the duties of the moral law. But, instead of this, they rejected Christ, and sat down upon the poor performances of the ceremonial law, ver. 6. without faith and love. So they transgressed the covenant, and broke it, Jer. xxxi. 32. Heb. viii. 9.

2. Whom they resembled in transgressing the covenant. In this they acted, *like men,* as our translators and others carry it; that is, vain, light, fickle, and inconstant, like men. But the Vulgate, Tigurine, Castalio, Arias Montanus,

tanus, Rabbi Solomon, Grotius, and the Dutch tranflation, and our own tranflation in the margin, read, *like Adam*. There is nothing about the Hebrew word to weaken this: on the contrary, at this rate the word is taken in its proper fenfe, and this reading is evidently the more forcible of the two: and therefore is the preferable and genuine one, agreeably enough to the context. Befides, as I fhewed before, the original word does but twice more occur in the fcripture, *viz.* Job xxxi. 33. Pfal. lxxxii. 7.; and in both thefe places it is taken the fame way. So the fenfe is, *They, like their father Adam, have tranfgreffed the covenant*, for fo the word is. He broke covenant with God, and fo have they: he the covenant of works, they the covenant of grace, which they externally entered into. God fet down Adam in paradife, in covenant with him, the end of which was to make him completely happy; but he perverted the end of the covenant, preferred the fruit of a tree to his moral duty to God, fo broke the covenant, and was caft out of paradife: and God fet Ifrael down in Canaan, in covenant with him, the end of which was to lead them to Chrift, as the end of the law; but they perverted the end of that covenant, and, preferring ceremonial obfervances to Chrift and moral duty, tranfgreffed the covenant, and therefore muft be caft out of Canaan. The tree of the knowledge of good and evil was, by God's appointment, a feal of the covenant, fitted to help man to the keeping of it; but he ufed it the quite contrary way: the ceremonial law was, by God's appointment, for fealing the covenant of grace, and leading the Jews to Chrift; but they ufed it the quite contrary way; and fo it was a ftumbling-block to them.

From the text thus explained, the following doctrine is clearly deducible;

DOCT. *Our father Adam broke the covenant of works.*

In difcourfing from this doctrine, I fhall,

I. Confider the fatal ftep by which that covenant was tranfgreffed and broken.
II. How this fatal ftep was brought about.
III. How the covenant of works was broken by it.
IV. Apply the fubject.

The

The fatal step by which the covenant of works was broken.

I. I shall consider the fatal step by which that covenant was transgressed and broken. I think I need not stand to prove, that this covenant was broken by Adam. The truth of Moses's narration, Gen. iii. puts it beyond controversy; as also doth the doleful experience of his posterity, Rom. v. 12. Our father Adam was once in a flourishing condition, had in his hand a noble portion of holiness and happiness for every one of his children; and he had more in hope for himself and them, which would have made them eternally and completely happy. He had a goodly stock to set up with at first; and a trade with heaven to improve his stock in, which, rightly managed, would have made all his family happy for ever; the which trade was opened to him by this covenant. But, alas! the whole family is ruined, we are all born beggars, we have nothing left us; nay, we are pursued for our father's debt as well as our own, Rom. v. 18. *By the offence of one judgement came upon all men to condemnation;* and we are in hazard of dying in prison for evermore. A plain evidence, that our father was broke, his trade mismanaged, and he run in debt, the communication with heaven was stopt; and so, that the covenant was broken. Besides, the Lord's making a new covenant, a covenant of grace, with Christ as the second Adam, for the salvation of lost sinners of Adam's family, is a plain proof that the covenant of works was broken, and they ruined, by the first Adam. But what was the fatal step?

It was the eating of the forbidden fruit, Gen. iii. 6. *When the woman saw that the tree was good for food,* &c. *she took of the fruit thereof, and did eat, and gave also unto her husband with her; and he did eat.* This was it by which the covenant was broken, and man ruined. No wonder eating and drinking is the destruction of many to this day: that engine of ruin had too much success in the hand of the great destroyer, not to ply it still. God gave Adam a dominion over the creatures, to use them soberly for his own comfort and God's glory. He *put all things under his feet;* he only kept one tree from him, that he might not taste of the fruit thereof, and that for
the

the trial of his obedience. He was difcharged, under the pain of death, to meddle with it; to which he confented: and yet, over the belly of the folemn covenant, he laid hand on it, ate of it, and broke the covenant. Here, for the underftanding of this fin aright, confider the progrefs, the ingredients, and the aggravations of it.

The progrefs of the fin of breaking the covenant of works.

FIRST, Confider the progrefs of this fin. It is not to be imagined, that Adam and Eve were innocent till they had the forbidden fruit in their mouths; the coveting of it in their hearts behoved of neceffity to be before that: but the eating of it was that whereby their fin and apoftafy from God was completed. The beginning of their fin was unbelief and doubting. At the fuggeftion of Satan, they doubted the truth of God in the threatening, Gen. iii. 4. 5. 6. So, in this fatal battle, their faith got the firft ftroke. And it being once foundered, their heart plied to the temptation, and the luft after the forbidden fruit arofe, and then the fin was completed by actual eating, Gen. iii. 6. The eye of the mind was firft blemifhed; a mift arofe from hell, which they admitted, that by degrees darkened their underftanding, fo that they firft doubted, and then difbelieved the threatening of the covenant. Then their will was eafily conquered to a compliance with the temptation, and turned away from the command, the rule of duty. A luft and corrupt affection to the fruit of the tree feizeth them, difcovering itfelf at the eye, in a luftful looking at it, Gen. iii. 6. So the hand took it, and the mouth ate it, and the fatal morfel was lodged within the body.

Thus the coal of temptation raifed a flame, which quickly fpread itfelf over the whole foul and body. The which is often reacted, in the cafe of their finful pofterity, who by this means are frequently caft down from their excellency as it were in a moment, and plunged into a gulf of mifery.

There is more ill in doubting and unbelief, than men are aware of. It was the devil's mafter-piece for the ruin of souls under the covenant of works; and so it is still under the covenant of grace, Mark xvi. 16. *He that believeth not, shall be damned.* Men were first ruined by their doubting and unbelief of the threatening of the first covenant: now they are ruined by their doubting and unbelief of the promise of the second covenant: If. liii. 1. *Who hath believed our report?* says the prophet. And what that report is, see 1 John v. 10. 11.——*This is the record, that God hath given to us eternal life: and this life is in his Son.* Though doubting may consist with faith, so that it be not reigning; yet it belongs not, but is contrary, to the nature of faith, which in itself is a firm persuasion, more or less firm, according to the strength of it.

The ingredients of this sin.

SECONDLY, Let us consider the ingredients of this sin. If it is opened up, one may see it to be a complication of evils; not a little sin, but a great one, and in some sort the greatest sin.

1. Horrid unbelief was in it. By it the truth and faithfulness of God to his word, was questioned, disbelieved, and denied: the lie was given to the God of truth, 1 John v. 10. And to make the affront the blacker, the devil was believed in his contradiction to God. God said, Yea; Satan said, No: and the decision was in favour of the latter.

2. Pride, ambition, bold presumption, and curiosity, took place in this sin. No less was attempted by it, than to be like God himself: Gen. iii. 5. *Ye shall be as gods,* said the serpent. God had set them in paradise; but they would, in a manner, ascend above the height of the clouds, and set their throne above the stars, as the proud monarch of Babylon said, If. xiv. 13. 14. They had full liberty as to the use of all that was in paradise; only God locked up from them that one tree: and they boldly force the lock, and eat that which God forbade them to touch; as if nothing was to be hid to them.

3. There was in this sin monstrous ingratitude, and discontentment with their condition. They wanted nothing for necessity, convenience, or delight, beseeming their state of trial. A bountiful God had heaped favours

on them: they bore God's image, were fit to be companions of angels, were the envy of devils, had the dominion of the lower world, and were God's confederates. But all this was funk and loft in unthankfulnefs; and they were fo little contented, that they would needs have what in very deed they had no want of, as is often the cafe with their children.

4. This fin carried in it contempt of God, rebellion againft him, and downright apoftafy from him, going over to the devil's fide. Thus it was a renouncing of the covenant, and a confpiring with Satan againft God. They carry themfelves as if they had been decoyed into a foolifh bargain: and forgetting the majefty of God, and their own dependence on him, they break his bands, and caft his cords from them; pretending they would fee better to themfelves, and fo caft off his yoke at one touch.

5. *Laftly*, In one word, this fin was a breaking of the whole law of God at once. By this one deed, not only was the pofitive law trampled under foot, but the natural law written in their hearts was broken in all the ten commandments of it at once, as I have fhewn elfewhere *.

The aggravations of this fin.

THIRDLY, Let us view the aggravations of this fin. Confider,

1. The perfon who did it; righteous Adam: one who was not tainted with original fin, as others now are; but was endued with original righteoufnefs: one in whom Satan had nothing, till he winded it in by his fubtilty. There was no blindnefs of mind, perverfenefs of will, or unholinefs of affections, to graft his temptation on. So having thefe advantages, the fin was, in that refpect, of all fins the moft hainous. And therefore he having found mercy, is a pattern of mercy to all that will believe in Chrift.

2. The object by which he was enticed, and for which he broke God's law. It was not a wedge of gold, as in Achan's cafe; nor thirty pieces of filver, as in that of Ju-

---

* Fourfold ftate of man, ftate 2. head 1. under the title, *How man's nature was corrupted.*

das; but a morsel of fruit. The smaller the thing was, the greater the sin; and the more inexcusable the sinner, whom Satan catched with so sorry a bait. What need had he of it, who had enough besides? But when once the mind is bewitched with temptation, it is enough to stir up a longing after fruit, if it be but forbidden; as the wayfaring man in Nathan's parable, was entertained by the rich man with his poor neighbour's lamb, though he had a flock of his own.

3. The nature of the thing. Though it was a small thing, yet it was a sacred thing, set apart for a holy use, not to be touched. This sin was theft, and theft of the worst kind, namely, sacrilege. It was a profanation of holy things, and that of the worst kind; a profanation of a sacrament, a seal of the covenant. No wonder it brought on a curse.

4. The place where it was committed. In *paradise*, where every flower was proclaiming the glory of God, where he wanted nothing necessary for him, but was surrounded on every hand with tokens of the Lord's kindness to him. Eden was the pleasantest spot of the virgin earth, and paradise the pleasantest spot of Eden. But there the rebellion was begun against God, who set him in that delightful place. In the presence-chamber, as it were, rebel-man, by this act of his, struck at his Sovereign Lord. So it was aggravated like the murder of Zacharias, who was slain *between the temple and the altar*, Matth. xxiii. 35.

5. The time when it was committed. He had not been long in the world, till he lift up his heel against his Creator. He had stood short while, till, being giddy with pride and ambition, he fell into disgrace. What time Adam fell, is a question. It is the common opinion, that he fell the same day he was created. Some think he stood longer, supposing the events recorded about him, Gen. ii. and iii. to require more time than one day. And the Deists improve that against the credit of Moses's history, but entirely without ground. I think the common opinion is true. The devil's envy and malice would set him a-work on the first occasion to ruin man; and, for all that appears, whenever he tried it, he carried

his

his point. If our firſt parents had ſtood longer, the bleſſing of marriage would have taken place, in a ſtate of innocence. The ſcripture ſays, Satan was *a liar, and a murderer from the beginning,* John viii. 44. Pſal. xlix. 12. *Yet Adam in honour could not night : he became like as the beaſts they were alike.* From this text the Hebrew doctors gather, that the glory of the firſt man did not night with him; and the ancient tranſlators underſtand it of Adam. The work of redemption is the more illuſtrious, that man could not ſtand one day without the Mediator's help.

6. *Laſtly,* The effects and conſequents of this ſin. Theſe are all evils that came on Adam himſelf, and on his poſterity to this day, and that will come, even to the end of the world. Hereby all mankind was ruined. That ſin was the wide gate at which ſin and death entered into the world. It ſpread its malignant influence over the creation, looſed the pins of the fabric of the world, which it will pull down at length for altogether, according to the import of the threatening.

How the fatal ſtep, of breaking the covenant of works, was brought about.

II. I ſhall conſider how this fatal ſtep was brought about. For clearing of this, three things are to be conſidered; (1.) Satan's tempting to it; (2.) God's leaving man to the freedom of his own will, in the matter; and, (3.) Man's abuſing this freedom of will, and complying with the temptation.

Of Satan's tempting to this ſin.

Firſt, Satan tempted to it. God created all the angels holy ſpirits, yet mutable, as the event in ſome of them proved. Some of them were elected to eternal happineſs from eternity, and ſome of them not elected; hence the apoſtle makes mention of *the elect angels,* 1 Tim. v. 21. They were all created the firſt day, as appears from Gen. i. 1. 2. compared with Job xxxviii. 7. In the former it is ſaid, *In the beginning God created the heaven and the earth.* And in the latter place it is ſaid, that, when God

laid

laid the foundations of the earth, the morning stars sang together, and all the sons of God shouted for joy. The reprobate angels were not fallen before the sixth day; for it is said, Gen. i. 31. that, on that day, God saw every thing that he had made, and behold, it was very good. On the sixth day man was made, and the same day he fell, as has been shewn before. The reprobate angels were fallen before him, and therefore they fell on the sixth day too. And it seems they lost no time, but immediately, with the first occasion, one of them sets to work against man, and gained his point, by temptation, John viii. 44. forecited.

Concerning this temptation, we may remark,

1. The instrument of the temptation, was a serpent, Gen. iii. 1. And,

(1.) It was a true and real serpent, as appears from Moses comparing it with the rest of the beasts, Gen. iii. 1. *Now the serpent was more subtil than any beast of the field.* What sort of a serpent it was, is not determined. Some think it to have been a beautiful creature of a shining colour; for there are serpents mentioned Deut. viii. 15. called in the original text *Seraphim*, which is a name given to angels. And so possibly Eve might take the serpent to have been acted by one of the good angels, or Seraphims. Whatever sort it was of, serpents have been of great note in the kingdom of the devil since. The Egyptians worshipped serpents. The genius of a place was painted as a serpent. And in the old Greek mysteries, they were wont to carry about a serpent, and cry, *Evah.* A memorial of the extraordinary service it had done the devil.

(2.) It was acted by the devil. For since serpents could not speak, and far less reason, neither of which was wanting in this case, one may surely conclude, that it was the devil who abused the body of the serpent to his wicked purpose, and therefore is called *that old serpent, the devil and Satan,* Rev. xii. 9. & chap. xx. 2.

2. Satan set upon the woman first, the woman the weaker vessel, that having once overcome her, he might by her means the more easily conquer the man. And thus he readily manages his temptations still, observing

where

where the wall is weakest, that there he may make his attack with the more success. And he chose the time, when she was alone, not with her husband, from whom she seems to have had the knowledge of the covenant God entered into with him. Had they been together, they might have jointly withstood him, who conquered both, one after another.

3. He moveth a doubt concerning the command, Gen. iii. 1. *Yea, hath God said, Ye shall not eat of every tree of the garden?* And this he doth subtilly and ambiguously. He does not at first bring forth the whole venom of the temptation, but pretends, as one in doubt, that he would be informed by the woman. It is hard to tell, whether he meant this of God's forbidding to eat of any, or only not of every, tree of the garden. It is the design of the tempter, to draw us into a contempt of the commands of God. The woman, however, gives him a round answer, wherein she makes a very ample profession of the truth, ver. 2. 3. *And the woman said unto the serpent, We may eat of the fruit of the trees of the garden: but of the fruit of the tree which is in the midst of the garden, God hath said, Ye shall not eat of it, neither shall ye touch it, lest ye die.* They may resist at first, who are afterwards overcome.

4. Quitting the attack on the command, which he perceived her to adhere to, Satan falls on the threatening, and contradicts it, Gen. iii. 4. *And the serpent said unto the woman, Ye shall not surely die.* He tells her, it was not so sure as she imagined, that God would punish them at that rate. He puts her in hope of escaping punishment. Thus Satan resisted, flies; but where one method fails, he will try another; and, through hopes of impunity entertained in one's heart, he often gains his purpose.

5. He proceeds as one that wished well to her and her husband, and pretends to shew how they might both arrive at a high pitch of happiness speedily; even to be as gods, and that in knowledge or intellectual delights: insinuating withal, that by the very name of the tree, the truth of what he said might appear. *For* (said the serpent) *God doth know, that in the day ye eat thereof, then your eyes shall be opened: and ye shall be as gods, knowing good*

and

and evil. Thus the liar and murderer still ruins men, pretending to make them happy, while he carries on their destruction.

6. *Lastly,* She being ensnared, he makes use of her to tempt her husband, and prevails, Gen. iii. 6. *And when the woman saw that the tree was good for food, and that it was pleasant to the eyes, and a tree to be desired to make one wise; she took of the fruit thereof, and did eat, and gave also unto her husband with her; and he did eat.* And thus he often conveys his temptations to us, by those whose interest in us and affection to us we doubt not, and whom therefore we suspect not; and so rents men with wedges of their own timber, making one a snare to another.

God's leaving man to the freedom of his own will.

Secondly, God left man to the freedom of his own will, in this matter. He was not the cause of his fall: he moved him not, nor could he move him to it: James i. 13. *For God cannot be tempted with evil, neither tempteth he any man.* Such is the holiness of his nature. He gave him a power to stand if he would, and he took not away from him any grace given; but, for his trial, left him to his freedom of will, with which he was created. God made him good and righteous, and the natural set of his will was to good only, Eccl. vii. 29. But it was liable to change, yet only to change by himself: he could only be made evil or sinful by his own choice.

If it be asked, Why man was not set beyond the possibility of change? It is to be remembered, that absolute immutability is the peculiar prerogative of God himself; and every creature, in as far as it is a creature, is incapable of being so immutable. Yet the creature may be in some sense made immutable, that is, so as it shall not be possible for it actually to fall from its goodness, though there is still a changeableness in its nature. Now, if man had been created without so much as a remote power in himself to change himself, he had not been a free agent: but God might have so established him, as that he could not actually have fallen; yet that would have been owing to confirming grace. The which why the Lord did not bestow

bestow on him, it belongs not to us to define: only he was no debtor to him for it.

Man's abusing the freedom of his will.

Thirdly, Man abused his own liberty or freedom of will, and complied with the temptation, and so broke the covenant. He only himself was the true and proper cause of his own falling: not God, for he can never be the author of sin; not the devil, nor Eve, for they could only tempt and entice, but not force him. It was his own choice, he did it freely without coaction or compulsion; and he could have stood if he would. And thus was the fatal step made, whereby the covenant was broken.

How the covenant of works was broken, by this fatal step.

III. I shall consider how the covenant of works was broken, by this fatal step. We may take up this in three things.

1. The command was violated. The covenant required perfect obedience, but it was not given; perpetual obedience, but man did soon come to a stand in the course of obedience, and went no further. Here he disobeyed, here he shook off the yoke, here he sinned against his God. Thus the condition of the covenant was broken.

2. The right and title to the promised benefit by that covenant was undermined. The promised life was lost, man had no more any pretensions to it; he could no more plead the reward, which was to be given him in hand; and the prospect of the reward, which before his disobedience, he had in hope, was entirely cut off. Thus failing in his performance of the condition of the covenant, he rendered the promise of the covenant null and void, as if it had never been made.

3. He fell under the penalty of the covenant, became liable to death in its utmost extent. As he had no more ado with the promise, the threatening now bound him to bear the wrath threatened for the satisfaction of divine justice. The blessing of the covenant being lost, the curse of it seized him, and he was bound with the cords of death; the which was let out as a flood, at that gap, that breach which was made in the covenant, and overflowed,

Cov. I.   I   (1.) The

(1.) The soul of man, so that it died spiritually, losing the image of God, and losing the favour of God. Man turning from God as his chief end, the image of God in his soul was defaced, Gen. v. 1. 3. His saving knowledge was lost; witness the cover of fig-leaves, which our first parents prepared for covering of their nakedness, and their pretending to hide themselves from the presence of God, Gen. iii. 7. The righteousness of his will was lost; witness their aversion to God, hiding themselves from him, their excusing of their sin, transferring of their guilt, the man laying the blame on the woman, the woman on the serpent; nay, Adam not obscurely reflected on God himself. The holiness and regularity of their affections went off; they were filled with disorder, confusion, and shame. They lost God's favour; were seized with horror of conscience, Gen. iii. 8.; were driven out of paradise, like a divorced woman out of the house of her husband; declared incapable of communion with God; and debarred from the tree of life, the seal of the covenant.

(2.) The body of man became mortal, death working within it, and without it, from that moment the covenant was broken. He was condemned to toil and weariness for life, and then to return to the dust at length, the frame and constitution of man's body having become deadly from the moment of his breaking the covenant. And sorrow and pain in breeding and bringing forth of children, was laid on the female sex, as a particular mark of displeasure with the first sin. And the ground was cursed for man's sake, because of the dependence of the life of man upon it.

(3.) *Lastly*, Soul and body both were subjected and bound over to eternal death in hell. For this was comprehended in the threatening of the covenant of works, as has been already shewn.

Thus was the covenant of works broken. Yet man was not, and could not thereby be freed from that covenant: still he was bound to obedience, according to the command of it, and to satisfaction, according to the threatening. Only God was no more obliged to fulfil his promise, since it was conditional, and the condition was broken.

Application

Application of the doctrine of the breach of the covenant of works.

USE I. Here is a memorial, which we have need ever to carry about with us, while we live in this world: A memorial,

1. Of the nothingness of the creature, when left to itself. God left some of the angels to themselves, and they turned devils; he left innocent Adam to himself, and he turned apostate. O the need of continual supplies of grace! There was no bent and inclination to evil naturally in them; but in us there is a natural propensity to depart from God. What need have we then to cry, *Lead us not into temptation!* What need of continual dependence on the Lord by faith!

2. Of the hopelessness of salvation by works. That was the way which man was first set on, and that is the way which man naturally is set to follow unto this day. But what hope can there be that way? Adam was able to work for life, having sufficient strength laid to his hand, and yet he miscarried in it: How can it prosper in our hands, who are without strength, and whose work arm is broken? He had less to do, than we have now; only perfect obedience was required of him at first: but of us now is required not only perfect obedience, but satisfaction for sin done. More work, and less strength, than Adam had when he fell a-working for heaven, which was marred in his hand, may justly make us to despair of salvation that way. He could not stand: how shall we that are fallen, raise up ourselves? How unlikely is it, that self-destroyers shall be their own saviours?

USE II. Here is a watchword which we are never to forget.

1. Watch and pray, that ye enter not into temptation. The devil still goes about seeking whom he may devour. No state, while ye are here, can secure you from temptation. Though ye be in a state of friendship with God, he will attack you. No place, though a paradise, can protect you. He has malice enough to drive you to the greatest sins; subtilty and long experience to manage the temptation, so as it may best take. Do not parley with temptation:

listening to the tempter may bring on doubting, doubting will bring on disbelieving, and disbelieving will bring on full compliance. O therefore watch!

2. Take heed of forgetting the covenant of your God. When men lose the sense of the bond of the covenant, they cannot long forbear the breaking of it. We see this in Adam our father; and we may see it daily in mens personal covenants, and the national covenants these lands are under the bonds of. The impression of them is worn off, and so the duties of them are cast behind mens backs. No wonder that this is the sin of the land, and of particular persons, seeing we are all children of the great covenant-breaker Adam.

Use III. *Lastly*, Here is a demonstration of the absolute necessity of being united to the second Adam, who kept the second covenant, and thereby fulfilled the demands of the first covenant. See your absolute need of him; prize him, and flee to him by faith. Behold him with an eye of faith, who has repaired the breach. The first Adam broke the first covenant, by eating of the fruit of the forbidden tree; Christ has repaired the breach, by hanging on a tree, and bearing the curse, for his people. Adam's preposterous love to his wife made him sin: Christ's love to his spouse made him suffer and satisfy. In a garden Adam sinned, and therefore in a garden Christ was buried. Eating ruined man, and by eating he is saved again. By eating the forbidden fruit all died; and by eating Christ's flesh, and drinking his blood by faith, the soul gets life again, John vi. 57. O then have recourse to Christ; and thus shall you be saved from the ruins of the fall, and have an interest in the covenant made with Christ, the condition of which being already fulfilled by him, can never be broken, and they who are once in it, can never fall out of it again.

And thus far of the *breach* of the covenant of works.

HEAD III.

Of the IMPUTATION *of Adam's firſt Sin, of breaking the Covenant of Works, to his Poſterity.*

ROMANS V. 19.

For as by one man's diſobedience many were made ſinners: ſo by the obedience of one ſhall many be made righteous.

YE have heard of the *making* of the original contract betwixt God and man, the covenant of works; as alſo of the *breaking* of it by our father Adam. This text ſhews *our* concern in the breach of that covenant: and it is neceſſary we be ſenſible of it, that we be not eternally ruined thereby, but being convinced of that debt lying on our head, may flee to, and make uſe of the great Surety, for removing it from us.

In this chapter, ver. 14. the apoſtle ſhews Adam to have been a figure or type of Chriſt; and from ver. 12. and downwards, he inſtitutes a compariſon betwixt theſe two, the common heads and repreſentatives of mankind, though Chriſt's repreſentation is not ſo extenſive as Adam's: but each of them repreſented his ſeed; Adam all his natural ſeed; and Chriſt all his ſpiritual elect ſeed. Adam by his diſobedience broke the firſt covenant; Chriſt by his obedience to the death fulfilled the ſecond covenant. The diſobedience of the one brings condemnation and death on thoſe that are his; the obedience of the other brings juſtification and life to all that are his. The reaſon of both is given in the text; namely, That by the one, all his are made ſinners, and ſinners are juſtly condemned and die: by the other, all his are made righteous, and the righteous muſt, according to the covenant, be juſtified and live.

So the text is a compariſon made betwixt the effect of Adam's *diſobedience*, and the effect of Chriſt's *obedience*.

The

The causes are quite contrary the one to the other, as light and darkness; and so are the effects redounding from them to those who are respectively affected by them. The former makes men *sinners*, the latter makes men *righteous*. It is the former that concerns our present purpose: *By one man's disobedience many were made sinners*. Where consider,

1. The malignant cause, to which all evil among men is owing; *one man's disobedience*. This is the impure fountain of all, the original of all evils. Here two things must be cleared. (1.) Who that *one man* was. Who, but Adam, the *first* man? Him the apostle had expressly named, ver. 14. as the great transgressor, the head of the rebellion, the fountain of sin, opposed to Christ Jesus as the fountain of righteousness; and unto him our text in the Greek expresly points, which saith not simply, *By one man*, &c. as ver. 12. but, *By that one man's disobedience*, that man Adam whom he had mentioned before. (2.) What that *disobedience* was. No question but Adam was guilty of many acts of disobedience through the whole of his life, after his fall: but the text speaks of this disobedience emphatically, and as such by way of eminency, *that disobedience*, plainly referring to the first sin of Adam. That was the sin which first broke into the world, and opened the sluice to death, ver. 12.; *the* transgression of Adam, Gr. ver. 14.; *that* offence or fall, ver. 15. So then, this disobedience is Adam's breaking of the covenant of works, by his eating of the forbidden fruit. The transgression of Adam, was his transgressing of the covenant, which set him the bounds he was to keep within, on pain of death, Rom. v. 14. compared with Hos. vi. 7. He set off in a course of covenant-obedience, running for the prize; but he stumbled and fell in breaking of the covenant. Though he was a son by creation, he was God's hired servant by covenant; but by his disobedience to his Master, he broke the covenant.

2. The answerable effect: *Many were made sinners*. The poisonous fountain being opened, the waters kill where-ever they come. Here also two things are to be cleared. (1.) Who these *many* are. Even the *all* mentioned before, ver. 12. All Adam's natural seed comprehended

hended with him in the first covenant; as the *many* made righteous, are all Christ's spiritual seed, comprehended with him in the second covenant. But the apostle uses the term *many* here, though *all* are meant, not only because *all* are *many*; but, because *one man*, viz. the man Christ, is excepted: so, in strict propriety of expression, Adam's disobedience touched not *all men* simply, but *many*, there being one man excepted: and also because the scope of the apostle here is to shew, that many shall be made righteous by the obedience of *one*; to prove which, proceeding on that principle, That the deed of one may be imputed to many, he instanceth in Adam's disobedience, who being *one* man, yet his deed was imputed to many; and he being a type or figure of Christ in that respect, it plainly follows, that as by his disobedience many were made sinners, so by the obedience of Christ shall many be made righteous. (2.) How by Adam's disobedience they were *made sinners*. There are but three ways how, by the sin of another, we may be made sinners. [1.] By adopting it through consent and approbation: so Ahab was a murderer of Naboth, though not he, but the magistrates of Jezreel did the deed, 1 Kings xxi. 19. But this is not the way we are made sinners by Adam's disobedience: for infants, and many in the world who never heard of Adam or his sin, and therefore are incapable of adopting it at that rate, are yet made sinners by it. Or, [2.] By imitation, as Pelagians would have it. So indeed one may be made a sinner by imitating of sinners. But this cannot be it neither in this case: 1.) Because infants, who are not capable of imitation, are involved here as well as others, Rom. v. 14. where *death* is said to have *reigned even over them that had not sinned after the similitude of Adam's transgression*. So also are Pagans concerned here, who know nothing of the copy, that Adam cast us. 2.) Because we are made sinners by Adam's disobedience, as we are made righteous by Christ's obedience. But it is not by imitation, but imputation of Christ's obedience we are made righteous: Therefore it is not by imitation, but imputation of Adam's disobedience we are made sinners. 3.) All men, of all ages, sexes, conditions, &c. are made sinners. But it is incredible, that, if imitation were the way, there should never

never have been so much as one mere man, to refuse to imitate the ruining example. Therefore, [3.] It necessarily follows, that we are thereby made sinners by imputation: even as we are made righteous by Christ's obedience, the same being reckoned our obedience, though not done by us in our own persons. We are not only made liable to punishment by this disobedience, but we are made sinners by it. Not only is the guilt ours, but the fault is ours: we not only die in Adam, 1 Cor. xv. 22. but we sinned in him as our federal head, Rom. v. 12.; we broke the covenant in him; that breach in law-reckoning is ours, and is reckoned ours, because it is ours by virtue of our being one with him, in his loins, as our natural and federal head.

The text affords the following doctrine, plainly founded upon it.

DOCT. *Adam's breaking of the covenant of works, by his eating of the forbidden fruit, is our sin, our breaking of it, as well as his.*

For the illustration of this doctrine, I shall,

I. Consider the extent of this sin which is ours.

II. Shew how Adam's sin of breaking the covenant of works is our sin, our breaking of it, as well as his.

III. Evince the truth of the doctrine, and prove the imputation of Adam's first sin, the sin of breaking the covenant of works, by eating the forbidden fruit, to his posterity.

IV. Shew the ground and reason why this first sin is ours.

V. Lastly, Improve the subject.

Of the extent of Adam's first sin.

I. I shall consider the extent of this sin which is ours. There is a twofold breaking of the covenant of works.

First, There is a private and personal breaking of it, by such persons as are still under it. And thus it is to this day broken every day; John vii. 19. *Did not Moses give you the law,* said Christ to the Jews, *and yet none of you keepeth the law?* Let none imagine, that the covenant of works

works being broken by Adam, was laid by as an useless thing, which men were no more concerned in. It is true, it is no more useful now as a way to salvation and happiness: but that is not from itself, but from man's weakness, whose weak head, heart, and legs, cannot serve him to walk in so high a way to heaven, from which he fell down headlong before in Adam, and received such a bruise as made him quite incapable for it afterwards. But the covenant itself stands firm still in all the parts of it. The promise of it stands still to perfect obedience, which now takes in suffering as well as doing: as appears from what passed between our Lord and a certain lawyer, Luke x. 27. 28. The lawyer had put the question to him, *Master, what shall I do to inherit eternal life?* Our Lord answered, *What is written in the law? how readest thou?* The lawyer having replied, *Thou shalt love the Lord thy God with all thy heart, and with all thy soul, and with all thy strength, and with all thy mind; and thy neighbour as thyself:* our Lord thereupon said, *Thou hast answered right; this do, and thou shalt live.* So that if any could answer the demands of that covenant, he should have the promised life. The threatening of it stands firm as mountains of brass, that without satisfying of it by one's self or Surety, none shall escape: for *without shedding of blood is no remission,* Heb. ix. 22. and *God will by no means clear the guilty,* Exod. xxxiv. 7. The commands of it are in as full vigour as ever; for the breaking of a law can never take away the binding force and authority of it; so that it demands perfect obedience of all that are under it, with as much authority still, as ever it did of Adam, Rom. iii. 19. *For what things soever the law saith, it saith to them who are under the law.* And all men continue under it, till they be ingrafted into Christ, be dead to it, and married to Christ, Rom. vi. 14. Wherefore, all ye Christless sinners are under it, and are breaking it every day, in every thought, word, and action of yours; and so the curse of it is raining down upon you incessantly, Gal. iii. 10. *Cursed is every one that continueth not in all things which are written in the book of the law to do them.* John iii. 36. *He that believeth not—, the wrath of God abideth on him.*

Some of you stand off from the sacrament of the Lord's supper, and from personal covenanting with God in embracing of the covenant of grace; and think ye do wisely to hold your necks out of the yoke of a covenant with God. But, poor soul, thou art hard and fast under covenant to God, the covenant of works, by which thou art bound to perfect obedience, under the pain of God's curse; and every sin of thine is covenant-breaking with God, laying thee under the curse of the covenant. So all this wisdom of yours amounts to a holding fast of the covenant of death, and refusing a covenant of life. But this breaking of the covenant of works, by violating the commands of it now, is not what we aim at.

Secondly, There was a public breaking of it by Adam the father of all mankind, standing as the representative of his posterity. This breach was made in paradise, where Adam broke the covenant by eating the forbidden fruit. And even this is our sin, and breaking of the covenant; *viz.* the first breaking of it is ours, and brings us under guilt.

The extent of this sin of breaking the covenant may be considered two ways; (1.) In reference to the persons to whom the guilt of it reaches, whose sin it becomes; and, (2.) In reference to the sin itself.

1. The extent of this sin may be considered in reference to the persons to whom the guilt of it reaches, whose sin it becomes. And thus we say,

(1.) It extended not to the man Christ. Adam's breaking of the covenant was not his: he sinned not in Adam, which the rest of mankind did. Though he was born of a woman, he was born sinless; hence the angel said unto Mary, Luke i. 35.—*That holy thing which shall be born of thee, shall be called the Son of God.* And Heb. vii. 26. he is said to be *holy, harmless, undefiled,* and *separate from sinners.* He came *to destroy the works of the devil,* 1 John iii. 8. and *to take away sin,* John i. 29.; which he could not have been fit for, if he himself had been one of the sinful multitude. If he had needed a sacrifice for himself, he could not have been an atoning sacrifice for us.

He was indeed a son of Adam, as appears from his genealogy brought up to Adam, Luke iii. And it was necessary he should be so, that he might be our near kinsman.

man, to redeem us; that man's fin might be expiated by man's fufferings, and fo juftice might be fatisfied of the fame nature that finned. But Adam was not the man Chrift's federal head, nor was he comprehended with him in the covenant of works; forafmuch as he did not come of Adam in virtue of the bleffing of fruitfulnefs given to the man and woman before the fall; but was the feed of the woman only, born by virtue of a fpecial promife made after the breach of the covenant of works. So the breach of that covenant could not be imputed to him, or counted his, by virtue of his relation to Adam.

Nay, he is another public perfon, as the firft Adam was; the federal head in the fecond covenant, erected to repair the ruins made by the breach of the firft: and fo he is called *the fecond Adam*, and is reprefented as the antitype to the firft Adam, Rom. v. 14.; unto whom the firft Adam, having mifmanaged his own headfhip, did as a private perfon commit himfelf for falvation, being in a myftical union by faith joined to Jefus Chrift, as the quickening Head in the fecond covenant. But,

(2.) It extends to all mankind befides Chrift, without exception of any one from the firft fon and daughter of Adam, to the laft child that fhall be born into the world, 1 Cor. xv. 22.—*In Adam all die.* It is the common portion of all the children of our father's family, from the eldeft to the youngeft; the common inheritance of the whole tribe of Adam, from the leaft to the greateft. The man a hundred years old may fay, " It is my fin;" and the child at its firft moving in the womb may fay, " It is " mine." The guilt of it is removed indeed from believers upon their union with Chrift; but once it lay upon them to condemnation alfo, as it ftill lies on all unregenerate perfons, Rom. v. 18.—*By the offence of one judgement came upon all men to condemnation.* The faints in heaven are finging Glory to him who wafhed them from it in his own blood, and the damned in hell are lying, and will lie for ever under the weight of it.

2. The extent of this fin of breaking the covenant may be confidered in reference to the fin itfelf. There is fomething in this fin peculiar to Adam's perfon, in fo far as though the whole mafs of mankind was concerned in it, yet there was

this difference betwixt Adam and his posterity, that he was the representative, they were the party represented; he sinned this sin in his own person, they only in him; and consequently he ruined not himself only, but all the world by it, they ruined themselves only by it. Wherefore, setting aside what was in this sin peculiar to Adam as the head of the covenant, otherwise

This sin of breaking the covenant of works is our sin in the whole compass and extent of it. We must look back to the state of innocence, and behold the human nature adorned with the glorious image of God in our father Adam, and us in his loins; taken into covenant with God, a covenant of life upon condition of perfect obedience, which we in him were able to give, and fenced with a threatening of death, which we were not liable to before we sinned. And we must consider with sorrow of heart, how we broke that covenant in Adam; and with bitter repentance, shame, and self loathing, lament over the eating of that forbidden fruit, and all the ingredients of it, our horrid unbelief, pride, ambition, presumption, and bold curiosity, our monstrous ingratitude, &c. The fearful aggravations of it must accent our lamentation, that it was in the state of righteousness of our nature the fact was committed, how small and sorry an object was the covenant broken for, a thing though small yet sacred, the place where, the time when, and the direful effects and consequents of it on ourselves. And we must apply to the Head of the second covenant for our reparation, pardon, and reconciliation with God.

Vain men who have never been deeply convinced of sin by the working of the Spirit on their hearts, but measure their religion more by their corrupt reason than God's word, will be apt to look on these things as idle tales; and to say in their hearts, Would God we may mourn for our own sins, the sins that we ourselves have been guilty of. Alas, Sirs, that sin, with all the ingredients and aggravations of it, as is said, is as really your own sin, as the lies ye have made with your own tongue, and the profane oaths ye have sworn with your own mouth, &c. Rom. v. 12. 19. *By one man sin entered into the world, and death by sin; and so death passed upon all men, for that all*

have

How Adam's first Sin is our Sin.

have sinned.—*By one man's disobedience many were made sinners.* And if it be not forgiven you, through the atoning blood of Christ, it will sink you into hell; and we know no sins that are forgiven, but they are repented of expressly, if known, and virtually, if unknown. We find David mourning over it, Psal. li. 5. *Behold, I was shapen in iniquity: and in sin did my mother conceive me.* And so ought all of us to mourn over it every day of our life, and have recourse to the blood of Jesus for pardon of it.

How Adam's sin, of breaking the covenant of works, is the sin of his posterity.

II. I shall shew how Adam's sin of breaking the covenant of works is our sin, our breaking of it, as well as his.

1. It is really ours in itself. It is not ours in its effects only, as a father's sin in riotously spending his estate, reaches his whole family, reducing them to poverty and want. Though the effects of that riotous spending, the poverty, misery, and want, be theirs; yet the riotous spending is the father's only. But so is it not in this case. It is true, the effects of it, the sinful and penal evils following this sin, are ours; we see them, we feel them, and the most stupid groan under them; but the sin itself is ours too. And,

(1.) The guilt of it is ours, Rom. v. 18 —*By the offence of one judgement came upon all men to* CONDEMNATION; that is, the guilt of sin whereby the soul is bound over to God's wrath, by virtue of the sanction of the law. Thus that word is used frequently in the scripture, as John iii. 18. *He that believeth on him, is not condemned; but he that believeth not, is condemned already:* Rom. viii. 1. *There is no condemnation to them which are in Christ Jesus:* though it is often mistaken for what we usually call *damnation*, by which is understood the full execution of the law's sentence after death. So the guilt of the eating of the forbidden fruit lies on all men naturally as their guilt: though but one man's mouth tasted it, the guilt of the crime seizes all men. Every man is bound over to God's wrath

for

for it, till the Lord Jesus, by an application of his blood to the soul, loose the cords of death.

(2.) The fault of it is ours, Rom. v. 12. *By one man sin entered into the world, and death by sin; and so death passed upon all men, for that* ALL HAVE SINNED, namely, in Adam. The fault lies in its contrariety to the holy commandment; this made it a faulty deed, a criminal action, a sin against God: and as such it is ours. We in Adam transgressed the law, broke through the hedge, and so broke the covenant. If the fault were not ours, a holy God would never punish us for it: but certain it is, that he does punish the children of Adam for it, Rom. v. 14. *Death reigned from Adam to Moses, even over them that had not sinned after the similitude of Adam's transgression.* It is true indeed, God may punish one that is not really faulty, for the fault of another, if he do voluntarily substitute himself in the room of the faulty, having a full power so to dispose of himself; and that was the case of Christ the Mediator: but that cannot be pretended to be our case, with respect to Adam's sin.

(3.) The stain and blot of it is ours. The whole nature of man was tainted with it, vitiated, and blackened, and, through defilement and loathsomeness thereby, rendered incapable of, and quite unfit for communion with God, Gen. iii. 24. This sin defiled the whole mass of man's nature, from our father Adam going through all his posterity, like leaven through the whole lump, 1 Cor xv. 22. *In Adam all die;* their souls die spiritually: his whole race by this sin became as dead corpses.

Thus Adam's sin, in itself, is really ours.

2. It is ours in law reckoning; God imputes it to us, charges it upon us all, once, in our natural state; though whenever a soul believes in Christ, it is disimputed to that soul: Rom. viii. 1. *There is now no condemnation to them which are in Christ Jesus.* But, by a sentence passed in the court of heaven, all mankind are decerned sinners, transgressors of the law, guilty of the first sin, and therefore liable to death, the penalty of the covenant, Rom. v. 12. 19.—*Death passed upon all men, for that all have sinned.* —*By one man's disobedience many were made sinners.* And forasmuch as the judgement of God is according to truth,

the

the matter muſt ſtand in itſelf, as it is found in that law-reckoning; that is to ſay, becauſe we are really ſinners in Adam, therefore we are reckoned in law to be ſo. So that the imputation of Adam's ſin to us, neceſſarily preſuppoſeth its being really ours.

Proof of the imputation of Adam's firſt ſin to his poſterity.

III. I ſhall evince the truth of the doctrine, and prove the imputation of Adam's firſt ſin, the ſin of breaking the covenant of works, by eating the forbidden fruit, to his poſterity.

1. The ſcripture plainly teacheth, that all ſinned in Adam, and were made ſinners by his firſt ſin, which was the breaking of the covenant of works, by eating the fruit of the forbidden tree, Rom. v. 12. 19. above cited. Where it is to be remarked, (1.) That the apoſtle ſpeaks of the firſt ſin in both texts: for as in the 19th verſe he calls it *that diſobedience*; ſo in ver. 12. *the* or *that ſin*, by way of eminency, as ver. 14. 15. in oppoſition to *that obedience*, by way of eminency, ver. 19.; whereas ſpeaking of ſin in general, ver. 13. he calls it ſimply *ſin*. Beſides, he ſpeaks of *that* ſin, by which death entered into the world; *As by one man that ſin entered into the world, and by that ſin death:* but it is evident, that it was by the firſt ſin that death entered into the world: Therefore it muſt be the firſt ſin which the apoſtle ſpeaks of here. This alſo is clear from the ſcope of this chapter, which is to account for the juſtification of ſinners by the obedience of Chriſt, which the apoſtle does by ſhewing that Chriſt died in our room and ſtead, ver. 7.—11. And he ſums up the whole matter in this concluſion, ver. 12. *Wherefore, as by one man ſin entered into the world, and death by ſin; and ſo death paſſed upon all men, for that all have ſinned;* which he afterwards enlarges upon. The words, it is plain, muſt have ſomething underſtood, to make up the ſenſe; and I conceive it is this: *Wherefore,* IT IS *even as by one man that ſin entered into the world,* &c. *i. e.* The matter of the juſtification of a ſinner before God, is even as the condemnation and death of ſinners by that ſin of one man, &c. (2.) That the apoſtle determines all men to have ſinned

that

that sin. *For that,* or *in whom* (as Mark i. 4.) *all have sinned.* But that this is the sense, however the words be read, appears, if it is considered, [1.] That death entered into the world by that sin, and so passed on all men: but, according to the apostle, it could not pass on all men for that sin, but for that all were the sinners; for where death comes, sin must needs be before; by the rule of justice, no man can die for a sin he is not guilty of. [2.] If all sinned, infants sinned too: but infants are not capable of having sinned otherwise than in Adam. The apostle teaches very plainly, that infants are comprehended among these *all,* and that they sinned, ver. 14. *that had not sinned after the similitude of Adam's transgression,* which clearly bears them to have sinned another way. [3.] By that sin we were *constituted* or *made sinners,* ver. 19. not by consent and approbation, nor by imitation, but by imputation, as was argued before; and consequently, since the judgement of God is according to truth, we sinned that sin.

2. All are under the guilt of that sin in Adam, till it be removed in justification by faith in Jesus Christ: they are, by virtue of that first sin, bound over to death, and the eternal wrath of God. This the scripture teacheth evidently, 1 Cor. xv. 22. *In Adam all die:* but how can they die in him, if they did not sin in him? Rom. v. 12. *By one man——death passed upon all:* sin then behoved in the first place by him to pass on all. ver. 15. *Through the offence of one, many be dead:* that offence therefore behoved to be their offence. ver. 18. *By the offence of one,* IT WAS (*viz.* the offence) *upon all men unto condemnation,* i. e. the guilt of eternal wrath: but how could they be condemned by a holy and just God for an offence that was not their offence, it being undeniable, that they did not substitute themselves, nor were they substituted by another, in the room of the offender? When the apostle tells us, that *there is therefore* NOW *no condemnation to them which are in Christ Jesus,* Rom. viii. 1. does he not plainly teach us, (1.) That all who are not in Christ, are under condemnation, whoever they be, whether guilty of actual sin in their own persons, or not, as infants and idiots? (2.) That even such as are *now* in Christ, were under condemnation,

condemnation, all along while they were not in him? Let men take a view of our guilty ſtate in Adam, that wrath which by nature we ſtand adjudged to, Eph. ii. 3. which the ſcripture plainly teaches; and then conſider the holy, juſt nature of God; they ſhall be obliged to own, that we ſinned in Adam, and that his ſin is ours as well as his, and that that wrath on that account is juſt. But corrupt unſubdued nature firſt frames to itſelf a notion of God's juſtice, according to its own principles, and then rejects this imputation as inconſiſtent therewith, and then puts a ſenſe on clear ſcripture-texts agreeable to its preconceived notions.

3. The univerſal depravation and corruption of human nature is a glaring evidence of this. Man is now deſpoiled of his primitive glory and integrity, the image of God, the rectitude of his nature, with which he was created; and inſtead of it, his whole nature is corrupted; there is in it a bent and propenſity to evil. His mind is darkened, his will is perverſe, his affections are altogether diſorderly. He is born in this caſe, corruption is woven into his nature from the time he has a being in the womb; Job xiv. 4. *Who can bring a clean thing out of an unclean? not one.* John iii. 6. *That which is born of the fleſh, is fleſh.* Gen. vi. 5.—*Every imagination of the thoughts of man's heart is only evil continually.* Pſal. li. 5. *Behold, I was ſhapen in iniquity; and in ſin did my mother conceive me.* There is a neceſſity of regeneration; without a man be born again, he is ruined for ever, John iii. 3. He is naturally dead in ſin, he muſt be raiſed from death; he is ſo marred, that he muſt be new-made, created to good works; elſe he will lie for ever void of ſpiritual life, utterly unable to do any thing but ſin, Eph. ii. 5. 10. Such a nature, and ſuch a frame of ſoul, is a ſin, a fountain of ſin. But without queſtion it is a miſery too, and the greateſt of miſeries human nature is capable of, as ſetting men at the greateſt diſtance from God, the chief good: Therefore it muſt be concluded to be a puniſhment of ſin too, and of ſome ſin previous to it, which can be none elſe but Adam's firſt ſin. And that ſin muſt be our ſin, the ſin of all mankind, ſince it is puniſhed at this fearful rate in us and all mankind. It is not poſſible to account

for the juftice of this difpenfation otherwife. It was inconfiftent with the nature of God to have created man in this cafe; yet thus we are from the time we have a being as men. Is this from the Creator otherwife than as a punifhment of fin? Muft it not be from ourfelves, (Hof. xiii. 9. *O Ifrael, thou haft deftroyed thyfelf*), as the true authors of our mifery, by finning againft God, namely, finning this fin, for no other can have place here? The law of natural generation without this will not falve the matter: for fo juftice would have required either the ftopping of generation, or elfe that even corrupt Adam fhould not have generated corrupt children: it is within the compafs of Omnipotency, though not the compafs of created power, to bring a clean thing out of an unclean, as was done in the cafe of the man Chrift: otherwife the greateft mifery and punifhment, which might have been averted, is inflicted upon mankind without any fault of theirs; which is more than abfurd.

4. Though men venture to deny fin in infants, who are without queftion incapable of actual finning in their own perfons, Rom. v. 14. & ix. 11.; yet it is undeniable they are liable to mifery, pains, ficknefs, and die as well as thofe who are grown perfons. The groans and tears of parents over the cradles, the moans and diftreffes of poor harmlefs babes, the graves of the fmalleft fize in the church-yard, are demonftrations of this. Yea, look to the old world fwept away with the flood, and there you will fee the infants drowned with the finner of a hundred years old. Look to the overthrow of Sodom, and you will fee them burnt in the fire from heaven with the luftful parents that begot them. Look to Jerufalem when it was deftroyed, and there you will fee them pining to death by famine, with the aged finners. Then look up to heaven, and behold a holy, juft God, who fent on thefe plagues, and confider if it be confiftent with his holy nature to treat innocent finlefs perfons at that rate. And after all, look into your Bible, and you will fee how God is juftified in all this. There you will fee the threatening of death annexed to the fin of breaking the covenant of works, Gen. ii. 17.; and feeing it execute upon them, ye muft needs conclude they are guilty. There you find,

that

that *death paſſes on all, for that all have ſinned*, Rom. v. 12. *reigns over them that had not ſinned after the ſimilitude of Adam's tranſgreſſion*, ver. 14. and thence you muſt conclude them ſinners. There it appears, that *the wages of ſin is death*, Rom. vi. 23.: they receive the wages, they have then wrought the work of ſin; not in their own perſons ſurely, for they were not capable; therefore they ſinned in Adam. As for the corruption of their nature, it juſtifies this procedure indeed: but then the propagation of it to them, is owing to this firſt ſin: and the diſpenſation of God in that matter muſt be juſtified, by their guilt of that ſin.

5. *Laſtly*, The compariſon ſtated in ſcripture betwixt Chriſt and Adam, plainly evinceth this. The apoſtle, Rom. v. 14. tells us, that Adam was a type or *figure* of Chriſt; and 1 Cor. xv. 45. he calls the one the *firſt Adam*, the other the *laſt Adam*. Whence it appears, that as Chriſt was the federal head in the covenant of grace; ſo Adam was the federal head in the covenant of works. Whence we may gather,

(1.) That as Chriſt, in his obedience and death, ſtood not as a private perſon, but what he did and ſuffered, he did and ſuffered as a public perſon, to be imputed to all his ſpiritual ſeed, 2 Cor. v. 21. *For he hath made him to be ſin for us, who knew no ſin: that we might be made the righteouſneſs of God in him:* ſo Adam ſinning, and breaking the covenant of works, did what he did, not as a private man, whoſe guilt remains with himſelf, but as a public perſon, whoſe deed was to be imputed to all his poſterity, or natural ſeed, Rom. v. 18.—*By the offence of one judgement came upon all men to condemnation.*

(2.) That ſince Adam was eventually a head of deſtruction and ruin to all his ſeed, and Chriſt a head of reparation and ſalvation to all that were his ſeed of the ſhipwrecked multitude, 1 Cor. xv. 22. *For as in Adam all die, even ſo in Chriſt ſhall all be made alive:* then as God laid on Chriſt the iniquities of all that are his, making them to meet on him, Iſ. liii. 6.; ſo Adam's ſin was from him diffuſed and came upon all that were his, Rom. v. 12.: for the one was to repair thoſe whom the other had deſtroyed;

stroyed; to pay their debts, which they had been involved in by the other.

(3.) As believers obeyed and satisfied in Christ their head in the second covenant; so all men sinned in Adam their head in the first covenant. The former is the doctrine of the scripture. *The righteousness of the law was fulfilled in them*, Rom. viii. 4. They were *crucified with him*, Gal. ii. 20.; which further appears, in that they were *raised up, and set in heaven in him*, Eph. ii. 6. Hence the latter is established:—We *broke* the law in Adam, and *sinned* against God in him.

(4.) *Lastly*, As we are made righteous by the obedience of Christ; so we are made sinners by the disobedience of Adam. So says the text. But we are made righteous through the obedience of Christ imputed to us, therefore we are made sinners through the disobedience of Adam imputed to us. Christ's righteousness is really ours, not in its effects only, but in itself, being that very righteousness on which we are acquitted and justified: so Adam's sin is really ours, not in its effects only, but in itself, being that upon which we are all by nature condemned persons, Rom. v. 18. As soon as we have a spiritual being in Christ, are united to him by his Spirit and by faith, so soon is Christ's righteousness ours: and as soon as we have a natural being as children of Adam, Adam's sin is ours.

So much for the proof of this doctrine, That Adam's first sin, the sin of breaking the covenant of works, by eating the forbidden fruit, is our sin, our breaking of it, as well as his.

The ground and reason of the imputation of Adam's first sin to his posterity.

IV. I shall shew the ground and reason why Adam's first sin, of breaking the covenant of works, is our sin, our breaking of it. This is the foundation of the imputation of that sin to us, and lies in these two things jointly.

1. He was our natural or seminal head, the natural root of all mankind, Acts xvii. 26. God set up the human nature in him pure and undefiled, blessed him with fruitfulness, Gen. i. 28. and from him all mankind derive their pedigree. So that as Levi being in the loins of Abraham,

ham, when Melchifedek met him, paid tithes in Abraham, Heb. vii. 9. 10.; fo we being in the loins of Adam, when the tempter met him, finned and broke the covenant in him. But,

2. Which is the main thing here, He was our federal head in the covenant of works, our reprefentative in that bargain. There was a proper covenant betwixt God and Adam; and in it Adam was not confidered as a private perfon, but ftood as the head of all mankind in it, acting for himfelf and for his pofterity whom he reprefented; even as the fecond Adam in the covenant of grace. And thus his fin was ours. Even as Abraham having the covenant made with him, was the federal as well as natural head of Levi, being the covenant head of the Jewifh nation; and therefore Levi in his loins is reckoned to have paid tithes to Melchifedek.

The fum of the matter lies here: All mankind being originally one in Adam, were made legally one in him and with him, by the covenant of works entered into with Adam, as the head of all mankind, conftituted by God himfelf, the infinitely-wife and abfolute Lord of all the creatures. By the bond of the covenant fuperadded to the natural tie betwixt him and us, we were made one with him, to all the purpofes of the covenant. And being thus one with him, his fin in breaking of the covenant was ours as well as his. The being of this covenant I have already proved, and have alfo accounted for the equity and juftice of this difpenfation.

The doctrine of the imputation of Adam's firft fin to his pofterity, applied.

USE I. This truth ferves to difcover, and fet before your eyes,

1. The malignant nature of fin. It is an infectious vapour, a plague, a peft to mankind, of a killing nature, where-ever it comes. One finner of mankind infected the whole race; one morfel of that leaven leavened the whole nature of man. It is the fpiritual peftilence in the world, that makes more dreadful havock than fire and fword; an emblem of which God is giving this day in France by a bodily peftilence, with which alfo he is threatening

ening thefe nations *. It is Solomon's obfervation, That *one finner deftroyeth much good*, Eccl. ix. 18. This is lively reprefented to us in the cafe of Adam, and often in the cafe of many particular finners among us, whofe fphere of activity is more narrow ; but O what deftruction do they make within their bounds! This malignity of it appears,

(1.) In its fpreading from the finner to all that are concerned in him, deftroying and breaking down like a flood where it comes. The peace and purity of the whole world was marred by Adam's fin ; and the peace and purity of leffer focieties is ftill marred with the fins of others. Heb. xii. 15. the apoftle exhorts Chriftians to *look diligently, left any root of bitternefs fpringing up, trouble them, and thereby many be defiled.* How many fuch roots of bitternefs are fprung up in our land, wherewith the peace and purity of church and ftate are both marred together at this day! How many fuch have fprung up, and are ftill fpringing up among us, whofe pangs of luft mar the quiet of families, leave a blot on them, trouble many, make the congregation a reproach, and to ftink in the noftrils of the fober part of their neighbours!

(2.) In that when the finner is dead and gone, his fin lives and works after him. It is long fince Adam died, but ftill his fin is working. Jeroboam finned fo in his life, as that he opened fuch a fluice, as ran for feveral generations after he was filent in the grave. And thus do the fins of many ftill live and deftroy much good, after they are gone. And therefore, befides the particular judgement at death, there is a general judgement at the end of the world, where people muft anfwer for the mifchief done by the current of their fin in the world, after they were gone out of it.

2. The awful and tremendous holy fovereignty of God, whofe judgements are always juft, but often unfearchable. When one confiders how God made the angels independent upon one another as to ftanding and falling, but comprehended the whole race of mankind under one federal head ; whom alfo, in the depth of his fovereign wif-

---

* This part of the fubject was preached in November 1721, at which time the plague raged in France. Happily Great Britain and Ireland efcaped that dreadful fcourge.

dom, he permitted to fall, when he could have held him up; fo as all mankind was ruined in him: muſt we not cry out, *O the depth of the riches both of the wiſdom and knowledge of God! how unſearchable are his judgements, and his ways paſt finding out?* Rom. xi. 33. The difpenfation was juſt, he can do us no wrong: it was becoming the divine perfections, and defigned for holy ends in the depth of wifdom. But in the mean time, there is need of a holy humble fpirit to adore the fovereignty of it.

3. The impoſſibility of our obtaining falvation by the way of this covenant. What hopes can we have of living by doing, when it has mifgiven in our hand already, when we were fitted for working and doing at another rate than we can pretend to be now? We have already broken that covenant, fallen under the penalty of it, the which we muſt needs difcharge, before we can have accefs to begin again on new ground, to look for life by keeping it better. And who of us is able to difcharge that debt to the juſtice of God? *Therefore by the deeds of the law, there ſhall no fleſh be juſtified in his ſight,* Rom. iii. 20.

4. The glory of the contrivance of the fecond covenant by the ever-bleſſed Trinity, and of the performance of it by the fecond perſon in our nature. Look here and behold the neceſſity of it for our falvation: What could they have done for themfelves, who had ruined themfelves, and were brought into the world in a ſtate of condemnation? There was a neceſſity of the obedience and death of Chriſt in that cafe, Luke xxiv. 26. *Ought not Chriſt to have ſuffered theſe things?*—Behold the fuitablenefs of it: Man was ruined by Adam's breaking the firſt covenant, and the remedy is provided by Chriſt's keeping the fecond covenant.—Behold the perfection of it: It takes away not only this fin, but all other fins too. How ſtrong is the grace of Chriſt, that is able to ſtop the torrent of Adam's fin, increafed with innumerable perfonal fins running with it in one channel? Rom. v. 16.

5. *Laſtly,* A notable confirmation of believers faith as to the imputation of Chriſt's righteoufnefs, obedience and death unto them, upon their embracing the covenant of grace. Is Adam's fin ours, by virtue of our union with him as the federal head in the covenant of works? Surely
Chriſt's

Chriſt's righteouſneſs, obedience and death, are no leſs ours, in virtue of our union with Chriſt, the federal head in the ſecond covenant. That God who imputes the one to all mankind for condemnation, will much more impute the other to believers for juſtification.

Use II. This doctrine ſerves to ſtir up to ſeveral duties. And,

1. Be convinced of this ſin as your ſin. Take it home to yourſelves among the reſt of the pieces of guilt, chargeable upon you before the Lord. God charges it on all mankind as their ſin: all men therefore ought to charge it on themſelves, ſince he is the Amen, the faithful and true Witneſs, and cannot charge any with guilt falſely, or by miſtake. It is hard to convince men of this: but when the Spirit of the Lord comes, to carry the work of conviction through, he will faſten this conviction on the conſcience among others: And how can one ſue for the pardon of that ſin, which he will not admit the conviction of?

2. Confeſs and mourn over this ſin before the Lord, Be humbled under the ſenſe of it, and anxiouſly inquire how ye may be ſaved from it, and the wrath and curſe of God due to you for it. Conſider ſeriouſly how this debt is on your head by nature, how ye are tranſgreſſors from the womb, breakers of covenant with God, fallen under the penalty of the covenant of works, by your not fulfilling the condition of it, but tranſgreſſing the covenant. Live no more unconcerned about it, but ſift your guilty conſciences in this point particularly before the Lord; and let that fear and ſorrow work in your ſouls on this head, that ought to be in the caſe of ſins committed by you in your own perſons.

Motive 1. Conſider that it is really your ſin, by which you have offended God, broken his covenant, and made yourſelves liable to eternal wrath. And ſhall it not lie heavy on your ſpirits, that you have thus ſinned? Rom. v. 19. If it be really your ſin, your debt ye are involved in by the miſmanagement of your firſt father; can it be ſafe to be unconcerned about it, while a holy juſt God is the party ye have to do with?

Mot. 2. It is the fountain of all the ſins and miſeries
that

that ever have been found with you. Ye are guilty before God of sins of heart, lip, and life; these must sometime be a terror to the soul. But whence did all these flow, but from your corrupt nature, averse to all good, and prone to all evil? And whence had you that nature, but from the guilt of this sin lying on you? Ye have been plunged in a gulf of miseries; even from the womb to this day, the clouds have been returning after the rain. Trace them to the spring-head, and ye will find they all issue from this sin. And what sin can ye truly mourn over to purpose, if ye do not mourn over the fountain of all? What calls more loudly for repenting and mourning than this leading sin?

Mot. 3. While the guilt of this sin lies upon you, ye lose all your labour in striving to get the guilt of other sins removed, or to get your lives reformed. That is but to shut the door while the grand thief is in the house; to labour to dry up the streams, while ye are at no pains to get the poisonous fountain stopt; the which is labour in vain. And it is the overlooking of this, that is the cause of the apostasy of many, who sometimes have made such a fair appearance; and is also the cause of the prevailing of a legal disposition so much at this day, among professors.

Mot. 4. *Lastly*, If ye get not the pardon of it, it will ruin you for ever, Rom. v. 18. Hereby ye are condemned; and a pardon only can reverse that sentence. Ye must then sue out the pardon of it; and if you come to God on that errand, be sure your souls will be humbled and broken within you for it.

And if ye would have your hearts duly affected with this sin, (1.) Labour to lay aside your carnal reasonings, and believe God's word as the word of truth and righteousness, which fixes this guilt on all mankind, and particularly on you. These reasonings in this matter are dangerous, and can tend to nothing but hardening the heart, and casting dishonour on God. (2.) Consider how ye naturally trace the steps of Adam in his breaking of the covenant, so bearing fallen Adam's image most lively, as I shewed elsewhere *. The consideration of this may serve

* Fourfold-state, state ii. head 1. under the title, *That man's nature is corrupted.*

Cov. I.   M   to

to prove the fact upon us, while we do so readily fall into the same way again, as far as we have occasion. (3.) Consider the righteousness of Christ, which is to be the same way imputed to all believers, and shall be imputed to you on your believing. There is a gift of righteousness to be imputed, as well as that debt of sin is charged upon you.

3. *Lastly*, Let this stir you up to quit your hold of the first Adam and his covenant, and flee for life and salvation to the second Adam in the second covenant, uniting with him by faith. The offer of the gospel is made to you: The Lord has made a grant of his Son as a quickening head to poor sinners: believe it, embrace the offer, accept Heaven's gift; otherwise ye will be ruined not only by the breach of the first covenant, but by despising of the second.

If ye be of those to whom that iniquity is forgiven, ye will highly prize the second Adam; for *unto them which believe he is precious*, 1 Pet. ii. 7. Ye will be holy and tender in your walk, the power of sin being broken where the guilt is removed, Rom. viii 1. Ye will be dead to the law, and denied to your own righteousness, making Christ's fulfilling of the covenant your only plea for life and salvation, Matth. v. 3. Phil. iii. 3.

Thus far of the *imputation* of Adam's first sin, in breaking the covenant of works, to his posterity.

HEAD

HEAD IV.

The STATE *of Men under the broken Covenant of Works; and their dreadful Condition under the Curse.*

GALATIANS iii. 10.

For as many as are of the works of the law, are under the curse: for it is written, Cursed is every one that continueth not in all things which are written in the book of the law to do them.

HAVING difcourfed of the *breaking* of the covenant of works by all mankind in Adam, we are next to inquire into the *ftate* and *cafe* of finners under that broken covenant. And that the text fhews to be a very lamentable, and dangerous one. In a fhipwreck, when the fhip is dafhed in pieces upon a rock, how heavy is the cafe of the crew among the raging waves? The fhip can no more carry them to the harbour, but failing them, leaves them to the mercy of the waves. If one can get a broken plank to hold by, that is the greateft fafety there; but that doth often but hold in their miferable lives for a little, till the paffengers are fwallowed up. Such, and unfpeakably worfe, is the cafe of finners under the broken covenant of works, which leaves them under the curfe, as we fee in the text. In which we have,

1. The covenant-ftate of fome of mankind, yea, of many of them. They *are of the works of the law:* it is the fame thing as to be *of the law of works;* that is, to be under the covenant of works. So *the works of the law,* are oppofed to *the hearing of faith,* Gal. iii. 2. that is, the law to the gofpel, the covenant of works to the covenant of grace. But the apoftle in our text intimates their covenant-ftate, by a phrafe which, in the firft place, defigns their habitual courfe and practice, *viz.* to feek life and falvation by the works of the law; but, in the next place,

place, designs the covenant they are under, whereof their practice is a plain evidence. They are opposed to those who are of faith, who being under the covenant of grace, by faith look for life and salvation by Christ's works.

The phrase, *As many as are of the works of the law*, imports, that there are others who are not under that covenant. In the scripture we read of *two covenants*, Gal. iv. 24. Each of these have their children: and so the world is divided into two sorts of men; some under the covenant of grace, others still remaining under the covenant of works; which the phrase, *under the curse*, doth also bear; for since they are under the curse of the law or covenant of works, they are surely under that law or covenant itself; for *whatsoever the law saith, it saith to them who are under the law*, Rom. iii. 19.

2. The state and case of men under that covenant: They *are under the curse*. The covenant is broken, and so they are fallen under the penalty: the duty of the covenant is neglected and cast off; and so they are under the curse of the covenant. As the blessing or promise, which they have lost, comprehends all good for time and eternity, on soul and body; so the curse comprehends all evil on soul and body, for time and eternity. To be under the curse, is to be by the law's sentence separated and destined to evil, according to the threatening, Gen. ii. 17.—*In the day that thou eatest thereof, thou shalt surely die.*

3. The proof and evidence of this their miserable state and case: *For it is written, Cursed is every one that continueth not in all things which are written in the book of the law to do them.* There is an extract of the sentence of the law, which is standing against them, Deut. xxvii. 26. *Cursed be he that confirmeth not all the words of this law to do them.* That sets the matter in full light, from whence the conscience of every man under that covenant may conclude him under the curse.

And hence from the text ariseth these two weighty truths. 1. *There are some, yea many, of mankind, who are still under the broken covenant of works.* 2. *Man in his natural state, being under the broken covenant of works, is under the curse.* Of both which we shall speak in order.

DOCT. I.

DOCT. I.

There are some, yea many, of mankind, who are still under the broken covenant of works.

In prosecuting of this subject, I shall,

I. Evince the truth of the doctrine, That there are some, yea many, of mankind, who are still under the broken covenant of works.

II. Inquire who they are that are under this broken covenant.

III. Shew what is the effect of the broken covenant of works upon them.

IV. Shew why so many remain still under this broken covenant.

V. Lastly, Apply the subject.

Proof of the doctrine, that there are many still under the broken covenant of works.

I. I shall evince the truth of this doctrine, That there are some, yea many, of mankind, who are still under the broken covenant of works. This will clearly appear, if ye consider,

1. That there are but *few that shall be saved*, Matth. vii. 14. Christ's flock is but *a very little flock*, Luke xii. 32. But all who are brought from under the covenant of works, are brought into the covenant of grace, Rom. vi. 14.; and all who are within the bond of the covenant of grace, are of Christ's flock, and shall be saved, Heb. viii. 10. Hence it follows, that the most part of mankind are left under the covenant of works. The truth is, all men by nature are under it, and so are born under the curse, Eph. ii. 3. And many live and die under it; and therefore the sentence against the whole wretched herd of the condemned world runs in these terms, *Depart from me, ye cursed*, &c.

2. The scripture is plain on this head. The apostle tells us, that there are some *under the law*, Rom. iii. 19. to whom the law doth say, what it says for conviction and condemnation; and that is under the law as a covenant of works,

works, for otherwise all are under it as a rule of life. It curseth and condemneth many, Gal. iii. 10. *Cursed is every one,* viz. who is under the law; for its curse cannot reach others, viz. *them which are in Christ Jesus,* Rom. viii. 1. It condemns all unbelievers, John iii. 18.—*He that believeth not, is condemned already,* viz. by the sentence of the law as the covenant of works; for the covenant of grace condemns no man: John v. 45. said our Lord to the Jews, *Do not think that I will accuse you to the Father: there is one that accuseth you, even Moses, in whom ye trust.* Chap. xii. 47. *And if any man hear my words, and believe not, I judge him not: for I came not to judge the world, but to save the world.*

3. As all men in Adam were taken into the covenant of works, so no man can be freed from the obligation of it, but they who are discharged from it by God, who was man's party in it. This is evident from the general nature of contracts. And none are discharged from it, but on a full answering of all it could demand of them; as says our Lord, Matth. v. 18. *Till heaven and earth pass, one jot or one tittle shall in no wise pass from the law, till all be fulfilled.* This no man can attain unto, but by faith in Jesus Christ, whereby the soul appropriates and applies to itself Christ's obedience and satisfaction offered in the gospel; and so pleading these, gets up the discharge; for, *being justified by faith, we have peace with God, through our Lord Jesus Christ,* Rom. v. 1. But certain it is, all men have not faith, nay few have it: therefore few are discharged from the covenant of works, but most part are still under it.

4. Freedom from the covenant of works is such a privilege, as requires both price and power, each of them infinite, to invest a sinner with it. The sinner is by nature under the covenant of works, bound to perfect obedience to its commands, to complete satisfaction of its sanction: none but Christ was able to purchase the sinner's freedom from that covenant, since none but he could answer its high demands. When the sinner's freedom is purchased, he is so loath to part with that covenant, that none but the Spirit of Christ, in his day of power, can make him willing to come away from under it. So it is the peculiar

privilege

That many are still under the broken Covenant. 95

privilege of the elect, for whom Christ died; yea, of believers, whom the Spirit of Christ has translated from the kingdom of darkness into the kingdom of God's dear Son, Rom. vii. 4. Gal. ii. 19.

5. There are many who still live as they were born; in the same state wherein their father Adam left them, when he broke; who were never to this day in any due concern, how to be discharged of the debt he left upon their head, or of the band of the covenant of works which in him they entered into. How can it be then, but that the debt remains, and the bond is uncancelled as to them? In one of the two Adams all mankind stand to this day; some in the first Adam, bearing the image of the earthy, sin and death; others in the second Adam, bearing the image of the heavenly, life and salvation The translation from the first to the second, none meet with in a morning-dream; both law and gospel have a part to act in their souls, ere this work can be effected.

6. *Lastly*, There are but two covenants, *viz*. of works and grace, Gal. iv. 24. as there never were but two ways of life and salvation, by works and by grace; and but two federal heads of mankind, the first and second Adam. Under one of these covenants, and but under one of them, every son and daughter of Adam must be, Rom. vi. 14. The covenant of grace has not been so much as externally revealed or preached to many in the world; and among those to whom it is, how few are there who have really and truly embraced it? how do many stand at a distance from it, as they would do from fetters of iron? Since therefore but few are within the bond of the covenant of grace, it is evident that most men are under the covenant of works.

Hence the case of many, yea most men, is most miserable, they are under the curse.

Those who are under the covenant of works described.

II. The second thing proposed was, to inquire who they are that are under the broken covenant of works? This is a weighty inquiry; it is in effect, who are they that are under the curse? because all that are under that covenant,

covenant, now that it is broken, are under the curse. And therefore take heed to it, and apply what may be offered on this head. I premise these four things, to make this the more clear.

1. Men may be under the covenant of works, and yet living under the external dispensation of the covenant of grace. There is a great difference betwixt one's visible church-state, and the state of their souls before the Lord. The covenant of grace was preached to Adam in paradise, Gen. iii. 15. yet was he in hazard of running back to the covenant of works, ver. 22. The Jews had the dispensation of the covenant of grace among them, and the ceremonial law clearly held out the way of salvation by the Messiah, yet most of them were under the covenant of works, being sons of the bond woman. So under the gospel dispensation to this day, many to whom the covenant of grace is offered, continue under the covenant of works. It is one thing to hear the new covenant proclaimed, another thing to accept of it by faith.

2. Men may receive the seals of the covenant of grace, and yet be under the covenant of works. Circumcision was a seal of the covenant of grace, yet many who received it, were still sons of the bond-woman, to be cast out from inheriting with the children, Gal. iv. 24. 25. 30. And so will many who are baptized in the name of Christ, and have partaked of the Lord's table, yet be disowned at the last day, by the Head of the second covenant, as none of his, Luke xiii. 26. forasmuch as they never truly came into the bond of that covenant.

3. Men may be convinced in their consciences of the impossibility of obtaining salvation by Adam's covenant of works, and yet remain under it still. Where are they that are so very stupid, as to think that they can obtain salvation by perfect obedience to the law? The Pharisees of old, and the Papists to this day, will not venture their salvation on the absolute perfection of their own obedience; yet the former lived, and the latter do live under that covenant. Let no man deceive himself here; such a conviction as hardly any man can shun, is not sufficient to divorce a man from the law or covenant of works.

4. *Lastly*, Men, upon the offer of the covenant of grace made

made to them, may aim at accepting of it, and so enter into a personal covenant with God, and yet remain under the covenant of works. Many miss their mark in their covenanting with God, and instead of accepting God's covenant of grace, make a covenant of works with God, upon other terms than Adam's covenant was, for which there is no warrant in the word. The Galatians did not cast off Christ's righteousness altogether, but only mixed their own works with his: And thus do many still, looking on their faith, repentance, and obedience, such as they are, to be the fulfilling of a law, upon which they are to be accepted of God.

But more particularly, and directly,

1. All unregenerate persons are under the covenant of works. Where is the unconverted man or woman, living in the state of irregeneracy, strangers to a saving change on their souls? That man or woman is yet a branch of the old Adam, growing on the old stock, a stranger to the new covenant, because not in Christ the head of the covenant: for *if any man be in Christ, he is a new creature: old things are passed away, behold, all things are become new*, 2 Cor. v. 17. Such an unregenerate person is still under the covenant of works. This is evident, in that the death contained in the threatening of that covenant has full sway over them, so that they are *dead in trespasses and sins*, Eph. ii. 1. 5. They lie yet without spiritual life, as the first Adam left them. They have no communion with the second Adam, else they had been quickened; for he is a quickening head, as the other was a killing one.

2. All that have not the Spirit of Christ dwelling in them, are under the covenant of works: hence says the apostle, Rom. viii. 9. *If any man have not the Spirit of Christ, he is none of his.* Compared with Gal. v. 18. *But if ye be led by the Spirit, ye are not under the law.* It is one of the first promises of the covenant of grace, the giving of the Spirit, Ezek. xxxvi. 27. *I will put my Spirit within you.* And the Spirit of Christ once entering into a man, never changes his habitation; as Christ himself saith, John xiv. 16. *I will pray the Father, and he shall give you another Comforter, that he may abide with you for ever.*

ever. Wo to thofe then that have not the Spirit of grace, they are under the curfe. And fuch are all prayerlefs perfons, Zech. xii. 10 ; ignorant, unconvinced finners, who have not yet feen their loft and ruined ftate, John xvi. 8. ; refractory and rebellious ones, who will not be hedged in within the Lord's way, Ezek. xxxvi. 27. ; carnal men, who are under the government of their own lufts and unruly paffions, Gal. v. 16.

3. All unbelievers, John iii. 18. Whofoever is deftitute of faving faith, is under the covenant of works: for it is by faith that one is brought within the bond of the covenant of grace, is married unto Chrift, being dead to the law. Every foul of man is under one of the two hufbands, Chrift or the law. All believers have their Maker for their Hufband; and all unbelievers have the law as a covenant of works for theirs, a rigorous hufband, a weak one, who can do nothing for their life and falvation, but for their ruin and deftruction. Faith unites the foul to Chrift, Eph. iii. 17. The unbeliever, what though he go about the duties of religion, walk foberly and ftrictly ? he is not joined to Chrift, therefore he remains under the covenant of works, under the curfe.

4. All unfanctified, unholy perfons, Rom. vi. 14. The doctrinal ftaking finners down under, and wreathing about their necks the yoke of the law as a covenant of works, is fo far from being a proper method to bring them to holinefs and good works; that contrariwife they fhall never be holy, never do one good work, till fuch time as they are fairly rid of that yoke, and fit down under the jurifdiction of grace. So that true holinefs is an infallible mark of one delivered from the law; and unholinefs, of one that is yet hard and faft under it, Gal. v. 18. forecited. Legalifm is rank enmity to true holinefs, it is but a devil transformed into an angel of light, and never prevails fo in the church, as in a time of apoftafy, growing unholinefs, untendernefs, regardleffnefs of the commands of God, when all flefh has corrupted their ways. Take for an example Popery, the grand apoftafy. What fet of men that call themfelves Chriftians, fet up for the law and good works in their doctrine, more than they do ? and among

among whom is there less of these to be found? How can they be but unholy, who are under the covenant of works? For there is no communion with God in the way of that covenant now; so sanctifying influences are stopt, and they must wither and pine away in their iniquity. Whereas when once the soul is brought out from that covenant into the covenant of grace, the course of sanctifying influences is opened, the clean and cleansing water flows into their souls: the Head of the covenant is a holy Head, conveying holiness to his members; the Spirit of the covenant is a sanctifying Spirit; the promises of the covenant are promises of holiness; the blood of the covenant is purifying blood: and, in a word, every thing in the covenant tends to sanctifying and making holy the covenanters.

5. All profane, loose, and licentious men, are under the covenant of works, Rom. vii. 5. & viii. 2. These men of Belial are under that heavy yoke: for under that covenant being broken, sin and death have the force of a law upon the subjects, as the worms, stench, and rottenness domineer in the grave without control. When one sees so many profane livers, unclean, drunkards, swearers, liars, thieves, cheaters, oppressors, and others walking after their own lusts; he may conclude all these to be evidences and consequents of the curse of the broken covenant on them: even as when ye go through a field full of briers, thorns, thistles, nettles, &c. ye may sigh and say, These are the product of the curse laid on the earth. These people think they walk at liberty; but what liberty is it? Even such as that madman enjoyed, Mark v. 4. *who had been often bound with fetters and chains, and the chains had been plucked asunder by him, and the fetters broken in pieces; neither could any man tame him.* The truth is, they are the arrantest slaves on earth, who are slaves to their own domineering lusts and passions: 2 Pet. ii. 19. *While they promise them liberty, they themselves are the servants of corruption: for of whom a man is overcome, of the same is he brought in bondage.* Such kindly slaves are they of the worst of masters, that they have lost all just notion and sense of true liberty, Psal. cxix. 45.

6. All

6. All mere moralists, such as satisfy themselves with common honesty and sobriety, living in the mean time strangers to religious exercises, and without a form of godliness. These are under the covenant of works, as seeking justification and acceptance with God, by their conformity (such as it is) to the letter of the law, Gal. v. 4. These are they, who please themselves, in their wronging no man, doing justly betwixt man and man, and in their pretended keeping of a good heart towards God; while in the mean time the rottenness of their hearts appears, in their ignorance of God and Christ, and the way of salvation by him, their estrangedness from the duty of prayer, and other holy exercises. Some of these have that scripture much in their mouths, Micah vi. 8.—*What doth the Lord require of thee, but to do justly, and to love mercy, and to walk humbly with thy God?* little considering that the last clause thereof writes death on their foreheads. They are under the covenant of works with a witness, having betaken themselves to their shreds of moral honesty, as so many broken boards of that split ship.

7. *Lastly*, All formal hypocrites, or legal professors, these sons and daughters of the bond-woman, Gal. iv. 24. 25. These are they, who have been convinced, but never were converted; who have been awakened by the law, but were never laid to rest by the gospel; who are brought to duties, but have never been brought out of them to Jesus Christ; who pretend to be married to Christ, but were never yet divorced from, nor dead to the law; and so are still joined to the first husband, the law as a covenant of works. Though they be strict and zealous professors, and therein go beyond many; they are as really enemies to Christ, as the profane are, Rom. x. 3. *For they being ignorant of God's righteousness, and going about to establish their own righteousness, have not submitted themselves unto the righteousness of God.* Though they will not let an opportunity of duty slip, but take heed to their ways, and dare not walk at random, as many do; all that they do is under the influence of the covenant of works, and therefore God regards it not, but they remain under the curse.

Of the effect of the covenant of works, upon those who are under it.

III. I proceed to shew what is the *effect* of the broken covenant of works, upon those who are under it.

Of the commanding power of the covenant of works.

First, It has and exercises a *commanding* power over them, binding them to its obedience, with the strongest bonds and ties of authority. Its commands are contained in the fiery law delivered from mount Sinai, out of the midst of the fire, Deut. v. 22. The obedience of them, which it binds unto, is perfect obedience, every way perfect, Luke x. 27. 28. It has its full commanding power over them all that are under it. It has become a question, Whether or not believers are set free from the commanding power of the covenant of works, as well as from the condemning power of it? We own the ten commands, which were delivered on mount Sinai, to be the eternal rule of righteousness, and that these are given of God in the hand of Jesus Christ to believers, for a rule of life to them; that they require of them perfect obedience, and have all the binding power over them, that the sovereign authority of God the Creator and Redeemer can give them, which is supreme and absolute. But that believers are under that law as it stands in the covenant of works, that these commands are bound on believers by the tie of the covenant of works, or that the covenant of works has a commanding power over believers, we must deny. For believers are dead to the law as a covenant of works, Rom. vii. 4. And therefore as a husband cannot pretend to command his wife after she is dead, and the relation dissolved; so neither can the law as a covenant maintain its authority over believers, after they are dead to it, and the relation betwixt them is dissolved. They are not under it, Rom. vi. 14. how then can it have a commanding power over them? They are not under its jurisdiction, but under that of grace: so though the commands be the same as to the matter, yet they are not to take them from the covenant of works, but from the law as in the hand of Christ.

Christ. Our Lord Jesus did in the name of all his people put himself under its commanding power, and satisfied all its commands, to deliver his people that were under it, Gal. iv. 4. 5.—*God sent forth his Son made of a woman, made under the law, to redeem them that were under the law.* And shall they dishonour him, by putting their necks under it again? After Christ has got up the bond, having fully paid all the law's demands, shall we pretend to enter in payment again?

Let us take a view of the commanding power of the covenant of works, which it has over all that are under it.

1. It commands and binds to perfect obedience, under pain of the curse; Gal. iii. 10. *Cursed is every one that continueth not in all things which are written in the book of the law to do them.* Every the least duty is commanded with this certification, and this is the risk they run upon every the least slip. The law in the hand of Christ unto believers commands obedience too, and that under a penalty. But it is a soft one in comparison of that, *viz.* strokes of fatherly anger; as appears from Psal. lxxxix. 30.—33. *If his children forsake my law, and walk not in my judgements; if they break my statutes, and keep not my commandments: then will I visit their transgression with the rod, and their iniquity with stripes. Nevertheless, my loving kindness will I not utterly take from him,* &c. This penalty is not the curse of a wrathful Judge, Gal. iii. 13. *Christ hath redeemed us from the curse of the law, being made a curse for us.* But the covenant of works has no less certification, it cannot speak to its subjects in softer terms; so that though the stroke in itself be never so small, yet there is a curse in it, if it were but the miscarrying of a basket of bread, Deut. xxviii. 17.

2. It commands without any promise of strength at all to perform. There is no such promise to be found in all the Bible, belonging to that covenant. It shews what is to be done, and with all severity exacts the task; but furnisheth not any thing whereof it is to be made. So the case of men under that covenant is represented by Israel's case in Egypt, Exod. v. 18. *Go therefore now and work,* said Pharaoh to that people; *for there shall no straw be given you, yet shall ye deliver the tale of bricks.* Under the

the covenant of grace, duty is required, but strength is promised too, Ezek. xxxvi. 27. *I will put my Spirit within you, and cause you to walk in my statutes, and ye shall keep my judgements, and do them.* And the commands in the hands of the Mediator are turned into promises; as appears from Deut. x. 16. *Circumcise the foreskin of your heart, and be no more stiff-necked.* Compared with chap. xxx. 6. *And the Lord thy God will circumcise thine heart, and the heart of thy seed, to love the Lord thy God with all thine heart, and with all thy soul, that thou mayst live.* Yea, the Mediator's calls and commands to his people bear a promise of help, Prov. x. 29. *The way of the Lord is strength to the upright.* But there is no such thing in the covenant of works; the work must be performed in the strength that was given; they must trade with the stock that mankind was set up with at first: but that strength is gone, that stock is wasted; howbeit the law can neither make it up again, nor yet abate of its demands.

Of the debarring power of the covenant of works.

Secondly, The broken covenant of works has a *debarring* power over them that are under it, in respect of the promise; it bars them from life and salvation, as long as they are under its dominion, Gal. ii. 16. *For by the works of the law shall no flesh be justified.* While Adam kept this covenant, it secured eternal life to him: but as soon as it was broken, it set it beyond his reach; and neither he, nor any of his posterity, had ever seen life, if another covenant had not been provided. The broken covenant of works fixeth a great gulf, betwixt its territories and life and salvation; so that no man can pass from the one to the other. If any would be at heaven, they must get out from under the law, and get into the covenant of grace; so shall they have life and salvation; but no otherwise.

There are two bars which this broken covenant draws betwixt its subjects and life and salvation.

1. There is no life to the sinner, without complete satisfaction to justice, for the wrong he has done to the honour of God and his law, Heb. ix. 22. *Without shedding of blood is no remission.* The terms of the covenant were,
—*In*

—In the day that thou eatest thereof, thou shalt surely die, Gen. ii. 17. Now the covenant is broken, the penalty must be paid, in the true sense and meaning of the bond: the sinner must die, and die infinitely, die till infinite justice be satisfied. Can the sinner get over this bar? Is he able to satisfy, can he go to that death, a sacrifice for himself, and return again? Can he pay the penalty of the bond? No, no. In his blindness and ignorance, he thinks perhaps to get over it by his mourning and afflicting himself for his sin, by bearing as well as he can the afflictions God lays on him. But all his sufferings in the world are but an earnest of what he must suffer hereafter: for at best they are but the sufferings of a finite being, which cannot compensate the wrong his sin has done to the honour of an infinite God: and besides, he sins anew in his suffering too; he cannot bear a cross without some grudge against God, and some impatience, which are new sins. So the sinner in this does but attempt to wash himself in the mire. Wherefore he can never get over this bar. And if he were over it, there is yet a

2. Second bar betwixt him and life and salvation, namely, There is no life and salvation without perfect obedience to its commands for the time to come, Matth. xix. 17. *If thou wilt enter into life,* says Christ to the young man there, *keep the commandments.* This was the condition of the covenant; and it is not enough that a man pay the penalty of a broken contract, but he must perform the condition of it, ere he can plead the benefit. Perfect obedience to the commands of God is the terms of life in that covenant: no less was proposed to Adam, who broke it: no less to Christ, who fulfilled it in the room of his elect, Gal. iv. 4. 5. forecited. As there was a necessity of passive obedience to it, Luke xxiv. 26. *Ought not Christ to have suffered these things?* so was there of active obedience, Matth. iii. 15.—*It becometh us to fulfil all righteousness.* And there is no less proposed to all that are under it.

Is the sinner able to get over this bar? His stock of strength is gone; the fall in Adam has so bruised him, that his arm is broken, he cannot work for life: he is not fit to be God's hired servant now, for life; for till he get

life

life of free grace in Chrift, he can do nothing, John xv. 5. He muſt be ſaved before he can work one good work, ſaved from ſin, the guilt and power of it, ſaved from the ſpiritual death he is lying under as the penalty of the covenant of works: how then can he work for ſalvation? The ſcripture is expreſs on this head, not only that we are not juſtified by works, but that we are not ſaved by works: *For by grace are ye ſaved,* ſays the apoſtle, *through faith; and that not of yourſelves: it is the gift of God: not of works, leſt any man ſhould boaſt: for we are his workmanſhip, created in Chriſt Jeſus unto good works, which God hath before ordained that we ſhould walk in them,* Eph. ii. 8. 9. 10. *Not by works of righteouſneſs, which we have done, but according to his mercy he ſaved us by the waſhing of regeneration, and renewing of the Holy Ghoſt,* Tit. iii. 5.

I know the ſinner, in his blindneſs, will think to pleaſe God by his doing as well as he can; by his pretended ſincerity, though he cannot attain to perfection; by the will, where he cannot reach the deed. But alas! he conſiders not, that the covenant of works will admit of none of theſe, all which are rejected by that one ſentence of the law, *Curſed is every one that continueth not in all things which are written in the book of the law to do them.* Beſides that there is not one thing he does that is well done, while he is not in Chriſt; there is no ſincerity with him, but ſelfiſhneſs; no will, but ſelf-will.

And as there is no getting over either of theſe bars, ſo there is no removing them out of the way, that ſo the ſinner may have a paſſage, without concerning himſelf with them, Matth. v. 18. Some fancy to themſelves a removing of them by mere mercy. God knows that we cannot anſwer theſe demands of the covenant of works, ſo, think they, mercy will paſs them for the ſafety of the ſinner. But has not God ſufficiently declared the contrary, in the ſending of his own Son, who, before he could redeem the elect, behoved to get over them both, by perfect obedience and ſatisfaction in their ſtead, Rom. viii. 32.? If the terms of life and ſalvation could have been abated, might not God's own Son have expected the abatement in his favour, while he ſtood in the room of elect ſinners?

Cov. I.   O   but

but he got no abatement; how can ye expect it then? See Exod. xxxiv. 7.

Of the condemning power of the covenant of works.

Thirdly, The broken covenant of works has a *cursing* and *condemning* power over them that are under it, in respect of the threatening: Gal. iii. 10. *For as many as are of the works of the law, are under the curse: for it is written, Cursed is every one that continueth not in all things which are written in the book of the law to do them.* Compare Rom. iii. 19. *Now we know that what things soever the law saith, it saith to them who are under the law: that every mouth may be stopped, and all the world may become guilty before God.* Every man and woman under it, is in a state of condemnation; they are condemned persons, bound over to the wrath of God in time and eternity, John iii. 18. *He that believeth not, is condemned already.* So that there has never any come to Christ, but with the rope about their necks, as condemned criminals. Christ's kingdom is the jurisdiction of grace, where grace, life, and salvation reign through Jesus Christ: it is peopled by fugitives out of the dominion of the law; and they that flee thither, are all such as find there is no living for them at home; they are such as the sentence of death is passed upon, and there is no access for a remission to them under the dominion of the law. And they never think of fleeing into the jurisdiction of grace, till once the sentence of death is intimated unto them, by their own consciences, and they begin to see they are in hazard every moment of being drawn to death: for till then, they will not believe it. Then they bethink themselves of making their escape out of the law's dominion.

This power the law as a covenant of works has over them by sin, forasmuch as it was a clause in the covenant, that man sinning should *die the death*, Gen. ii. 17. It had no such power over man, till once sin entered; but upon the breach of the command, the penalty took place. And since every man is born a sinner, he is also born a cursed and condemned man by the sentence of the law, which abides on him so long as he continues under that covenant. And upon every sin committed, the yoke is wreathed

wreathed faster and faster about his neck; so that upon every sin committed by men while in that state, there is a new band by which they are bound over to wrath.

Of the irritating power of the covenant of works.

Lastly, The broken covenant of works has an *irritating* influence upon all that are under it, so that instead of making them better, it makes them worse, stirring up their corruptions, like a nest of ants being troubled by one's touching of them, Rom. vii. 5. 10. 11. *For when we were in the flesh,* says the apostle, *the motions of sins which were by the law, did work in our members to bring forth fruit unto death.—And the commandment which was ordained to life, I found to be unto death. For sin taking occasion by the commandment, deceived me, and by it slew me.* Men under this covenant, whose corruptions lie dormant after a sort, while the law is not applied to their consciences, when once the law is brought home to their souls, and they are touched with it, their corrupt hearts swell and rage in sin, like the sea troubled with winds. See a notable instance of it, Acts vii. 54. in the case of the Jews after Stephen's speech to them, *When they heard these things, they were cut to the heart, and they gnashed on him with their teeth.* And hence is that direction of our Saviour, Matth. vii. 6. *Give not that which is holy unto the dogs, neither cast ye your pearls before swine, lest they trample them under their feet, and turn again and rent you.* You may see another instance, Hos. xi. 2. *As they called them, so they went from them: they sacrificed unto Baalim, and burnt incense to graven images.* And thus it is, that by the law sin abounds, and becomes exceeding sinful.

Now, this is accidental to the law as the covenant of works; for it is holy, and just, and good; and therefore can never bring forth sin as the native fruit of it: but it is owing to the corruption of mens hearts, impatient of restraint, Rom. vii. 12. 13. *Wherefore the law is holy; and the commandment holy, and just, and good. Was then that which is good, made death unto me? God forbid. But sin that it might appear sin, working death in me by that which is good; that sin by the commandment might become exceeding sinful.* While the sun shines warm on a garden, the flowers send forth a pleasant smell: but while it shines so on the dunghill, it smells more abominably than at other times. So it is here. There are two things here to be considered in the case of the law.

1. It lays an awful restraint on the sinner with its commands and threatenings, Gal iii. 10. The unrenewed man would never make a holy life his choice; might he freely follow his own inclination, he would not regard what is good, but give himself a liberty in sinful courses. But the law is as a bridle to him: it crosseth and contradicteth his sinful inclinations; it commands him to obey under the pain of the curse, and threatens him with death and damnation, if he shall transgress the bounds it sets him. It is to him as the bridle and spur to the horse; as the master and his whip to the slave. So that the sinner can never cordially like it; but all the obedience it gets from him is mercenary, having no higher springs, than hope of reward, and fear of punishment.

2. In the mean time it has no power to subdue his corruptions, to remove his rebellious disposition, to reconcile his heart to holiness, or to strengthen him for the performance of duty: *For the law was given by Moses, but grace and truth came by Jesus Christ*, John i. 17. As it finds the man without strength, so it leaves him, though it never ceases to exact duty of him. Though no straw is given to the sinner by it, yet the tale of the bricks it will not suffer to be diminished. Hence,

(1.) The very restraint of the law, as the covenant of works, awakens, and puts an edge upon the corruption of the heart, Rom. vii. 11. forecited. It breeds in the corrupt heart a longing after the forbidden fruit, though it have nothing more to commend it than allowed fruit, but that it is forbidden. The sinner perceiving the thorn-hedge of the law betwixt him and sin, conceives a keenness to be over the hedge. And hence it is, that many are never so ready to break out into extravagancies, as after their consciences have been most keenly plied by the word. And thus many never give such a loose to their lusts, as after solemn occasions of communion with God.

(2.) In

(2.) In the encounter betwixt the law and lusts, lusts gather strength by the law's crossing them. They are irritated, provoked, and stirred up the more, that the law goes about to hold them down, Rom. vii. 5. They swell, they rally all their forces, to make head against their enemy, that they may get the victory. The sinner, the more he is plied by the law to hold him back, runs the more fiercely down the steep place into the sea, like the swine possessed by the devil. If the law come into the heart, without gospel-grace to water the soul; it shall be like one with a besom sweeping a dry floor; the more forcibly one sweeps, the more thick will the dust fly up, and fly about into every corner. The sinner is like the unruly horse, which the more he is checked with the bit, rages the more. And hence the issue often is that, Hos. iv. 17. *Ephraim is joined to idols: let him alone.* And Psal. lxxxi. 11. 12. *But my people would not hearken to my voice: and Israel would none of me. So I gave them up unto their own hearts lust: and they walked in their own counsels.*

(3.) The sinner finding the case hopeless, hardens himself, and goes on: Jer. ii. 25. *Thou saidst, There is no hope. No, for I have loved strangers, and after them will I go.* He looks to the height of the law's commands, and finds himself incapable to reach them; and he looks to the terror of the law's threatenings, and finds them unavoidable. So he gives up with hope, sits down hardened in secret despair, using all means to stop the access of light from the law for his conviction and disquietment. Thus he is like a tired horse, that bears the spur, but will not answer it; or if he be moved by it, turns back to bite the rider, but goes not one foot faster for all it.

(4.) *Lastly,* Hence the heart is filled with the hatred of the holy law, and of the holy God who made it, and holds by it. This is the fearful issue of the matter, Prov. i. 29. *They hated knowledge, and did not chuse the fear of the Lord.* Rom. i. 30.—*Haters of God.* As the condemned criminal hates the judge and the law, so do they. They cannot bring up their hearts to the purity the law requires, and cannot get the law brought down to the impurity of their hearts, but still it reads their doom: hence the heart cannot miss to rise against the law, being girded with the

cords

cords of death by it; and against God in secret grudges at his holiness and justice, secret wishes that he were not such a one as he is.

This is a short account of what is called the *irritating power of the law*; from which alone one may see, what a fearful case it is to be under the law as it is the covenant of works. It tends to make the heart of man a very hell: and the truth is, in hell it comes to its height; and so they are held like wild bulls in a net.

Reasons why so many still remain under the broken covenant of works.

IV. I now proceed to shew, why so many do still remain under this broken covenant of works. As for those who never heard of, nor had the offer of the covenant of grace, we need not inquire much. The case is plain; they know no other way. But men to whom the covenant of grace is proclaimed, and yet remain under the covenant of works; they will still hang on about Sinai for all the thunders and lightnings there, and will not come to Sion. The following reasons of this conduct may be given.

1. The covenant of works is natural to men, being made with Adam, and us in his loins: it is ingrained in the hearts of all men naturally. *Tell me*, says the apostle, Gal. iv. 21. *ye that desire to be under the law, do ye not hear the law?* And there are impressions of it to be found on the hearts of all, among the ruins of the fall. The law as a covenant of works was the first husband that human nature was wedded to; and so it is natural to men to cleave to it. And we have a clear proof of it,

(1.) In men left to the swing of their own nature; they all go this way in their dealing with God for life and favour. Look abroad into the world, and behold the vast multitudes embracing Paganism, Judaism, Mahometism, and Popery. All these agree in this, That it is by doing man must live, though they hugely differ in the things that are to be done for life. Look into the Protestant churches, and you shall see readily, that the more corrupt any of them are, the more they incline to the way of this covenant.

covenant. Confider perfons among us ignorant of the principles of true religion, who, not having received inftruction, fpeak of the way of life and falvation as nature prompts them, and you fhall find them alfo of the fame mind. Finally, confider all unrenewed men whatfoever, having the knowledge, and making profeffion of the expectation of life and falvation in the way of the covenant of grace; yet they in practice ftumble at this ftumblingftone, Matth. v. 3.

(2.) In men awakened and convinced, and in moral ferioufnefs feeking to know what courfe they fhall take to be faved, and plying their work for that end. They all take this principle for granted, That it is by doing they muft obtain life and falvation, Matth. xix. 16. *Good Mafter, what good thing fhall I do, that I may have eternal life?* Luke x. 25. *Mafter, what fhall I do to inherit eternal life?* And this prevails when they are pricked to the very heart, and the law as the covenant of works has wounded them to the very foul. They never think of a divorce from the law, that they may be married to Chrift; but how they fhall do to pleafe the old hufband, and fo be faved from wrath; as appears in the cafe of Peter's hearers, Acts ii. 37. when they faid, *Men and brethren, what fhall we do?* and the Philippian jailor, Acts xvi. 30. when he faid, *Sirs, what muft I do to be faved?*

(3.) In the faints, who are truly married to Jefus Chrift. O what hankering after the firft hufband! how great the remains of a legal fpirit? how hard is it for them to forget their father's houfe, Pfal. xlv. 10.? Adam having embraced the promife of the Meffiah, yet was in hazard of running back to this covenant. There is a difpofition to deal with God, in the way of giving fo much duty, for fo much grace and favour with God, in the beft, that they have continually to ftrive with. Self-denial is one of the moft difficult leffons in Chriftianity.

2. The way of that covenant is moft agreeable to the pride of man's heart. A proud heart will rather ferve itfelf with the lefs, than ftoop to live upon free grace, Rom. x. 3. Man muft be broken, bruifed, and humbled, and laid very low, before he will embrace the covenant of grace. While a broken board of the firft covenant will do them

them any service, they will hold by it, rather than come to Christ; like men who will rather live in a cottage of their own, than in another man's castle. To renounce all our own wisdom, works, and righteousness, and to cast away all these garments as filthy rags, which we have been at so much pains to patch up, is quite against the grain with corrupt nature, Rom. vii. 4.

3. It is most agreeable to man's reason in its corrupt state. If one should have asked the opinion of the philosophers, concerning that religion which taught salvation by a crucified Christ, and through the righteousness of another; they would have said, it was unreasonable and foolish, and that the only way to true happiness was the way of moral virtue. The Jewish Rabbi's would have declared it *scandalous*, 1 Cor. i. 23. Gr.; and would have maintained the only way to eternal life to be by the law of Moses. To this day many learned men cannot see the reasonableness of the gospel-method of salvation, in opposition to the way of the covenant of works: and therefore our godly forefathers who reformed from Popery, and maintained the reformed truth against Popery by their heroic zealous wrestlings even unto blood, while they shewed that acquaintance with practical godliness and real holiness, whereof there is little in our day, are in effect looked upon as a parcel of well-meaning simple men, whose doctrine must be reformed over again, and rendered more agreeable to reason. A rational religion is like to be the plague of this day. But assure ye yourselves, that where ever the gospel comes in power, it will make the reason of the wisest sit down at its feet, and learn, and give over its questions formed by Hows and Whys, 2 Cor. x. 5. *Casting down imaginations, and every high thing that exalteth itself against the knowledge of God, and bringing into captivity every thought to the obedience of Christ.*

Even unlearned and simple men, in whom this appears less, because they do not enter deep into the thought, will be found sick of the same disease, when once they are thoroughly awakened, and take these matters to heart. How will they dispute against the gospel-method of salvation, against the promise, against their believing their
welcome

welcome to Christ, who are so sinful and unworthy! The matter appears so great, as indeed it is, that they look on the gospel-method as a dream, and they cannot believe it.

4. Ignorance and insensibleness of the true state of that matter, as it now is. There is a thick darkness about mount Sinai, through the whole dominion of the law; so that they who live under the covenant of works, see little but what they see by the lightnings now and then flashing out. Hence they little know where they are, nor what they are.

(1.) They do not understand the nature of that covenant to purpose, Gal. iv. 21. Any notion they have of it is lame and weak, without efficacy. They see not how forcibly it binds to perfect obedience and satisfaction, how rigorous it is in its demands, and will abate nothing, though a man should do to the utmost of his power, and with cries and tears of blood seek forgiveness for the rest. They are not acquainted with the spirituality of the law, and the vast compass of the holy commandment, but stick too much in the letter of it. Hence they are *alive without the law*, Rom. vii. 9. They narrow the demands of it, that so they may be the more likely to fulfil them.

(2.) They are not duly sensible of their own utter inability for that way of salvation: John v. 45.—*There is one that accuseth you, even Moses, in whom ye trust.* They know they are off the way, and that they have wandered from God; but they hope they will get back to him again by repentance; while in the mean time, their heart is a heart of stone, and they cannot change it; and *the Ethiopian shall* be able as soon to *change his skin, or the leopard his spots, as they may do good, that are accustomed to do evil,* Jer. xiii. 23.; and there is no coming to God but by Christ, John xiv. 6. They know they have sinned, and provoked justice against them: but they hope to be sorry for their sin, to pray to God for forgiveness, and bear any thing patiently that God lays on them; while in the mean time they see not, that none of these things will satisfy God's justice, which yet will have full satisfaction for every the least sin of theirs, ere they see heaven. They know they must be holy: but they hope to serve God better than ever they have done; while in the mean time they

they confider not, that their work-arm is broken, and they can work none to purpofe till they be faved by grace.

Application of the doctrine, that there are many ſtill under the broken covenant of works.

This doctrine may be applied for *information* and *exhortation*.

Use I. of *information*. Hence learn,

1. That fome, yea many of mankind are under the curfe, bound over to wrath. For that is the cafe of all under that covenant. Their necks are under a heavy yoke; they are liable in payment of a penalty, which they will never be able to difcharge, and to put off their heads. They may pay more or lefs of it, in this world; but if they get not rid of it another way, it will not be paid out through all the ages of eternity.

2. See here whence it is that true holinefs is fo rare, and wickednefs and ungodlinefs fo rife in the world. Moſt men are under that covenant, under which fin and death reign; and there is no holinefs, no good works under it, Rom. vi. 14. It has, being broken, barred communion betwixt God and finners under it; and therefore of neceffity there muſt be a pining away in iniquity while one is under it. It is only in the way of the fecond covenant that fanctifying influences are had.

3. Here ye may fee the true fpring of legalifm in principles as well as in practice. Many are really under that covenant; no wonder then there be many to fet up for that way. It is the way that backfliding churches in all ages have gone. It foon began in the primitive apoſtolical churches; and that myſtery of iniquity wrought till it iffued in Popery, the grand apoſtafy under the New Teſtament.

4. See whence it is that the doctrine of the gofpel is fo little underſtood, and in the purity of it is looked at as a ſtrange thing. It is like other things which are not known in the country that one is bred in, and therefore ſtared at, and often miſtaken. Hence it gets ill names in the world. When Chriſt himſelf preached it, he was called a
friend

friend of publicans and sinners; when Paul preached it, they would not believe but he made void the law by it, and that he opened a door for licentiousness of life, Rom. iii 8.

USE II. Be *exhorted* then seriously and impartially to try what covenant ye are under. It is true, there is a covenant of grace made, proclaimed and offered unto you, and ye are all under the outward dispensation of the covenant of grace: but yet many are notwithstanding really under the covenant of works still. As ye love your own souls, try impartially, whether ye be under it, or not, but under the covenant of grace. For motives, consider,

Mot. 1. Ye are all born under the covenant of works, being *by nature children of wrath*, Eph. ii. 3. It is in the region of the law, that we all draw our first breath. And no man will get out from its dominion in a morning-dream. We owe it to our second birth, whoever of us are brought into the bond of the covenant of grace; but that is not our original state. The law is the first husband to all and every one of Adam's children. I would have you try whether ye be dead to it, and divorced from it, or not.

Mot. 2. Till once ye see yourselves under the covenant of works, and so lost and ruined with the burden of that broken covenant on you; ye may hear of the covenant of grace, but ye will never take hold of it in good earnest, Gal. ii. 16. Here lies the ruin of the most part who hear the gospel; they were never slain by the law, and therefore never quickened by the gospel; they never find the working of the deadly poison conveyed to them from the first Adam, and therefore they see no beauty in the second Adam for which he is to be desired.

Mot. 3. Your salvation or ruin turns on this point, What covenant ye are under. If thou be within the bond of the covenant of grace, thou art in a state of salvation: *He that believeth, shall be saved*, Mark xvi. 16. David could say, *God hath made with me an everlasting covenant, ordered in all things and sure: for this is all my salvation*, 2 Sam. xxiii. 5. If thou art under the covenant of works, thou art in a state of death: for, says the text, *as many as are of the works of the law, are under the curse*. And is this

this so light and trivial a matter, as that thou shouldst be unconcerned which of these covenants thou art under?

Mot. 4. There is no ease for a poor sinner, but severity and rigour, under the covenant of works. One may easily see that we are not able to abide that now, when we are become weak and guilty: Psal. cxxx. 3. says the psalmist, *If thou, Lord, shouldst mark iniquities; O Lord, who shall stand?* But while thou remainest under the first covenant, thou canst expect no mitigation or favour. There is no pardon under that covenant; the law-statute is, *In the day that thou eatest thereof, thou shalt surely die,* Gen. ii. 17. The sinner must die the death. That ever we heard of pardon, is owing to the second covenant, which secures pardoning mercy to those who come under the bond of it: For *by him* [viz. Christ] *all that believe are justified from all things, from which they could not be justified by the law of Moses,* Acts xiii. 39. Though there is no question but the covenant of works requires repentance, a turning to God under pain of the curse; yet there is no grace for helping the sinner to it, under this covenant; and suppose one could win at it, it could not help him. There is no accepting the will for the deed under it. It is not good will, but perfectly good works that will satisfy it.

Mot. 5. While ye are under that covenant, ye are *without Christ,* Eph. ii. 12. As a woman cannot, by the law of God, be married to two husbands at once; so one cannot be under the covenant of works, and married to Christ, at once. The first marriage to the law must be dissolved by death or divorce, ere the soul can be married to Christ, Rom. vii. 4. And being without Christ, ye have no saving interest in his purchase.

Lastly, All attempts you make to get to heaven, while under this covenant, will be vain. The children of that covenant are, by an unalterable statute of the court of heaven, excluded from the heavenly inheritance: so that do what you will, while ye abide under it, you may as well fall a-ploughing the rocks, and sowing your seed in the sand of the sea, as think to get to heaven that way: For *what saith the scripture? Cast out the bond-woman and her son: for the son of the bond-woman shall not be heir*

with

with the son of the free-woman, Gal. iv. 30. The way to heaven by that covenant is blocked up to sinners; the angel with the flaming sword guards the tree of life, so that there is no accefs to falvation that way, but under a condition impoffible for you to perform.

Now, to set this matter in a due light to you, I will,

1. Give fome marks and characters of thofe that are under this covenant.

2. Difcover the vanity of fome pleas that fuch have, to prove that it is not to their own works they truft for falvation, but to Chrift.

FIRST, I will give fome marks and characters of thofe that are under this covenant.

Firft, They have never yet parted with the law, or covenant of works, lawfully, which all the faints have done. There are two ways of parting with that covenant. One is by running away from it; and thus we may apply to this cafe, Nabal's tale concerning David, 1 Sam. xxv. 10. *There be many fervants now-a-days that break away every man from his mafter.* They break its bonds, and caft away its cords, value neither its commands nor threats; for they look on it like an almanack out of date, as a thing that they are not concerned with. This is no lawful parting, and therefore it cannot diffolve the relation betwixt them and it. A fervant or a wife that is run away, is a fervant or a wife for all that ftill. And the mafter can bring back the one, and make him ferve or fuffer; and the hufband the other. And fo will this covenant deal with fuch, and make them fenfible they are under it ftill, in the ftraiteft bonds. It will take them by the throat here or hereafter, faying, *Pay what thou oweft.*

The other is a parting with it, after fair count and reckoning with it, and payment inftructed; a parting with it upon a divorce obtained, after a fair hearing given it before the Judge of all the earth. It is brought about in this manner. There is a fummons given at the inftance of the law or covenant of works, to the confcience of the fecure finner, to compear before the tribunal of God. Hereby the confcience being awakened, it compears and ftands trembling at the bar: in the mean time the King's Son offers himfelf in a marriage-covenant to the guilty foul,

with

with his righteousness, obedience, and satisfaction. The law appears and pleads,

1. So much and so much owing by the sinner, for his breaking of its commands. Mountains of guilt appear, innumerable items in its accounts; and the charge must be owned just, for it is just, in every particular. Here the sinner betaking himself to Christ, pleads by faith the satisfaction of Christ for him; and embracing the gospel-offers, he sets betwixt him and the law, the death and sufferings of Christ as full payment of that debt.

2. So much to be done before the sinner can be saved, according to the condition of the covenant, perfect obedience owing to it by all the children of Adam. The sinner cannot deny the debt; but pleads by faith the Mediator's payment of it, by his obedience even to the death. He counts up on this score unto the law, all that Christ the Son of God did for the space of about thirty-three years on the earth, in the perfect obedience of all its commands.

Thus the sinner embracing Christ, has wherewith to answer it. And the plea of payment that way is sustained, and the soul is declared free from the law or covenant of works, and so lawfully parted from it. What experience have ye of this? This will for the substance of it pass in every soul freed from the covenant of works. But alas! how many are there, (1.) Who were never troubled about that, how to get a discharge of that bargain, from the Judge of all the earth, but have lived at ease without it? (2.) Who never saw a necessity of reckoning with the law, in order to their getting clear of it? (3.) Who have still aimed at putting off the demands of the law, with their own obedience and suffering, such as they were?

Secondly, They are of a legal spirit, and have not the Spirit of the covenant of grace. Caleb and Joshua had another spirit than the rest of the spies; so have those who are within the bond of the covenant of grace, Gal. iv. 24. In the saints indeed there are wretched remains of that spirit, but it does not reign in them as in others.

1. They are of a slavish spirit, who are under that covenant; whereas the saints are acted by a son-like spirit. *For,* says the apostle, Rom. viii 15. *ye have not received the spirit of bondage again to fear; but ye have received the*

the Spirit of adoption, whereby we cry, Abba, Father. As the slave is moved with fear, not with love; so is it with them. This slavish spirit appears in them thus.

(1.) They are driven from sin, and to their duty, by the fear of hell and wrath, rather than drawn from the one to the other, by any hatred of the one and love of the other, in themselves; like the Israelites of old, of whom it is said, Psal. lxxviii. 34. *When he slew them, then they sought him: and they returned and inquired early after God.* It is the influence of the covenant of works in its terrible sanction, that moves them. Take away that, secure them but from hell and damnation, and they would give themselves the swing in their lusts; they have no other kind of principle to move them to holiness; all is selfish about them.

(2.) They content themselves with the bare performance of duty, and abstaining from any sin, without regarding the true principle, end, and manner of doing: even as the slave who is concerned for no more, but to get his task over, Is. xxix. 13. It is not their business to get their hearts wrought up to the love of God, concern for his glory, and to the doing of their work in faith; but to get the work done, Luke xviii. 11. It may be they dare not neglect duty, but it is not their concern to find Christ in duty, nor is it their grief if they do not find him.

(3.) Under terror of conscience, they do not flee to the blood of Christ, but to their work again, to amend what was done amiss, or make it up by greater diligence, Acts ii. 37. Are not the consciences of men under that covenant affrighted sometimes? But consider how they are pacified again. Not by the sprinkling of Christ's blood on them by faith, Heb. ix. 14. but by resolves to do better in time to come, by prayers, mourning, &c. And hence it is that their corruptions are never weakened for all this, for the law makes nothing perfect; but the believing application of the blood of Christ not only takes away guilt, but strengthens the soul.

2. They are of a mercenary spirit; they are acted by the spirit of a hireling, who works that he may win his wages. The covenant of works is so natural to us, that
we

we naturally know no other religion, but to work and win, do good works that we may win heaven by them. Hence the prodigal would be put among the hired servants, when he thought of returning: but when he returned, he insists not on that. This spirit appears in those under the covenant of works, thus.

(1.) Their work is for reward, to obtain God's favour and salvation by their works, Rom. x. 3. Whereas the saints look for salvation and the favour of God only through the obedience and death of Jesus Christ, Tit. iii. 5. *Not by works of righteousness, which we have done, but according to his mercy he saved us.* I own the saints may have an eye to the gratuitous reward promised to them, to crown their work and labour of love, as Moses is said to have *had respect unto the recompense of the reward,* Heb. xi. 26.; and they may be thereby influenced in their duty. But then they look for that reward as coming to them, not for the sake of their work, but for the sake of Christ's work. They are sons, and have a more noble principle of obedience to God, Heb. vi. 10. as God's own children, Rom. viii. 15. who having the inheritance secured to them another way than by their working, are prompted to obedience by their love to God, and desire to please him. The truth is, those under the broken covenant of works, being destitute of saving faith, are void also of true love to God, 1 Tim. i. 5. It is themselves mainly, if not only, that they seek in their duties: and were it not the hope of gain to themselves by them, they would not regard them. In a word, they serve God, not out of any kindly love to him, but that thereby they may serve themselves.

(2.) The more they do, and the better they do, they look on God to be the more in their debt; like Micah, who said, *Now know I that the Lord will do me good, seeing I have a Levite to my priest,* Judg. xvii. 13. For it is according to their own doing, not according to the interest in Christ's blood, that they expect favour from the Lord. The publican, Luke xviii. 13. pleads mercy through a propitiation, *Be propitious to me,* according to the Greek; but the Pharisee pleads upon what himself had done more than many others, ver. 11, 12. *God, I thank thee,* says he, *that*

I

I am not as other men are, extortioners, unjust, adulterers, or even as this publican. I fast twice in the week, I give tithes of all that I possess. Hence their hearts rise against God, if they find not their works regarded and rewarded, according to the value themselves put upon them; like the Jews of old, who said, *Wherefore have we fasted, and thou seest not? wherefore have we afflicted our soul, and thou takest no knowledge?* If. lviii. 3. Hence ariseth a very considerable difference betwixt the children of the two covenants: Those of the first covenant, the better they do their duty, their hearts are the more filled with conceit of themselves, their duties like wind puff them up, as in the case of the Pharisee, Luke xviii. 11. just now cited. But those of the second covenant, the better they do, they are the more humble, and low in their own eyes; as David, 1 Chron. xxix. 14. *Who am I, and what is my people, that we should be able to offer so willingly after this sort? for all things come of thee, and of thine own have we given thee:* and Paul, 2 Cor. xii. 11. *In nothing am I behind the very chiefest apostles, though I be nothing.*

(3.) Their duties make them more easy and secure in some one sin or other; like the adulterous woman, Prov. vii. 14. 15. *I have peace-offerings with me; this day have I paid my vows. Therefore came I forth to meet thee, diligently to seek thy face, and I have found thee.* The Jews, as profane as they were in Isaiah's time, brought a multitude of sacrifices to God's altar, If. i. 11. Why did they do so, but because they expected that these would make all odds even betwixt God and them? Just so do many with their duties; they pray to God, and do many good things: so they can with the more ease do and say many ill things. By their duties they seem to themselves as it were to pay the old, and they can the more freely take on the new. Thus they *bless God, and curse men, with the same tongue. Out of the same mouth proceedeth blessing and cursing*, Jam. iii. 9. 10. They use their duties for an occasion to the flesh, and turn the grace of God into lasciviousness; than which there cannot be a more speaking evidence of one under the broken covenant of works. Publicans and harlots will enter into the kingdom of heaven before such persons.

Thus you have some characters of those who are under this covenant, and may perceive that they deal with God in the matter of his favour and salvation in the way of that covenant, and not in the way of the covenant of grace. But it is hard to convince men of this: therefore,

SECONDLY, I will discover the vanity of some pleas that such have, to prove that it is not to their own works they trust for salvation, but to Christ.

1. They are so far, say they, from trusting to their own works in this matter, that they really wonder how any body can do it. I answer, That this is rather a sign of the ignorance of the corruption of man's nature, and unacquaintedness with the deceitfulness of your own heart, than of your freedom from that corrupt way of dealing with God. Hazael said so in another case, *Am I a dog to do this thing?* Yet was he such a dog as to do it. Ye know not, it seems, what spirits ye are of. That way of dealing with God, is as natural to us, as to fishes to swim in the sea, and birds to fly in the air. The godly themselves are not quite free from it; the disciples needed that lesson, *When ye shall have done all those things which are commanded you, say, We are unprofitable servants: we have done that which was our duty to do,* Luke xvii. 10. They are too apt to think much of any little they do; like Peter, *Behold, we have forsaken all,* said he, *and followed thee; what shall we have therefore?* Matth. xix. 27. The difference then lies here: The godly feel this corrupt bias of their hearts, they wrestle against it, loathe themselves for it, and would fain be rid of it; whereas it reigns in others, and has quiet possession.

2. This is rank Popery, and they are true Protestants, believing that we are not saved for our works, but for the sake of Christ. *Answer.* It is indeed the very life and soul of Popery. But what is Popery, but the product of man's corrupt nature framing a way of salvation, according to the covenant of works? So even Protestants have Popish hearts, by nature. A floating principle in the head, received by means of education, or other external teaching, will never be able to change the natural bent of the heart: it is the teaching of the Spirit, with power, which only can do that. It is an article of the profane

Protestant's

Protestant's religion, That there is a heaven and a hell: yet they live, as if there were neither of them.—That the grace of God teacheth to deny ungodliness, and worldly lusts, and to live soberly, righteously, and godly in this present world: yet their life and practice is as far from this principle, as the east is distant from the west. Men do not always live according to their professed principles: therefore, in this point, the head may look one way, and the heart another.

3. They are persuaded, that of themselves, without the grace of God, they can do nothing; that there is no strength in them. *Answer*. Many have this in their mouths, who never to this day were let into a view of their own utter inability to help themselves. They take up that principle, rather to be a cover to their sloth, and a pretence to shift duty; than out of any conviction of the truth of it, in their own souls. Hence none are readier to delay, and put off salvation-work from time to time, than they; as if they could really do all, and that at any time. But whatever be of that, this is an insignificant plea: the proud Pharisee might have pleaded that as well as you, and yet he stood upon his works with God, Luke xviii. 11. The matter lies here; they profess they can do nothing without the help of grace; but when by the help of grace they have done their duty, they think God cannot but save them, who so serve him; as if God's grace helped men to purchase their own salvation.

4. They are convinced that they cannot keep the law perfectly, but when they have done all they can, they look to Christ to supply all wherein they come short. *Answer*. The truth is, no body is so far from doing all they can, as such men are who pretend most to it: there are many things they never do, which yet are within the compass of their natural powers. But the Pharisees, who, no body doubts, dealt with God in this way of works, were convinced as well as you, that they did not keep the law perfectly; but then the ceremonial law afforded them a salve, in their apprehension, for their defects in the duties of the moral law. Just so is the case in this plea; where the deceit lies, in that the man lays not the whole stress of his acceptance with God, and his salvation, on

the obedience and death of Chrift; but partly on his own works, partly on Chrift; thus mixing his own righteoufnefs with Chrift's, which the apoftle rejects, Gal. iii. 12. *The law is not of faith: but, The man that doth them, shall live in them.* Chap. v. 4 *Chrift is become of no effect unto you, whofoever of you are juftified by the law; ye are fallen from grace.*

5. *Laftly,* They truft in Chrift for the acceptance of all their duties, and are perfuaded they would never be accepted but for Chrift's fake. *Anfwer.* Men may do this, and yet ftill keep the way of the covenant of works. Being perfuaded that the beft of their duties are not without fome imperfection, they look to get them accepted as they are for Chrift's fake, fo as God will thereupon juftify and fave them, give them his favour, pardon their fin, keep them out of hell, and give them heaven. Thus they make ufe of Chrift, for obtaining falvation by their own works, juft as fome Papifts teach, that our works merit by virtue of the merit of Chrift; and that they merit not, but as they are dipt in his blood. But the way of the fecond covenant is to look to Chrift alone, for the acceptance of our perfons, to juftification and falvation; and then our perfons being accepted, to look to him alfo for the acceptance of our works, not in point of juftification, but of fanctification only. This was Paul's way, Phil. iii. 8. 9. *Yea doubtlefs, and I count all things but lofs, for the excellency of the knowledge of Chrift Jefus my Lord: for whom I have fuffered the lofs of all things, and do count them but dung that I may win Chrift, and be found in him, not having mine own righteoufnefs, which is of the law, but that which is through the faith of Chrift, the righteoufnefs which is of God by faith.*

O deal impartially with yourfelves in this matter, and be not too eafy in this important point. The heart of man is a depth of deceit: and if you are not exercifed to root up this weed of legality, and have felt the difficulty of fo doing; it is a fhrewd fign ye are yet under the covenant of works; the mifery of which condition I am now to open up to you, in the fecond doctrine from the text.

DOCT. II.

DOCT. II.

Man in his natural state, being under the broken covenant of works, is under the curse.

Here is the case in which Adam left all his children, the case of all by nature. Behold here as in a glass the doleful condition of sinners by the breach of the first covenant, they are *under the curse.* I shall consider this dreadful condition,

I. More generally.
II. More particularly.
III. *Lastly,* Apply the subject.

A general view of mens dreadful condition under the curse.

I. I shall consider the dreadful condition in which men in their natural state are, under the curse, more generally. And here let us consider,
1. What that curse is which they are under.
2. What it is to be under the curse.
3. Confirm the doctrine, That man in his natural state, being under the broken covenant of works, is under the curse.

What the CURSE *is which natural men are under.*

FIRST, I shall consider what that *curse* is which men in their natural state are under. It is the sentence of the law as a covenant of works, binding over and devoting the sinner to destruction. Thus the covenant being made with the awful sanction of death, Gen. ii. 17. upon the transgressing of it, the curse is pronounced, Gen. iii. And so it is,

First, GOD's curse, as the sinner's Lawgiver and Judge; it is his sentence of death against the transgressor, the doom pronounced by him on the malefactor, that has not continued in all things which are written in the book of the law to do them. It is expresly called *the curse of the Lord,* Prov. iii. 33. and those under it, *the people of his curse,* Is. xxxiv. 5. Man's curse is often causeless, so it miscarries, it comes not, it does no more harm than

a

a bird flying over one's head, Prov. xxvi. 2. But God's curse is ever on a valid weighty cause, so his justice requires; and it cannot miss, by reason of his truth, to come, and lie heavy where it doth come, by reason of his almighty power, John iii. 36.

Secondly, It is the curse of the *law*, Gal. iii. 13. the curse of the broken covenant of works, whose penalty is death. So it runs in our text, *Cursed is every one that continueth not in all things which are written in the book of the law to do them.* The law is armed with a curse against the disobedient, and therefore when obedience is not performed, it is poured out, Dan. ix. 11. Of old when men entered into a covenant, they cut a beast in twain, and passed betwixt the parts, to signify the curse on the breaker, that he should be like that beast. Hence the Lord threatens covenant-breakers, Jer. xxxiv. 18. *And I will give the men that have transgressed my covenant, which have not performed the words of the covenant which they had made before me, when they cut the calf in twain, and passed between the parts thereof,* &c. Compare Matth. xxiv. ult. *And shall cut him asunder, and appoint him his portion with the hypocrites,* &c. As for the curse of the gospel, as the scripture mentions no such thing, it is needless; the law secures the curse, and a double curse on those who despise the gospel.

Now, in this curse there are these three things to be considered.

1. The revenging wrath of God is in it, Matth. xxv. 41. *Depart from me, ye cursed, into everlasting fire, prepared for the devil and his angels.* It is the breathing of fiery indignation by vindictive justice against the sinner. Sin is so opposite to the nature of God, that he cannot endure it; but his wrath (may I say it with reverence) takes fire against the sinner, at the very sight of it, and makes the curse to fly against him. See this awfully represented, Deut. xxix. 20. *The anger of the Lord, and his jealousy shall smoke against that man, and all the curses that are written in this book shall lie upon him.*

2. A binding over of the sinner unto punishment for the satisfaction of offended justice, Gal. iii. 13. As the judge, by his sentence of death, binds over the criminal

to death; fo God, by his curfe, binds over the finner unto death in its whole compafs, as in the threatening of the covenant of works. Thus he is bound to fuffer till juftice is fatisfied, which being without the finner's reach, the punifhment comes to be eternal. It is not a punifhment for the amendment of the party, as under the covenant of grace; but for reparation of the honour of the Lawgiver and law.

3. A feparating of the finner unto deftruction, though not of his being, yet of his well-being, Deut. xxix. 21. *And the Lord fhall feparate him unto evil,—according to all the curfes of the covenant, that are written in this book of the law.* Hereby the finner is exterminated and excommunicated from the fociety of God's favourites, and fet up as a mark for the arrows of wrath. As accurfed things were to be deftroyed, and not kept for ufe; fo the curfe on the finner is a devoting of him to deftruction, as a veffel of wrath, in which juftice may be glorified, 2 Theff. i. 9. *Who fhall be punifhed with everlafting deftruction from the prefence of the Lord, and from the glory of his power.*

What it is to be under the curfe.

SECONDLY, Let us confider what it is to be *under* the curfe. Man in his natural ftate, being under the broken covenant of works, is under the curfe; and fo,

1. He is under the wrath of God; *a child of wrath by nature,* Eph. ii. 3. *The wrath of God abideth on him,* John iii. 36. God is difpleafed with him; he is not, and cannot be pleafed with him; *Without faith it is impoffible to pleafe God,* Heb. xi. 6. God is ever angry with him, Pfal. vii. 11. angry with him *every day,* however he fpend the day, better or worfe. He cannot endure the fight of him; *The foolifh fhall not ftand in thy fight,* Pfal. v. 5. That black cloud of the wrath of God, is over his head from the moment of his being a living foul, and all along, during his continuance in his natural ftate, under the broken covenant of works. He may be well pleafed with himfelf, and others may be fo too, faints as well as finners; but God is ftill wroth with him.

2. He is bound over to revenging juftice. It has him by

by the throat, saying, *Pay what thou owest;* though perhaps he neither feels the gripe, nor hears the terrible demand, because his conscience is asleep, and all his spiritual senses are fast bound up: Rom. iii. 19. *Now we know* (says the apostle) *that what things soever the law saith, it saith to them who are under the law: that every mouth may be stopped, and all the world may become guilty before God; guilty* (Gr. compare Acts xxviii. 4.), that is, under revenging justice. The holiness of God gave out the holy commandment in the covenant, justice annexed the threatening of death to the breach of it, truth secures the accomplishment of the threatening, and so lays the sinner *under justice,* without relief. So that there is no parting of them, till the utmost farthing be paid (2 Thess. i. 9. Gr.) by the sinner himself, or a cautioner.

3. He stands as a mark for the arrows of vengeance; he is a devoted man in law, tied to the stake, that the law and justice of God may disburden all their arrows into him, and that in him may meet all the plagues flowing from avenging wrath: *If he turn not,* says the psalmist, *he* [God] *will whet his sword; he hath bent his bow, and made it ready. He hath also prepared for him the instruments of death; he ordaineth his arrows against the persecutors,* Psal. vii. 12. 13. Job complains that he was set as a mark for God's arrows, Job xvi. 12. 13.; but natural men have better reason for that complaint. They are in law devoted heads, on which the law has laid its hand as on the head of a sacrifice, as a signal for cutting off; Psal. xciv. *ult. He shall bring upon them their own iniquity, and shall cut them off in their own wickedness; yea, the Lord our God shall cut them off.* Psal. xxxvii. 22. *They that be cursed of him, shall be cut off.*

O, if men did believe this to be their condition under the broken covenant of works, what rest could they possibly have while in that state? How would they anxiously inquire, what way they might be discharged from that broken bargain? But alas! as the unbelief of the threatening was the cause of the desperate adventure to break the covenant; so the unbelief of the curse following thereupon, is the cause why they are easy under it. Therefore I shall next confirm the truth of the doctrine.

That

That man, being under the broken covenant of works, is under the curse.

THIRDLY, I am to confirm the doctrine, That man in his natural state, being under the broken covenant of works, is under the curse.

1. This is evident from plain scripture-testimony. Our text is express. Therein it is proven from the records of the court of heaven, as to this process; *It is written, Cursed is every one that continueth not in all things which are written in the book of the law to do them.* This sentence is extracted out of Deut. xxvii. 26. *Cursed be he that confirmeth not all the words of this law to do them.* And the apostle plainly designs the persons against whom it is passed, namely, those that are *under the law*, Rom. iii. 19. compared with chap. vi. 14. Who then can make any doubt of it? It is as firm as the truth of God can make it, in his word, and under his hand and seal.

2. It is evident from the consideration of the justice of God, as supreme Rector and Judge of the world; by which he cannot but do right, and give sin its due. Two things will clear this.

1st, The breaking of that covenant, whereof all under it are guilty, deserves the curse. They broke it in Adam, and they are breaking it every day; and so they deserve the curse. Now, sin's deserving of the curse, doth not arise from the threatening of eternal wrath annexed for a sanction to the commands in the law, as our new divinity would have it; that is framed for bringing believers under the curse of the law too. But it ariseth from sin's contrariety to the command of the holy law; for it is manifest, that sin does not therefore deserve a curse, because a curse is threatened against it; but because it deserves a curse, therefore a curse is threatened.

Now look at sin in the glass of the holy commandment, and you will see it deserves the curse. For the commandment is,

(1.) An image of the sovereign God's spotless holiness; *The law is holy; and the commandment holy,* Rom. vii. 12. When God would let out the beams of his own holiness to man, he gave him the law of the ten commandments, as a tranfcript of it, and wrote them in his heart; and afterwards, the writing being much defaced, he wrote them to him in his word. So the commandment is holy without fpot, as God is. So that the creature rifing up againft the commandment, rifeth up againft God.

(2.) It is an image of his righteoufnefs and equity, whereby he does juftly to all; *The commandment is—juft*, Rom. vii. 12. The commandment is all right in every part, and of perpetual equity: *I efteem all thy precepts concerning all things to be right*, Pfal. cxix. 128. Look to it as it prefcribes our duty to God, to our neighbour, and to ourfelves, Tit. ii. 12. it is of fpotlefs and perfect righteoufnefs, as that God is, whofe righteous nature and will it reprefents to us.

(3.) It is an image of his goodnefs; *The commandment is—good*, Rom. vii. 12. It is all lovely, lovely in every part; lovely in itfelf, and in the eyes of all who are capable to difcern truly, what is good and what evil, Pfal. cxix. 97. *O how love I thy law!* Conformity to it is the perfection of the creature, and its true happinefs, as rendering the creature like unto God, 1 John iii. 2.

Thus the breaking of the covenant, by doing contrary to the holy commandment, is the tranfgreffing of the holy, juft, and good will of our Sovereign Lord; a defacing of, and doing violence to his image, who is the chief good and infinite good. Therefore fin is the chief or greateft evil, and confequently deferves the curfe.

2*dly*, Since it deferves the curfe, the juftice of God, which gives every thing its due, enfures the curfe upon it, Gen. xviii. 25. *Shall not the Judge of all the earth do right?* 2 Theff. i. 6. *It is a righteous thing with God to recompenfe tribulation to them that trouble you.* If fin did not lay the finner under the curfe, how would the rectoral juftice of God appear? He will rain a terrible ftorm on the wicked, not becaufe he delights in the death of the finner, but becaufe he *loves righteoufnefs*, Pfal. xi. 6. 7. and his righteoufnefs requires it.

3. It appears from the threatening of the covenant, Gen. ii. 17. *In the day that thou eateft thereof, thou fhalt furely die.* That threatening being a threatening of death

in its whole extent, enſures the curſe on the ſinner whenever he tranſgreſſeth the command. And the truth of God requires that it take effect, and be not like words ſpoken to the wind. Here is the caſe then, man came under the covenant of works, wherein death was threatened in caſe of tranſgreſſion: now the covenant is broken. It behoved then of neceſſity, that that moment man ſinned, he ſhould be bound over to the revenging wrath of God, or fall under the curſe. And in that caſe all natural men lie. And thus the ſentence of the law paſſeth immediately on ſinning, Gal. iii. 10. *Curſed is every one that continueth not*, &c. in the preſent time; agreeable to the tenor of the threatening, *In the day that thou eateſt thereof, thou ſhalt ſurely die.*

4. If man had once run the courſe of his obedience, being come to the laſt point of it, he behoved to have been juſtified and adjudged to eternal life, according to the tenor of the covenant, *That the man which doth thoſe things, ſhall live by them*, Rom. x. 5.; the ſentence of the law would immediately have paſſed in his favour, according to the promiſe. And therefore man having once broken the covenant, falls under the curſe, and is adjudged to eternal death: for the curſe bears the ſame relation to the threatening, that law-juſtification bears to the promiſe. Hence it is that the unbeliever is declared to be *condemned already*, John iii. 18.

5. *Laſtly*, Chriſt's being made a curſe for ſinners, is a clear evidence of ſinners their being naturally under the curſe, Gal. iii. 13. *Chriſt hath redeemed us from the curſe of the law, being made a curſe for us.* He took their place in the broken covenant of works, Gal. iv. 4. 5. that bearing the curſe due to them, they might be ſet free upon their union with him. Hence they who by faith are united to Chriſt, having his ſatisfaction imputed to them, are delivered from the curſe, as borne for them, and away from them, by their Surety: but all others remain under it, as not being reputed to have ſatisfied it.

Thus far in the general, concerning this dreadful condition. But,

II. We

II. We must take a more particular view of the dreadful condition of the natural man, under the curse of the broken covenant of works. And here opens the most terrible scene, that men are capable of beholding, in time or in eternity. Happy they who timely behold it so, as to be thereby stirred up to flee to Christ. It comprehends both the sinfulness and the misery of a natural state, the curse being the chain by which the sinner is bound over to death in its full latitude, as it stands in the threatening of the covenant, Gen. ii. 17. and by which he is staked down under that death. And we shall take a view of this the natural man's condition, by the breach of the covenant of works, *in this life*, and *after this life*.

The condition of the natural man under the curse,
IN THIS LIFE.

FIRST, The natural man's condition under the curse of the broken covenant, is very terrible in that part of it, which takes place *in this life*. The execution of the curse is not quite delayed to another world: it is begun in this life, carried further on at death, and full and final execution comes at the last day. As to that part of this condition which takes place in this life, we shall have the more distinct view of it, if we take it up in these following parcels; viz. the condition of his *soul*, his *body*, and his *whole man*.

The condition of the natural man's SOUL *under the curse.*

FIRST, Let us view the condition of his *soul* under the curse. The natural man's soul is under the curse: it is the most noble part of the man, but the heaviest part of the curse lies upon it. And therefore Christ's soul-sufferings, when he was made a curse for us, were the most terrible of all his sufferings. That is the inward man into which the curse sinks, like water or oil, Psal. cix. 18. In the moment man sinned, his soul fell under the curse. And so,

1. His soul was separated from God, in favour with whom its life lay, Psal. xxx. 5. Deut. xxix. 21. The course of saving influences was stopt, the sun went quite

down

down on him, and he loſt God, his friend, his life, the ſoul of his ſoul. Thus natural men live without God, Eph. ii. 12. ſeparated from him, Iſ. lix. 2. There is no ſaving intercourſe betwixt God and them, more than there is betwixt us and our friends now lying in the grave, Pſal. v. 5. Amos iii. 3. They hear his word preached; but, alas! they hear not his own voice, John v. 37. They pray to him, but he hears them not neither; John ix. 31. *God heareth not ſinners.* They hang on about the poſts of his doors, but they never get a ſight of the King's face. Be where they will, in the church or in the tavern, in duty or out of it, they are ever at a diſtance from God. The reaſon is, they are under the curſe, which is as a great gulf fixed betwixt God and them, that there can be no communication between them; none by any means, but what can dry up the gulf, or remove the curſe; which the blood of Chriſt only applied to the ſoul can do.

2. Hence man's ſoul beauty was loſt; death ſeizing on him by ſin, his beauty went off. As when Chriſt curſed the fig-tree, it withered away; its bloſſoms went up as duſt, its verdure and greenneſs were loſt: ſo the curſed ſinner was ſtript of his original righteouſneſs, the light of his mind, the rectitude of his will, the orderlineſs of his affections, and the right temper of all the faculties of his ſoul, Gen. iii. 7. 8. Thus under the curſe the natural man's ſoul lies in ruins, *dead in treſpaſſes and ſins,* Eph. ii. 1. dead to God, dead to righteouſneſs, dead to its primitive conſtitution and frame, though in a living body.

A dead corpſe is an awful ſight, where the ſoul is gone. But thy dead ſoul, from which God is gone, O natural man, is a more awful one. Couldſt thou ſee thy inward man, as well as thou ſeeſt the outward, thou wouldſt ſee a ſoul within thee of a ghaſtly countenance, the eyes of its underſtanding ſet, its ſpeech laid, all the ſpiritual ſenſes now locked up, no pulſe of kindly affection towards God beating any more; but the ſoul lying ſpeechleſs, moveleſs, cold, and ſtiff like a ſtone, under the curſe.

3. Hence the whole ſoul is corrupted in all the faculties thereof, Gen. vi. 5. *God ſaw that the wickedneſs of man was great in the earth, and that every imagination of the thoughts of his heart was only evil continually.* Jer. xvii. 9.

9. *The heart is deceitful above all things, and desperately wicked, who can know it?* As the soul being gone, the body corrupts; so the soul being divested of its original righteousness, is wholly corrupted and defiled, having a kind of verminating life in it, Psal. xiv. 3. *They are all together become filthy.* And as when the curse was laid on the earth, the very nature of the soil was altered; so the souls of men under the curse are quite altered from their original holy constitution; the which appears in all the faculties thereof.

(1.) Look into the mind, framed at first to be the eye of the soul; there is a lamentable alteration upon it under the curse. *O how is the fine gold become dim!* There is a mist upon it, whereby it is become weak, dull, and stupid in spiritual things, and really incapable of these things, 1 Cor. ii. 14. *The natural man receiveth not the things of the Spirit of God: for they are foolishness unto him: neither can he know them, because they are spiritually discerned.* Darkness has sit down on it, Eph. v. 8. *Ye were sometimes darkness*; and there spiritual blindness and ignorance reign, not to be removed by man's instruction, or any power less than what can take off the curse. This cursed ground is fruitful of mistakes, misapprehensions, delusions, monstrous and mishapen conceptions, in divine things: doubtings, distrust, unbelief of divine revelation, grow there, of their own accord, as the natural product of the cursed soil; while the seed of the word of the kingdom sown there doth perish, and faith cannot spring up in it; for such is the soil that they cannot take with it.

(2.) Look into the will, framed to have the command in the soul, and it is in wretched plight. Its uprightness for God is gone, and it is turned away backward from him. It is not only under an inability for good, having lost all power to turn itself that way, Rom. v. 6. Phil. ii. 13. but it is averse to it, as the untrained bullock is to the yoke, Psal. lxxxi. 11. *My people would not hearken to my voice; and Israel would none of me.* Luke xix. 14. *We will not have this man to reign over us.* John v. 40. *Ye will not come to me, that ye might have life.* It is set in direct opposition and contrariety to the will of God, Rom. viii. 7. *The carnal mind is enmity against God: for it is*
not

not subject to the law of God, neither indeed can be. It is a heart of stone, that will break, ere it bow to the will of God; and will remain refractory and contumacious against him, till the curse be removed, and the nature of the soul changed, though it should be plied with all the joys of heaven, and all the terrors of hell. It is prone to evil, having a fixed bent unto sin, Hof. xi. 7. *My people are bent to backsliding from me*; and this proneness to sin nothing can alter, but an omnipotent hand.

(3.) Look into the affections, framed to be the arms and feet of the soul for good, and they are quite wrong. Set spiritual objects before them to be embraced, then they are powerless, they cannot embrace them, nor gripe them stedfastly; they presently grow weary, and let go any hold they have of them: like the stony-ground hearers, who, because they had not root, withered away, Matth. xiii. 6. But as for carnal objects agreeable to their lusts, they fly upon them, they clasp and twine about them; they hold so fast a gripe, that it is with no small difficulty they can be got to let go their hold. Summon them to duty, they are flat, there is no raising of them, they cannot stir: but on the least signal given them by temptation, they are like Saul's hungry soldiers, flying on the spoil.

(4.) Look into the conscience, framed to be in the soul God's deputy for judgement, his spy, and watchman over his creature; and it is miserably corrupted, Tit. i. 15.— *Their mind and conscience is defiled.* It is quite unfitted for its office. It is fallen under a sleepy distemper, sleeping and loving to slumber. So it is a dumb conscience, often not meddling with the work of directing, informing of the will of God, warning against sin, and exciting to duty: and thus men are left as when there was no king in Israel, every one doing that which is right in their own eyes. Sometimes being consulted, it gives quite wrong orders, calling darkness light, and light darkness, having lost its right judgement; like those of whom our Lord speaks, John xvi. 2.—*The time cometh, that whosoever killeth you, will think that he doth God service.* And accordingly it excuseth, where it should accuse; and accuseth, where it should excuse. And if it be once thoroughly awakened, it driveth towards despair.

(5.) *Lastly*,

(5.) *Lastly*, Look into the memory, framed to be the storehouse of the soul, and the symptoms of the curse appear there too. Things agreeable to the corruption of nature, and which may strengthen the same, stick fast in the memory, so that often one cannot get them forgotten, though they would fain have their remembrance razed. But spiritual things natively fall out of it, and are soon forgotten; the memory like a leaking vessel letting them slip.

4. Man being in these respects spiritually dead, the which death was the consequent of the first sin; the curse lies on him as a grave-stone, and penally binds it upon him, that he cannot recover. So he is in some sort, by the curse, buried out of God's sight. Thus sinners are said to be *concluded in unbelief*, Rom. xi. 32. shut up as in a prison, *under the law*, viz. with its curse, Gal. iii. 23. So when Christ comes to sinners with his offers of life and salvation, he finds them bound in a prison, Is. lxi. 1.— *He hath sent me—to proclaim liberty to the captives, and the opening of the prison to them that are bound.* They are under chains of darkness, even the chains of the curse on all the faculties of the soul; which they can no more shake off them, than a dead man can loose and throw off him his dead cloaths, and hoise up his grave-stone, and come forth to the light. The curse cuts off the communication between God and the sinner, and so closeth up all door of hope, while it remains, but by that which can remove the curse.

5. Hence that corruption of the soul groweth more and more. As the dead corpse, the longer it lies in the grave, it rots the more, till devouring death has perfected its work in its utter ruin: so the dead soul under the curse grows worse and worse, in all the faculties thereof, till it is brought to the utmost pitch of sin and misery in hell, 2 Tim. iii. 13. Sin continuing its reign in the soul, must needs gather strength; and the longer the corruption of nature continues, the stronger it grows. And hence it is, that ordinarily the longer one has lived in an irregenerate state, the pangs of the new birth are the more severe.

6. And hence the corruption of nature shoots forth itself in innumerable particular lusts, according to its growth, Mark vii. 21. 22. 23. *For from within, out of the heart of men,*

men, proceed evil thoughts, adulteries, fornications, murders, thefts, covetousness, wickedness, deceit, lasciviousness, an evil eye, blasphemy, pride, foolishness: all these evil things come from within, and defile the man. These all spring up in the soul under the curse, in such plenty as at length to cover the face of the whole soul, as the cursed earth brings forth thorns and thistles without the pains of the husbandman, and as nettles do the face of the sluggard's vineyard, Prov. xxiv. 30. 31. The man thinks himself very far from such a sin, as he has not been tried with; but when a fit temptation offers, he appears in his own colours; why? but because the soul under the curse was fit to conceive by such a temptation.

7. And these lusts grow stronger and stronger. The man who first *walks in the counsel of the ungodly*, proceeds to *stand in the way of sinners*, and at length *sits down in the seat of the scornful*, Psal. i. 1. The more corrupt one's nature grows, the more nourishment it sends forth to feed and flesh particular lusts. And these lusts acting according to their nature, gather strength by exercise: so that custom makes their acting so easy, and ready, that they come at length to refuse to be managed; like those of whom Peter speaks, 2 epist. ii. 14. *having eyes full of adultery, and that cannot cease from sin.* And the man must quit the reins to them, they are quite beyond his control, Jer. xiii. 23.

But this is not all the misery of the soul under the curse: there are additional plagues, which by the curse they are liable to, who are under it. These soul-plagues are of two sorts; silent strokes, and tormenting plagues.

First, Silent strokes, which make their way into the soul with no noise: but the less they are felt, they are the more dangerous; such as,

1. Judicial blindness, Eph. iv. 18. *Having the understanding darkened, being alienated from the life of God, through the ignorance that is in them, because of the blindness of their heart.* They are naturally blind, and love not to have their eyes opened, John iii. 19. However, some gleams of light get into their minds, while it shines in the word round about them. But they rebel against the light, shut their eyes upon it, and so make themselves

more blind, Job xxi. 14. *Therefore they say unto God, Depart from us; for we desire not the knowledge of thy ways.* Wherefore God, in his just judgement, causes the light to withdraw, that it shall not enter into their souls, and leaves them to Satan to be by him blinded more than ever, 2 Cor. iv. 3. 4. *But if our gospel be hid, it is hid to them that are lost: in whom the god of this world hath blinded the minds of them which believe not, lest the light of the glorious gospel of Christ, who is the image of God, should shine unto them.*

2. Strong delusions. Men living under the gospel light, having the truth clearly discovered to them, do often keep the truth prisoner, Rom. i. 18. *holding it in unrighteousness.* They receive the true principles into their heads, but they will not allow them to model their lives in conformity to the truth: so they receive not the truth in love. For avenging of which quarrel, they are given up to a spirit of delusion, 2 Thess. ii. 10. 11.—*Because they received not the love of the truth, that they might be saved.—For this cause God shall send them strong delusion, that they should believe a lie.* Thus is the curse beginning to work at this day, for the contempt of the glorious gospel; and how the fearful plague of delusion may spread ere it end, God only knows.

3. Hardness of heart, Rom. ii. 5. Mens hearts are naturally hard and insensible: but under softening means, they harden them more: and God hardens them judicially, Rom. ix. 18.; with holding his grace from them, as in Israel's case, *not giving them an heart to perceive, and eyes to see, and ears to hear,* Deut. xxix. 4.; blasting all means to them, whether providences or ordinances, whereby others are bettered, so that they do them no good, Hos. iv. 17.; exposing them in his holy providence to such objects, as their corruptions make occasions of sinning more, Deut. ii. 30.; giving them over to their lusts, leaving them to the temptations of the world, and to the power of Satan, and suffering them to prosper in an evil course. Whereby it comes to pass, that they are hardened in sin more than before.

4. A reprobate sense, Rom. i. 28. whereby men lose the faculty of discerning betwixt good and evil; as those who

who are deprived of the fense of tasting, know no difference betwixt bitter and sweet. Thus men who being wedded to their lusts, and can by no means be brought to part with them, but treat that light which discovers the evil of them as an enemy, are sometimes in the fearful judgement of God suffered to proceed this length, that they can see no evil even in gross sins, but vile abominations are in their eyes harmless things.

5. *Lastly*, Vile affections, Rom. i. 26. Many a time vile affections stir in the soul, and the grace of God in some, and reason and a natural conscience in others, do strive against them, and repress their fury. These are the product of the corruption of nature in all: but this soul-plague is more dreadful. In it the soul is given up to these vile affections, so that by them they are commanded, and ruled, and led, like beasts, without reason. A fearful case! reason and conscience are imprisoned, all power and rule over the soul is taken out of their hands: and the rabble of vile passions and affections manage all, without control. So that the soul is like a ship at sea without a governor, that is tossed hither and thither, being entirely under the management of the winds and waves.

Secondly, Tormenting plagues, which make the soul to feel them, to its great pain and uneasiness. Many are the executioners employed against the soul fallen under the curse, who together do pierce, rack, and rent it as it were in pieces. These are tormenting passions, which had never appeared in the soul had it not fallen into sin, and so under the curse. Such tormenting plagues, which the soul under the curse is liable to, are chiefly these following.

1. Discontent. This haunts the soul like a ghost, ever since man fell from God, sometimes in greater, sometimes in lesser measure. He would not rest contented in God, and from that time he could have no more contentment within himself. He must have all his will, otherwise he is discontented: and that he shall never get, till God's will be his will; and that will never be till he be delivered from under the curse. Hence wretched man is born weeping, lives complaining and discontented, and dies disappointed. What saws, axes, and harrows of iron, does

this discontent draw through the soul, in fretfulness, impatience, murmuring, grudging, repining, quarrelling with God and men; whereby men become a burden to the Spirit of God, a burden to others, and a burden to themselves? The discontented soul is ruffled and rankled with very small trials, like Ahab, Haman, &c. yea and often with it knows not what; only there is something wanting, and the mind is uneasy. The mystery lies here, the peace of God is not ruling in the heart, Col. iii. 15. Phil. iv. 7.

2. Wrath. This is a fire in the man's bosom, to burn him up; an arrow, a dagger, a sword piercing to the very soul, Job v. 2. *For wrath killeth the foolish man.* This fills him with rage and fury, and makes the whole soul like the troubled sea, when it cannot rest, but its *waves toss themselves,* and roll up and down, *casting out mire and dirt.* The proud heart with temptation swells; and this will no more be wanting to us while here, than the air will be free from midges in the heat of summer, that the man may travel undisturbed. The secret discontent in the soul, following on its loss of God, is the cause of this, as well as of other tormenting passions. Hungry folk are soon angry. The gnawing hunger in the soul after happiness and satisfaction, from which it is barred under the curse, makes them so peevish and wrathful.

3. Anxiety, whereby the soul is as it were stretched on tenter hooks, and is drawn asunder by divers thoughts, and put on the rack. Many are the grounds of this torture to the soul. Sometimes it is on the account of carnal things, which come under the name of *the cares of this life,* Luke viii. 14.; and so as many lusts as a man has to satisfy, so much anxiety how to get them satisfied falls to the share of the wretched soul. Ahab is racked how to get his covetousness satisfied, Haman is racked with his ambition and revenge, &c. Hence the man travelleth with iniquity, Psal. vii. 14. is in pain as a woman with child to bring it forth. Sometimes it is on the account of his soul's state before God, how to escape the wrath and curse of God, while the dreadful sound is in the man's ears; Acts ii. 37. *Now when they heard this, they were pricked in their heart, and said, ——Men and brethren, what shall we do?*
Chap.

Chap. xvi. 30. *Sirs, what muſt I do to be ſaved?* Which, though it comes to nought in many, yet the Lord makes uſe of for bringing the elect to Chriſt.

4. Sorrow of heart, which is a weight on the ſoul preſſing it down, the native fruit of ſin and the curſe. There is a flood of ſorrow let out on man under the curſe, which divides itſelf into two great ſtreams. (1.) The ſorrow of the world, 2 Cor. vii. 10. Here run over the ſoul, the floods of ſorrow ariſing from worldly loſſes, croſſes, diſappointments, which men meet with in worldly things, in their bodies, eſtates, reputation, relations, and the like. And this ſtream never dries up, every day has the evil thereof, Matth. vi. *ult.* And as if the evils coming on men themſelves mediately or immediately, could not ſufficiently cauſe theſe waters to ſwell; ſuch is the diſpoſition of the ſoul under the curſe, that the good which others meet with, often ſerves to increaſe them, by means of envy, ill will, and grudge at their proſperity, Job v. 2. *Envy ſlayeth the ſilly one.* (2.) The ſorrows of death, Pſal. cxvi. 3. ariſing from a ſight of the guilt of ſin lying on the ſoul before the Lord, which will make the moſt ſtout-hearted bow their heads under the weight, Matth. xxvii. 3. 4. Theſe are the moſt bitter waters cauſed by ſin and the curſe; and wo to him with whom they ſwell to the brim, if Chriſt be not a lifter up of the head to him.

5. Fear and terror, which ſeizing on the ſoul puts an end to its eaſe and quiet. This covereth the ſoul with blackneſs, darkneſs, and tempeſt; takes away its courage, ſtrikes a damp upon it, and makes it reſtleſs. And it is twofold, both effects of the curſe on the ſoul.

1ſt, Terror of heart, from the apprehenſion of danger and miſery approaching. Man having ſinned, is by the curſe denounced a rebel, yea and adjudged to death: hence he is in God's world, like a man under ſentence of death, wandering here and there within the King's dominions, ready to be frighted at every accident, and no where ſecure or in quietneſs, like Cain, Gen. iv. 14. How can they be fearleſs among God's creatures, to whom God is an enemy? Guilt is a mother and nurſe of fears; and hence it comes to paſs, that the ſinner ſometimes is made

to

to tremble at the shaking of a leaf. In a special manner, any token, presage, or likelihood of the approach of death, the king of terrors, fills the soul with tormenting fear. This is awfully described Deut. xxviii. 65. 66. 67. *And among these nations shalt thou find no ease, neither shall the sole of thy foot have rest: but the Lord shall give thee there a trembling heart, and failing of eyes, and sorrow of mind. And thy life shall hang in doubt before thee, and thou shalt fear day and night, and shalt have none assurance of thy life. In the morning thou shalt say, Would God it were even: and at even thou shalt say, Would God it were morning, for the fear of thine heart wherewith thou shalt fear, and for the sight of thine eyes which thou shalt see.*

2*dly,* Horror of conscience, arising from the sense of guilt, and apprehensions of God's wrath against the soul, Is. xxxiii. 14. *The sinners in Zion are afraid, fearfulness hath surprised the hypocrites: who among us shall dwell with the devouring fire? who amongst us shall dwell with everlasting burnings?* This is of all terrors in the world the greatest, and makes a deep wound in the soul, Prov. xviii. 14. *A wounded spirit who can bear?* Cain could not bear it, Gen. iv. 13. Judas could not endure it, Matth. xxvii. 3. 4. Jeremiah prays against it, Jer. xvii. 17. it made Pashur a terror to himself, chap. xx. 4. This is the dreadful workings of the curse in the soul, giving it a foretaste of hell. And we may observe three degrees of it.

(1.) A confused fear as to one's soul's state, making the person uneasy, with suspicions and jealousies that matters are all wrong betwixt God and the soul; like that of Herod, Matth. xiv. 1. 2. who hearing of the fame of Jesus, said unto his servants, *This is John the Baptist, he is risen from the dead,* &c. Conscience may sleep long very sound, and yet at length begin to speak, as it were betwixt sleeping and waking, so as it may fill the man with uneasiness, with its very *may be's.* For under the curse it can never be true to a man's ease, but will one time or other give alarms.

(2.) A sharp pang, though passing like a stitch in one's side; the which, while it lasts, fills the soul with horror, and makes the man's heart melt in him like wax, under clear apprehensions that God is his enemy. Such was

that

that of Felix, Acts xxiv. 25. *And as Paul reafoned of righteoufnefs, temperance, and judgement to come, Felix trembled, and anfwered, Go thy way for this time ; when I have a convenient feafon, I will call for thee.* He felt the fire kindled in his bofom, that it was too ftrong for him; and therefore immediately orders that there be no more fewel laid to it, left it fhould quite burn him up. Such one day fevers of confcience, no doubt, many natural men do feel under the curfe; though, by methods of their own, they find means to caufe the fit wear off.

(3.) A vehement and abiding horror, which they can no more fhake off, as in Judas's cafe, Matth. xxvii. 3. 4. Then the guilt that lay on the confcience, like brimftone is fired, and burns fo that they cannot quench the flame. The arrows of wrath dipt in the poifon of the curfe, and fhot into the foul, by an almighty hand, work fo as the poifon of them drinks up their fpirits. The beginnings of hell then are felt. The confcience is like mount Sinai, all in fire and fmoke. The terrors of God are round about them, as fet in battle-array againft them: and they become a terror to themfelves, and fometimes a terror to others too. The threatenings of the holy law, are no more looked on as fcarecrows, by the moft obftinate finner once brought to this pafs; their lufts then are bitter to them as death; and all the comforts of the world faplefs.

6. *Laftly*, Defpair, If. xvii. 11. This is the very height of the foul's torment in this world, and puts the copeftone on its mifery here: and no wonder, for it is the tormenting plague of the damned. A man may be under great horror of confcience, and yet there may be a fecret hope of an outgate which fupports him: but who can conceive, without experience, the torment of that foul on whom defpair hath feized, and hath fhut up all doors of hope? What a fearful cafe muft that foul be in, againft which the fea of the Lord's wrath fo fwells and rages, that it is in that cafe, Acts xxvii. 20. *And when neither fun nor ftars in many days appeared, and no fmall tempeft lay on us, all hope that we fhould be faved, was then taken away!* This leaves the foul no eafe at all, and fometimes hath a moft fearful iffue, as in Saul and Judas.

The condition of the natural man's BODY *under the curſe.*

SECONDLY, The natural man's *body* is under the curſe. The firſt ſin was completed by an action of the body: man ate the forbidden fruit, and with it ſwallowed down death, by virtue of the curſe, which followed ſin hard at the heels. God made man a compend of the univerſe, by his creating power raiſed a body, a beautiful fabric, out of the duſt, and lodged the ſoul, a ſpirit, an immortal ſubſtance, in it, as in a glorious and convenient habitation, and he bleſſed the houſe as well as the inhabitant, Gen. i. 28. But the houſe he commanded to be kept clean, being defiled by the ſoul, ſuddenly he curſed the ſoul's habitation, and the original bleſſing was ſucceeded with a heavy curſe, Deut. xxviii. 18. *Curſed ſhall be the fruit of thy body :* And ſurely the curſing of the fruit implies a curſe on the tree it grows on, *viz.* the defiled body. The condition of the body thus laid under the curſe, we may view in the following particulars.

1. It is liable to many defects and deformities in the very conſtitution thereof. Adam and Eve were at their creation not only found and entire in their ſouls, but in their bodies, having nothing unſightly about them. But O how often now is there ſeen a variation from the original pattern, in the very formation of the body! Some are born deaf, dumb, blind, or the like. Some with a want of ſome neceſſary organ, ſome with what is ſuperfluous. Some with ſuch a conſtitution of body, as makes them idiots, the organs of the body being ſo far out of caſe, that they are unfit for the actions of the rational life; and the ſoul is by them kept in a miſt during the union with that body. All this is owing to ſin and the curſe, without which there had been no ſuch things in the body of man. It is purely owing to mercy, that theſe things are not more frequent; for by the curſe all the ſons and daughters of Adam are liable to them; and it may be a humbling queſtion, therefore, to the moſt handſome and beautiful, 1 Cor. iv. 7. *Who maketh thee to differ from another ? and what haſt thou that thou didſt not receive ?* And God makes ſome ſuch inſtances, that all may ſee in them what by the curſe they are liable to, John ix. 3.

2. As the temperature of the body was by the firſt ſin altered, ſo as it diſpoſed to ſin, Gen. iii. 7.; ſo by the curſe that degenerate conſtitution of it is penally bound on, by which it comes to paſs, that it is a ſnare to the ſoul continually. The ſeeds of ſin are in it; it is *ſinful fleſh*, Rom. viii. 3. *a vile body*, Phil iii. 21.; and theſe ſeeds are never removed while the curſe lies on it, being a part of that death, to which it is bound over by the curſe. To this is much owing the croud of *fleſhly luſts which war againſt the ſoul*, 1 Pet. ii. 11.; ſuch as ſenſuality, gluttony, drunkenneſs, filthineſs, &c. which more and more drown the ſoul in deſtruction and perdition. And the ſad effects of this diſtemperature of the body are never wanting of one kind or another, in all the periods of life: and by means thereof, it comes to paſs, that the ſouls of many are in their bodies, as ſunk in and overwhelmed with a mire of fleſh and blood. Thus the caſe of the man muſt needs be very miſerable, while a ſinful ſoul and ſinful fleſh remain ſo cloſely knit together, in the neareſt relation, each a ſnare to the other: the ſoul diſpoſing the body to ſin, and the body the ſoul on the other hand, the corruption of the whole man muſt make fearful advances under the curſe.

3. It is under the curſe a veſſel of diſhonour. By its original make, it was a veſſel of honour, appointed for honourable uſes, and was ſo uſed by the ſoul before ſin entered; and every member had its particular honourable ſervice, ſerving the ſoul in ſubordination to God. But now it is brought down from its honour, and its *members are yielded inſtruments of unrighteouſneſs unto ſin*, Rom. vi. 13. and is abuſed to the vileſt purpoſes: and it is never reſtored to its honour, till the curſe being removed, it becomes the temple of God, by virtue of the purchaſe of it made by the blood of Chriſt. But while the curſe remains, its honour lies in the duſt, being bound to ſuch ſervice as it was at firſt put to, in looking to, taking, and eating the forbidden fruit. See a mournful deſcription of this, Rom. iii. 13. and downwards. It is made by the drunkard like a common ſink, by the glutton like a draught, and is often like a weary beaſt under the load of divers luſts. Every natural man's ſoul makes it a drudge: in ſome it muſt be a ſlave to the vanity of the mind, in others

others to covetousness, in others to wrath and revenge: in a word, its union with the sinful soul under the curse, is become a yoke of iron.

4. It is liable to many mischiefs from without, tending to render it uneasy for the time, and at length to dissolve the frame of it. From the heavens above us, the air about us, the earth underneath us, and all that therein is, it is liable to hurt. All the creatures are in a state of enmity to man, while he is an enemy to God; and the least fly that passeth through the air, is able to annoy him now. So that the natural man is ever in the midst of his armed enemies. The promise of the covenant was his guard, that while he kept the commandment, no evil could approach unto him: but now the guard is removed, and he is laid under the curse, having broken the covenant; whereby not only his covenant-defence is departed from him, but Heaven has proclaimed war against him, armed the whole creation against the men of his curse, and ordered them to be ready to attack them on a moment's warning. Hence the waters swallow up some, the fire hurts others, beasts wound and bruise others, and man is not safe from the stones of the field, yea, every creature's hand is against him. And not only so, but by the curse men are become mischievous one to another, fighting, beating, wounding, and killing one another.

5. There is a seed-plot of much misery within it. It is by the curse become a weak body, and so liable to much toil and weariness, fainting and languishing, under the weight of the exercise it is put to, Gen. iii. 19. And not only so, but it hath in it such seeds of corruption tending to its dissolution, as spring up in many and various maladies, which prove so heavy many times, that they make life itself a burden. By virtue of the curse, death works in the body, all along from the womb, as a mole under ground, till at length it lays the whole fabric in the dust, and leaves not, as it were, one stone on another, in the grave. No part of the body, without or within, is beyond the reach of diseases and torturing pains. The greatest care of the body cannot altogether ward them off. The curse has turned this world into an hospital, where some are groaning under one distemper, some under another; some at one time, some

some at another; and some in that respect are dying daily, knowing little or nothing of perfect health. The strongest are liable to be so weakened by diseases, as to be unable to turn themselves on a bed; those who enjoy the greatest ease, are subject to tormenting pains: the most beautiful may be a prey to loathsome diseases and sores; and the soundest constitution to infectious plagues.

6. *Lastly*, In all these respects the body is a clog to the soul in point of duty, often hanging like a dead weight upon it, unfitting it for, and hindering it from its most necessary work. The sinful soul is in itself most unfit for its great work, in this state of trial, by reason of the evil qualities of it under the curse. But the wretched body makes it more so. The care of the body doth so take up its thoughts with most men, that, caring for it, the soul is lost. Its strength and vigour is a snare to it, and its weakness and uneasiness often interrupt or quite mar the exercises wherein the soul might profitably be employed. And one may see the forlorn case of the soul of man in this body under the curse, how it is on every hand pulled back from salvation-work, in the case of many to whom health and strength is such a powerful snare, while it remains, that they will not, and when they are gone, trouble and distress of body do so fill their hand, that they cannot, mind their salvation-work to purpose.

But it may be objected, That by this account of the condition of those under the curse, the case of natural men and of believers in Christ is alike; since it is evident, that not only these bodily miseries, but many of these soul-miseries are common to both. I answer, Though it seem to be alike in the eyes of beholders, in regard these miseries are materially the same, on natural men and on the children of God; yet really there is a vast difference. On the former, they are truly effects of the curse; on the latter, they are indeed effects of sin, but not of the curse: for *Christ hath redeemed* them *from the curse of the law, being made a curse for* them, Gal. iii. 13. Sin entering into the world, was a fountain of miseries; and till it be dried up, there will be miseries on mens souls and bodies: but the poison of the curse is mixed with these bitter streams to some, but not to others; and that makes as

great

great a difference betwixt the case of the godly and ungodly, as betwixt the case of one man to whom poison, and another to whom medicine is administered. And,

(1.) The stream of miseries on soul or body to a natural man, runs in the channel of the covenant of works; but to a believer, in the channel of the covenant of grace. To the former it comes, by virtue of the threatening, Gen. ii. 17. *In the day that thou eatest thereof, thou shalt surely die:* To the latter it comes by virtue of that, Psal. lxxxix. 30. 31. 32. &c. *If his children forsake my law, and walk not in my judgements; if they break my statutes, and keep not my commandments: then will I visit their transgression with the rod, and their iniquity with stripes,* &c. Running in the channel of the first covenant, they bring the curse along with them; but in the channel of the second covenant, the curse is not to be found; the waters are healed, however bitter they may be, Is. liv. 9. When one has a slave, he punisheth him for his misdemeanors, by virtue of his masterly authority over him: but if he be freed and adopted for a son, he chasteneth him, but no more as a slave, but as a son.

(2.) There is revenging wrath in the one, but fatherly anger only in the other, Is. liv. 9. *For this is as the waters of Noah unto me: for as I have sworn that the waters of Noah should no more go over the earth; so have I sworn that I would not be wroth with thee, nor rebuke thee.* If it were never such a small stroke on the natural man, it is in part of payment of law-debt; for he is under the law, in its commanding, cursing and condemning power: if it were never such a heavy stroke on a child of God, it is no part of payment of law debt, which he is for ever discharged of in his union with Christ. An ungodly man's basket of bread miscarries; it is no great loss, one would think, he may bear it: but alas! there is an impression of wrath upon it, it miscarried by virtue of the curse, Deut. xxviii. 17. *Cursed shall be thy basket and thy store;* and so it is heavier than the sand of the sea, though he, being insensible of his case, feels not the weight of it. Good Eli falls from off his seat, and breaks his neck, 1 Sam. iv. 18. O heavy stroke! we are apt to say: yea but there was no worse in it than fatherly anger; the

covenant

covenant was not broken, though his neck was broken, Pſal. lxxxix. 34. *My covenant will I not break.* He got a ſoft fall, as hard as it appeared to ſpectators, he fell on a pavement of love, Cant. iii. 10.

(3.) The miſeries of the ungodly in this life are an earneſt of eternal miſery in hell: but thoſe of the godly are medicines, to keep back their ſoul from death, 1 Cor. xi. 32. *When we are judged, we are chaſtened of the Lord, that we ſhould not be condemned with the world.* Every ſtroke a man under the curſe gets, he may call it *Joſeph;* for *the Lord will add another.* The leaſt brook that runs, is making towards the ſea, as well as the deepeſt river: and the leaſt affliction by virtue of the curſe laid on a man, looks towards hell, as well as the greateſt ſtroke he meets with. Though a piece of money be but ſmall in itſelf, if it be an earneſt·penny of a great ſum, it is valued accordingly. And ſo the leaſt ſtroke would be frightful to a natural man, if he diſcerned the nature of it. But in the worſt afflictions of God's people, there is a ſeed of joy, Pſal. xcvii. 11. *Light is ſown for the righteous, and gladneſs for the upright in heart:* and the darkeſt night will have a fair clear morning. There was more of heaven in Heman's hell, Pſal. lxxxviii. 15. than there is in the greateſt eaſe, joy, and proſperity of the wicked.

The condition of the ſinner's WHOLE MAN *under the curſe.*

THIRDLY, The *whole man* is under the curſe. The ſinner fallen from God, fell under the curſe; and like a deluge it has gone over him, and ſurrounded him on every hand. Hence our Lord Chriſt, being made a curſe for us, was beſet with ſorrows, Matth. xxvi. 38. *My ſoul is exceeding ſorrowful, even unto death;* like a man whom the devouring waves are compaſſing round about, and from every hand coming in upon him, ready to ſwallow him up. Thus ſtands the natural man under the curſe; it is upon him, it is round about him; go where he will, there is no ſhifting of it, all his days he wades through theſe waters; he is in the deep mire, where there is no firm ſtanding. He is curſed,

1. In his name and reputation: Iſ. xiv. 20. *The ſeed of evil-*

evil-doers shall never be renowned. Sin laid man's honour in the grave, and the curse lays the grave-stone upon it; and it can never rise again till the curse be removed, Is. xliii. 4. *Since thou wast precious in my sight, thou hast been honourable.* What of it appears before that, is but as it were a ghost, a spectre of honour, that vanisheth away, which vain men please themselves with a little, as with illusions of fancy. The sinner's name may shoot up and flourish a little: but it is blasted by the curse, with shame, contempt, reproach, and disgrace. And no heights of worldly grandeur can secure men against this; the curse is a worm at the root, which will work and cause to wither the sinner's name, whatever pains be taken to hold it green. A good name is better than precious ointment; but where the curse lies, the dead fly will be found there, to cause it send forth a stinking favour. Every man is desirous of a name, and the raising of it was the snare in which man was first caught, *Ye shall be as gods:* but since that time, man has been laid open to many and deep wounds in it, while, by the curse, the tongues of those of his own kind, have been as arrows shot from a bent bow against it, Psal. lvii. 4.

2. In his employment and calling in the world; Gen. iii. 19. *In the sweat of thy face shalt thou eat bread, till thou return unto the ground.* Man is put to sore toil, weariness, and distress in his worldly employment; and when he has done, O what fruitless pains and travel is he made to see! How often do men labour as in the very fire! and all the issue is, they weary themselves for very vanity. There is sore and hard travel; and after all men must say, *We have as it were brought forth wind* The husbandman toils in labouring the ground, and the earth, by virtue of the curse, often gives him but a poor reward of his labour. The storemaster is diligent to know the state of his flocks, and looks well to his herds; but oft-times it is seen, that that will not effect it, the curse works against him, and all goes to wreck, Deut. xxviii. 17. *Cursed shall be— thy store.* The tradesman is early and late at his work, but often has much ado to get bread to his mouth and his family. The merchant carefully watcheth occasions of advancing his interest; but how often seeking gain does he

find

find loss! and some unforeseen events discover a secret hand of providence working against him in the management of his affairs. See Hag. i. 6. *Ye have sown much, and bring in little: ye eat, but ye have not enough; ye drink, but ye are not filled with drink: ye clothe you, but there is none warm: and he that earneth wages, earneth wages to put it into a bag with holes.* The case of the labour of the mind, is in this respect no better than the labour of the hands. Solomon tells us, from his experience, the grievous toil of it, Eccl. i. 13. *I gave my heart to seek and search out by wisdom, concerning all things that are done under heaven: this sore travel hath God given to the sons of man, to be exercised therewith.* And he also tells the sorry issue of that toil, ver. 18. *For in much wisdom is much grief: and he that increaseth knowledge, increaseth sorrow.* No set of men have more remarkable symptoms of the curse on their employment, than those whose labour is the labour of the mind. The toil is sore, the success small, and the disappointments innumerable. The physician and the lawyer labour, the one to preserve the body, the other the estate; but after all their pains, their art fails, they mistake the case, or it is beyond their power to rectify it. The projects of statesmen laid in the depth of their wisdom, how often are they baffled, and by some small occurrence the whole frame thereof unhinged! The guides of the church, after all their contrivances for a steady management of her course; how often do they row her into deep waters, from whence they cannot bring her back, till she is dashed in pieces! Even in preaching of the gospel, while men shine, they burn and waste; and when all is done, they must sit down and say, *Who hath believed our report? I have laboured in vain, and spent my strength for nought and in vain.* Whence is all this, but that man has fallen under the curse, and it mars whatever he goes about to make.

3. In his worldly substance, Deut. xxviii. 17. *Cursed shall be thy basket and thy store.* Where ever he hath it, he hath the curse with it; whether it be in the field, Deut. xxviii. 16. or whether it be in the house, Prov. iii. 33. On the meat he eats, on the liquor he drinks, the cloaths he wears, and the house where he lodges, there is

a curse lying, because they are his. And under the weight of it they groan, as longing to be delivered out of the cursed hands, Rom. viii. 21. 22. And sometimes even providence recovers them out of their hands in this life, as men do goods out of the hands of unjust possessors, Hos. ii. 9. *I will return, and take away my corn in the time thereof, and my wine in the season thereof, and will recover my wooll and my flax given to cover her nakedness.* Thus under the curse men are liable to melancholy alterations and changes in their outward estate. Riches make themselves wings by virtue of the curse, and fly away, not to be called back again. The man is infatuated in his management, and so is not aware till he has run himself aground. He wants the hedge of the covenant-protection about what is his; and he sustains losses and damages at the hands of those with whom he has to do. Yea, he gathers and heaps up, and diligently watcheth it: but a fire unblown consumes it, and it melts away like snow before the sun; the curse like a moth eats it away, and he is wormed out of that on which he set his heart. Or if it stay with him, it is sometimes locked up from him so, as he has not the comfortable use of it, Eccl. vi. 2. *A man to whom God hath given riches, wealth, and honour, so that he wanteth nothing for his soul of all that he desireth, yet God giveth him not power to eat thereof,* &c. And so the man never has a blessed use of it, never has power to use it for the high and honourable ends it is appointed of God unto, when he gives it into their hands as stewards of it for him. The loss he has by it, as it turns to his hurt, is never counterbalanced by the gain. And all this comes on the natural man in virtue of the curse.

4. In his relations. Relations are the joints of society; and sin going through them all, they are all defiled, and the curse goes through them too, Deut. xxviii. 18. *Cursed shall be the fruit of thy body.* In them men promise themselves comfort; but there they find sorrow, pain, and smart. There they lean as it were to a wall, and a serpent doth bite them. In the state, magistrates often oppress, ensnare, and entangle the conscience, and prove a terror to those that do well. In the church, ministers are unfaithful, unwatchful, unconcerned for the good of souls,

or unsuccessful. In neighbourhood, men are unjust, selfish, and snares one to another. In the family, disorder and confusion are found, through every one's unfaithfulness in the duties of their respective relations. How many are there unequally yoked, companions of life, through their jarrings and discord, a burden and a cross to one another! Husbands such men of Belial, that their wives cannot speak to them; wives, as rottenness in the bones of their husbands; parents unnatural, and unfaithful to, and careless of their children; children froward, perverse, and stubborn; sons of youth hoped to be arrows in the hand of their parents, turning to be arrows to pierce them to the heart; daughters expected to be as corner-stones for their father's family, falling down on the heads of their parents, and crushing their spirits; masters unjust and unfaithful to their servants; and servants perverse, rebellious, and unconscionable in their service! For the curse has gone wide, and in every relation the weight of it is found; though most men that find the weight of it, know it not to be the curse indeed.

5. In his lot, whatever it is, afflicted or prosperous. Afflictions are cursed to the man who is under the curse; he is not bettered by them, though others are. He is not humbled by them, but his spirit is embittered; and instead of coming to God under them, he runs farther away from him: *Why should ye be stricken any more?* says the Lord to Israel; *ye will revolt more and more*, If. i. 5. God binds the man with these cords, but he crieth not. He may groan under the weight of his affliction, but he turns not unto the Lord; he saith not, *Where is God my Maker?* Job xxxv. 10. He remains stubborn, incorrigible, and impenitent; Jer. v. 3.—*Thou hast stricken them, but they have not grieved; thou hast consumed them, but they have refused to receive correction: they have made their faces harder than a rock, they have refused to return.* The man's prosperity in the world is a snare to his soul, and ruins him, Prov. i. 32. *The prosperity of fools shall destroy them.* If his ground bring forth plentifully, his barns are seen to, but his soul is neglected; as was the case with the rich man, Luke xii. 16. &c. If his family prosper, his house be in safety, and his stock thrive, *they say unto God,*

God, Depart from us; for we desire not the knowledge of thy ways. What is the Almighty, that we should serve him? and what profit should we have if we pray unto him? Job xxi. 8—14. 15. *If waters of a full cup be wrung out to them, they set their mouths against the heavens, and their tongue walketh through the earth.—And they say, How doth God know? and is there knowledge in the Most High?* Psal. lxxiii. 8. 9. &c. Youth, health, strength, and wealth together, prove ruining by virtue of the curse. Be the man's lot what it will, there is a curse on it to him, and it tends to his destruction.

6. In his use of the means of grace: Rom. xi. 8. *God hath given them the spirit of slumber, eyes that they should not see, and ears that they should not hear.* The man sits under the dropping of the gospel, but it does him no good. He is as the ground that often drinks in the rain, but brings forth no fruit meet for him by whom it is dressed. He stands cumbering the ground in God's vineyard, for there is a withering curse on him. Good grapes are expected from the pains bestowed on him, but behold only wild grapes appear. His praying, hearing, communicating, &c. are but like a withered hand that is never stretched out, nor reacheth to the throne. His convictions, and raised affections, quickly settle again, and these fair appearances come to nothing. The gospel that is a favour of life to some, is a favour of death to him, 2 Cor. ii. 16. and Christ himself, who is set for the rising of many, is eventually for his falling. Thus the curse turns every thing against the man, and all is death to him.

7. *Lastly,* In his person. Being a sinful man under the covenant of works, he is a cursed man: *For it is written, Cursed is every one that continueth not in all things which are written in the book of the law to do them.* The curse fixeth not only on what is his, but on himself; and it is for his sake that it is laid on other things. The curse, as you have heard, is on his soul, and on his body; for where-ever sin is found, under this covenant, there the curse also is. And,

(1.) The man is under the power of Satan, Acts xxvi. 18. Into the hand of this enemy man fell, when he broke the covenant of works. Satan having waged war

against

against Heaven, set on man Heaven's confederate, and gained the unhappy victory, gained him by temptation to renounce his allegiance to his rightful Lord by breaking the covenant, and so he fell under his power, as his captive taken in war, Is. xlix. 24. was brought under bondage to this worst of masters, 2 Pet. ii. 19. and is ruled by him at his pleasure, 2 Tim. ii. *ult.* The curse of the covenant falling on the covenant-breaker, he is thereby laid under condemnation, and adjudged to death according to the threatening: and so he falls under the power of him that has the power of death, that is the devil, Heb. ii. 14. Every natural man is shut up as in a prison, in his natural state; and there he lies in bonds, Is. lxi. 1. There are God's bands on him, the bands of the curse binding him over to death; and the devil's bands are on him, *viz.* the bands of strong lusts and corruptions, with which they are laden as a malefactor in prison is laden with irons. And Satan has the power of a gaoler over them. He keeps the keys of the prison, and narrowly watches the prisoners, that none of them escape. They are not all kept alike close; but none of them can move beyond the bounds of his jurisdiction, more than the prisoner can get out of the dungeon. Even when the King's word comes to deliver the elect, he will not yield them up; but the prison-doors must be broke open, and they forcibly taken out of his hand by a stronger than he.

(2.) The natural man being under the curse, is continually in hazard of utter destruction, of having the cope-stone put on his misery, and being set beyond all possibility of help. If his eyes were opened, he would see himself every moment in danger of dropping down into the pit of hell, Psal. vii. 12. *If he turn not, he will whet his sword; he hath bent his bow, and made it ready.* The man is ever standing before God's bent bow, and has nothing to secure him one moment from the drawing of it. The sentence of death is passed against him, John iii. 18. but no day intimate for the execution, but every day the dead warrant may be signed against him, and he led forth to death. His name may be *Mager-missabib, a terror round about,* Jer. xx. 3. Whither can he look, where he will not see his enemies, ready to ruin him, on a word of command from that God, under whose curse he lies? And what can he do for himself amidst his armed enemies? He is quite naked, Rev. iii. 17. and cannot fight them: he is without strength, Rom. v. 6. and cannot wield armour, though he had it: he is bound hand and foot, If. lxi. 1. and cannot flee: and if he could, whither could he flee for safety? heaven's gates are shut upon him; in the utmost parts of earth, or the most remote rock in the sea, God's hand would find him out. Justice is pursuing the criminals under the curse, crying for vengeance on the traitors; and their foot shall certainly slide in due time: the law is continually throwing the fire-balls of its curses on them, and will at length set them on fire round about: death is on the pursuit after them, and has gained much ground of them already; and the cloud of wrath hangs over their heads continually in the curse, and the small rain of God's wrath is still falling on them: how soon death may overtake them, they know not; and then the cloud breaks, and the great rain of his strength falls down upon them, and sweeps them away without hope for ever and ever.

The condition of the natural man under the curse,
AFTER THIS LIFE.

SECONDLY, The natural man's condition under the curse of the broken covenant of works, is very terrible in that part of it which takes place *after this life.* Then comes the full execution of the curse, and it is fixed on the sinner without possibility of deliverance. Then will be seen and felt by those who perish under it, what is in the womb of the curse of the broken covenant, whereof all that befals them in this life is but an earnest. The truth is, it cannot be fully represented in words from the tongues of men: but we shall briefly point at it, in the following particulars.

The condition of the natural man dying under the curse.

FIRST, The natural man under the curse, must not only die, but die by virtue of the curse. Death in any shape has a terrible aspect, it is the king of terrors, and can hardly miss to make the creature shrink, being a destruction

struction of nature, and carrying him into another world where he never was before, and putting him into a quite new state, which he has had no experience of before. But death to the natural man is in a singular manner terrible; it is death of the worst kind. The believer in Christ must die too; but Christ having died for them by virtue of the curse, and that death of his being applied to them by faith, they die not in virtue of the curse, Gal. iii. 13. *Christ hath redeemed us from the curse of the law, being made a curse for us.* It is a fatherly chastisement, a medicine to them, yea the most effectual medicine that cures them of all their maladies, 1 Cor. xi. 30. 32.

But the natural man dies by virtue of the curse of the broken covenant, agreeable to the threatening annexed thereto, Gen. ii. 17. *In the day that thou eatest thereof, thou shalt surely die.* Accordingly, upon man's sinning, the curse seized him; and continuing under that covenant, it is still working in him, till it works his soul and body asunder. Soul and body joined in sin against God, and by sin the man was separated from God: and, as a meet reward of the error, the companions in sin are separated by the curse at length; which would have remained eternally in a happy union, had not sin entered.

Now, that we may have a view of death to a sinner by virtue of the curse, consider,

1. It is the ruining stroke from the hand of an absolute God, proceeding according to the covenant of works against the sinner in full measure: *He shall be driven from light into darkness, and chased out of the world,* Job xviii. 18. It is the fatal wound, the wound of an enemy, for the sinner's utter destruction. To a saint, death is a friend's wound; a stroke from the hand of a Father, proceeding against his children in the way of the covenant of grace, for their complete happiness. But the ungodly in death fall into the hands of the living God, who then is, and ever will be, to them, a consuming fire. Having led their life under that covenant, they are then crushed in pieces by the curse for their breaking of it.

2. It is the breaking up of the peace betwixt God and them for ever; it is God's setting his seal to the proclamation of an everlasting war with them; after which no
message

message of peace is to go betwixt them any more for ever. It fixeth an impassable gulf, cutting off all comfortable communication with heaven, for the ages of eternity, Luke xvi. 26. Now the sinner under the curse, living within the visible church, has the privilege of offers of life and salvation: but then there is no more gospel, nor good tidings of peace, when once death has done its work. The curse which in life might have been got removed, by the sinner's embracing of Christ, is then fastned for ever on him without remedy. The door is shut, and that for ever.

3. It puts an end to all their comfort of whatsoever nature, Luke xvi. 25. It utterly quenches their coal, and puts out all their light, Job xviii. 18. forecited. To the godly death puts an end to their worldly comforts, but then it lets them into the full enjoyment of their Lord in heaven: but as for the ungodly, at death they leave all their worldly comforts behind them, and they have no comfort before them in the place whither they go. The curse then draws a bar betwixt them, and every thing that is pleasant and easy.

4. It is death armed with its sting, and all the strength it has from sin, and a holy just broken law. *The sting of death*, whereby it pierces like a stinged serpent, *is sin*, 1 Cor. xv. 56. *and the strength of sin is the law*. Now, when death comes on the ungodly man, all his sins are unpardoned; the guilt of them all, binding him, as with innumerable cords, over to eternal wrath, lies upon him. And these cords of guilt cannot be broken; for the law is their strength, which threatens sin with eternal wrath; and God's truth and faithfulness therein plighted, cannot fail. Thus is death armed against the unbeliever, and herein lies the truly killing nature of it. Where that sting is away, as it is to all in Christ, it can do them no real harm, whatever way they die, whether a lingering or sudden death, a violent or natural one, under a cloud, or in the light of comfort, 1 Cor. xv. 55. 56. 57.

5. *Lastly*, It is the fearful passage out of this world into everlasting misery, Luke xvi. 22. 23. It is a dark valley at best; but the Lord is with his people while they go through it, Psal. xxiii. 4. It is a deep water at best; but

where

where the curse is removed, the Lord Jesus will be the lifter up of the head, that the passenger shall not sink. But who can conceive the horror of the passage the sinner under the curse has, upon whom that frightful weight lies? It leads him as an ox to the slaughter; it opens like a trapdoor underneath him, by which he falls into the pit, and like a whirlpool swallows him up in a moment, and he is staked down in an unalterable state of unspeakable misery.

The condition of the natural man's soul before the tribunal of God, under the curse.

SECONDLY, He is immediately after death hauled before the tribunal of that God, under whose curse he lies; Eccl. xii. 7. *The spirit shall return unto God who gave it.* Compared with Heb. ix 27. *It is appointed unto men once to die, but after this the judgement.* There the soul is judged, according to its state, and the deeds done in the body: and there it must receive its particular sentence. And what can it be, but *Depart, ye cursed?* Where can such a soul expect to find its own place, but in the place of torment? Luke xvi. 23. The cause is already judged, the sinner is under the curse, bound over to hell by the sentence of the holy law. And those whom the law has power to curse, and does curse while they are in this world, God will never bless in the other world. Consider the sinner under the curse before this tribunal; and,

1. All his sins, of all kinds, in all the periods of his life, from the first to the last breathing on earth, are upon him. The curse seals them up as in a bag, that not one of them can be a-missing; Hos. xiii. 12. *The iniquity of Ephraim is bound up: his sin is hid.* Where a pardon takes place, the curse is removed, and being once removed, it never returns: so where the curse is, there neither is nor has been a pardon; for these are inconsistent, the one being a binding over of the sinner to wrath, the other a dissolution of that band, so that God will remember their iniquities no more. But where no pardon is, God has sworn he will not forget any of that sinner's works, Amos viii. 7. How fearful then must the case be, while the sinner stands before this tribunal with all his sins whatsoever upon him?

2. As

2. As the man's sins were multiplied, so the curses of the law were multiplied upon him; for it is the constant voice of the law, upon every transgression of those under the covenant of works, *Cursed is every one that continueth not in all things which are written in the book of the law to do them*, Gal. iii. 10. How then can such a one escape, while innumerable cords of death are upon him before a just Judge, with their united force binding him over to destruction? His misery is hereby ensured without all peradventure; and the more of these cords there are upon him, the greater must his punishment be.

3. There is no removing of the curse then; *when once the master of the house is risen up, and hath shut to the door*, Luke xiii. 25. The time of trial is over, and judgement is to be passed according to what was done in the flesh. When a court is erected within a sinner's own breast in this world, and conscience convicts him as a transgressor of the law, a covenant-breaker, and therefore pronounces him cursed; there is a Surety for the sinner to fly to, an Advocate into whose hands he may commit his cause, a Mediator to trust in and roll his burden on by faith. But before that tribunal there is none for the sinner who comes thither under the curse. As the tree fell, it must lie; that throne is a throne of pure justice to him, without any mixture of the grace he despised. By the law of works which he chose to live under, despising the law of grace, he must be judged.

4. *Lastly*, Wherefore he must there inevitably sink under the weight of the curse for ever, Psal. i. 5. *The ungodly shall not stand in the judgement.* He must fall a sacrifice for his own sin, who now slights the only atoning sacrifice, even Christ our passover sacrificed for us. In the course of justice sin must be satisfied for, and without shedding of blood is no remission. The satisfaction must be proportioned to the injury done to the honour of an infinite God by it. In the gospel Christ is set before the sinner, as the scape-goat before Aaron: he is called to lay his hand on the head thereof, by faith transferring the guilt on the Surety. Since the sinner did not so, but lived and died under the curse, his iniquity must fall and lie for ever on his own head.

The

The condition of the natural man's soul shut up in hell under the curse.

THIRDLY, The soul is shut up in hell, by virtue of the curse, Luke xvi. 22. 23.—*And in hell he lift up his eyes being in torments.* Thus, by the curse of the broken covenant, the sinner is cut asunder by the sword of death, and his soul receives its portion, where shall be weeping and gnashing of teeth, being hauled from the tribunal into the pit. Then falls the great rain of God's wrath on the men of his curse, the sinner being, to his own conviction, entered in payment of the debt which he can never discharge, and which can never be forgiven. The state of the separate soul, under the curse, after its particular judgement, who can sufficiently express the horror of? Consider these things following on that head.

1. Separate souls under the curse, after their particular judgement, are lodged in the place of the damned, called *hell* in the scriptures. Then the godly and the wicked change places, who lived together in this world as a mixed company: the soul which through faith received the blessing, is carried to heaven; and the soul which parted with the body under the curse, is carried to hell. This is evident from the parable of Dives and Lazarus, Luke xvi. 22. 23. In hell the souls of the wicked are lodged as in a prison, reserved to a further judgement against the great day, 1 Pet. iii. 19. And who can imagine what thoughts of horror must, at its entrance thither, seize the soul, which a little before was in the body in this world, but then goes into an unalterable state of misery, and hath the bars of the pit shut upon it, without hope of relief? O the fearful sudden change it will be to them who lived in wealth and ease, and to them who lived in poverty and distress here! Who can say to which of them it shall be the most frightful change?

2. The dregs of the curse shall there be wrung out to them, and they made to drink them, in the fearful punishment inflicted upon them for the satisfaction of offended justice, for all their sins original and actual. Then shall be more remarkably, than ever before, accomplished that, Psal. lxxv. 8. *In the hand of the Lord there is a cup, and*

Cov. I. X *the*

the wine is red: it is full of mixture, and he poureth out of the same: but the dregs thereof all the wicked of the earth shall wring them out, and drink them. The separate soul doth not sleep, nor is void of feeling, nor is it extinguished till the resurrection, as some have dreamed: no, no; it lives, but lives in misery; it feels, but feels nothing but anguish. It is laid under the punishment of loss, being at once deprived of all those things wherein it sought its satisfaction in this world, and of all the happiness of the other world: and it is punished also with the punishment of sense, the wrath of an angry God being poured into it, Luke xvi. 23. 24. which is expressed under the notion of being *tormented in a flame.* Then all the joys of the cursed soul are killed, plucked up by the root; and a flood of sorrows surrounds it, having neither brim nor bottom.

3. They are sensible of their lost happiness, Luke xvi. 23. They see it to their unspeakable anguish. Whatever they heard of heaven, and the happiness of those who die in the Lord, while they were on earth; they will get a more affecting discovery of it then, which will cause them rage against themselves, that ever they should have preferred the pleasures of sin and a vain world to such a blessed state. And how must it pierce the wretched soul, to think, that not only all is lost, but lost without possibility of recovery? Luke xvi. 26. O that men would be wise in time, and believe that the state of trial will end with them ere long, and so bend their cares and endeavours, that, amidst the throng of the world's business, cares, vanities, and temptations, they lose not their souls!

4. Their consciences are then awakened, never to fall asleep any more for ever. They will scorch them then like a fire that cannot be quenched, and gnaw them like a worm that never dieth, Mark ix. 44. Without question separate souls are capable of calling things past to remembrance, as is evident in the case of the rich man, Luke xvi. 25. where Abraham bids him remember what a portion he had in this life: and he remembers his five brethren, and what a life he and they led, ver. 28. The conscience that was seared till it was past feeling, will then be fully sensible. The evil of sin will then be clearly seen, because

becaufe felt: the threatenings of the holy law will no more be accounted fcarecrows, nor will there be any fuch fools there as to make a mock of fin. The foul there will be under continual remorfe, and rue for ever the ill-fpent life, where there is no place for repentance. The foul that would never fearch and try its ways, while there was occafion to mend what was amifs, will there go through the feveral fteps of life and converfation here; and every new fin that cafts up to it as done in the body, will pierce the foul like an envenomed arrow.

5. They will be filled with torturing paffions, which will keep the foul ever on the rack. Their finful nature remains with them, under the curfe, and they will fin againft God ftill, as well as they did in this life; but with this difference, that whereas they had pleafure in their fins here, they fhall have none in their fins there; they fhall be for ever precluded from acting that wickednefs that may give pleafure, and the reftraint upon them that way in their prifon may contribute to their torment; for no doubt the feeds of all fin remain ftill in them there under the curfe: but their fins there fhall be their felt mifery too. The fcripture holds out thofe torturing paffions which they will be filled with, by *weeping, and wailing, and gnafhing of teeth*; which intimates to us, that fouls there are overwhelmed with forrow, anguifh, and anxiety, with wrath, grudge, murmuring, envy, rage, and defpair.

6. *Laftly*, In this ftate they muft continue till the laft day, that they be reunited to their refpective bodies, and fo the whole man get his fentence at the general judgement, adjudging both foul and body to everlafting fire, Matth. xxv. For after they are gone out of this world, their wickednefs may be living behind them, and the ftream of it may be running when their bodies are confumed in the grave, and their fouls have been long in the pit of deftruction, like the fin of Jeroboam, who made Ifrael to fin; all which muft be accounted for. And hence it appears, that the expectation of the reuniting with their bodies, can be no comfortable thought to them, but a thought of horror, a fearful expectation.

The condition of the natural man's body in the grave, under the curse.

FOURTHLY, The body goes to the dust in virtue of the curse, Psal. xlix. 14. *Like sheep they are laid in the grave, death shall feed on them.* Man's body in the state of innocence was immortal, not subject to death: sin made it mortal, the curse bound it over to death, and to the grave, the dark territory of death, Rom. vi. 23. *The wages of sin is death.* Hence our Lord Jesus Christ becoming a curse for his own, was carried prisoner to the grave, Is. liii. 9. lay there for a time bound with the cords of death, Acts ii. 24.; but having fully discharged the debt, for which he was laid up, he disarmed death, and proved the destruction of the grave for all that are his, Hos. xiii. 14. But in the mean time, death and the grave remain as before to all those who have no saving interest in him: so that where-ever the dead bodies of the wicked are laid up, or however they are disposed of, whether consumed by the fire, eaten up by other creatures, or laid in a grave properly so called; where-ever they remain in the state of the dead: there they are laid up in virtue of the curse. But the bodies of the godly are not so.

The state of the dead body in the grave, under the curse, we may take up in these three things.

1. It is laid up there as in a prison, like a malefactor in a dungeon, to be kept there till the day of execution. Hence in the language of the Holy Ghost, Psal. xvi. 10. *hell* and the *grave,* or the state of the dead, go under one and the same name: so that article of the creed, that *Christ descended into hell,* is expounded of his continuing in the state of the dead. The bodies of the godly go to the grave too; but it is a place of rest to them, where they rest as in their bed, till the joyful morning of the resurrection, Is. lvii. 2. For death armed with the sting, poured out all its venom on Christ, when it had him there, in their room and stead. So it is a hiding-place to them, Job xiv. 13. whither they are carried from the evil to come, Is. lvii. 1. and where their eyes are held from beholding grievousness, and an end is put to their toil, Rev. xiv. 13. But in scripture-account it is not a place of rest to the ungodly.

ly. Remarkable to this purpose is that text, Job iii 17. 18. *There the wicked ceafe from troubling: and there the weary be at reſt. There the prifoners reſt together, they hear not the voice of the oppreſſor.* There are two forts of men spoke of here, who both go to the grave; ungodly men, troublers of others, perfecutors, oppreſſors; godly men, wearied with trouble, imprifonment, and oppreſſion. The ſtate of the former in the grave is, they are laid by from doing mifchief, cauſing their terror any longer in the land of the living: the ſtate of the latter is, they are at reſt. And as great a difference there is betwixt the two, though one cannot difcern it from the poſture of their duſt, as betwixt a man aſleep in his own bed, and a man bound hand and foot in a dungeon, If. lvii. 2. 1 Sam. ii 9. Pſal. xxxi. 17. And it is the removal or continuance of the curſe that makes the difference.

2. Their fin and guilt remains on them there, and that without further poſſibility of a removal, Job xx. 11. *His bones are full of the fin of his youth, which ſhall lie down with him in the duſt.* Sin is a dangerous companion in life; one had better live in chains of iron, than in chains of guilt: but happy they with whom fin parts, when foul and body part at death. That is the lot of believers in Chriſt, who at the Red ſea of death get the laſt fight of it. There the Lord ſays to the dying faint, whether he hears it or not, as Exod. xiv. 13.—*The Egyptians whom ye have ſeen to-day, ye ſhall ſee them again no more for ever.* But the man dying under the curſe, all his fins take a dead gripe of him never to be let go; and when he lies down in the grave, they lie down with him, and they never part. This is not to be diſcerned neither, in the duſt, by bodily eyes; but it is moſt certain, and as it is reprefented in the glaſs of the word, it makes a ſpectacle of unſpeakable horror, Nah. i. 14.—*I will make thy grave, for thou art vile;* like a vile, filthy, and loathſome thing, which one cannot endure to look at, and which there is no cleanſing of; but a hole is digged in the earth, wherein it is covered up with all its filthineſs about it. When a faint dies, there is (ſo to ſpeak) one grave made for him, and another for his vileneſs; and he is to rife again, but his vileneſs never to rife: but for the ungodly, there is but one where

he

he lies down and his vileness with him, both to rise together again.

3. All the ruin brought on their bodies there, is done by virtue of the curse, Job xxiv. 19.—*The grave consumes those which have sinned.* Death makes fearful havock where it comes: not only doth it separate the soul from the body; but separates the several parts of the body one from another, until it reduce the whole into dust, not to be discerned by the quickest eye from common dust. Thus it fares with the bodies of the godly indeed, as well as the bodies of the wicked: nevertheless great is the difference; the curse working these effects in the bodies of the latter, but not of the former; stinged death in the one, unstinged death in the other: so all these effects in the one are pieces of revenging wrath for the satisfaction of justice; in the other not so, but like the melting down of the crazy silver vessel, to be cast into a new mould.

The condition of natural men rising again under the curse.

FIFTHLY, They shall rise again, out of their graves, at the last day, under the curse, John v. 29. *And shall come forth,—they that have done evil, unto the resurrection of damnation.* Compare Matth. xxv. 41. *Depart from me, ye cursed,* &c. Our Lord Jesus Christ, who became a curse for all his people, was carried from the cross to the grave: but there the debt was fully paid, and the curse was exhausted; the cursing law and justice had no more to exact of him: so he was brought forth out of the prison of the grave, as a free person who had completely discharged the debt, which he was laid in prison for. And hence believers in Christ, though they fall down into the grave, as well as others; yet they do not fall down into it under the curse, far less do they rise again at the last day under it. But the natural man having lived and died, under the covenant of works, goes to the grave under the curse: and forasmuch as all that comes on him, in the state of the dead, cannot satisfy completely for his debt, therefore as the curse remains on him all along while he is there, so he rises again under it. And in this doleful event three things may be considered.

1. They

1. They shall rise again out of their graves by virtue of the curse. This is implied in that forecited John v. 29. When the end of time is come, the last trumpet shall sound, and all that are in the graves shall come forth, godly and ungodly: but the godly shall rise, by virtue of their blessed union with Christ, Rom. viii. 11.; the ungodly, by virtue of the curse of the broken covenant on them. As the malefactor is, in virtue of the sentence of death passed on him, shut up in close prison till the time of execution; and, in virtue of the same sentence, brought out of prison at the time appointed for his execution: even so the unbeliever is, in virtue of the curse of the law adjudging him to eternal death in hell, laid up in the grave till the last day; and, in virtue of the same curse, brought out of the grave at that day. Hence, by the by, one may see, that there is no force in that arguing, *viz.* The separation of the soul and body was not the sanction of the law; else why should the wicked be clothed with their bodies at the resurrection? It is true, that separation was not the whole of the sanction, but it was a remarkable part of it: and there is no inconsistency in the separation and the reuniting of soul and body, their being both comprehended in the sanction, more than in the laying up of the malefactor for, and bringing him forth to execution, their being both comprehended in the sentence of death. The same curse that separated soul and body at death, and separated each part of the body from another in the grave, shall, at the time appointed, have another kind of effect in bringing together the scattered pieces of dust, and joining them together in one body, and joining it again to the soul.

2. All their sin and guilt shall rise again with them: the body that was laid in the grave, a vile body; a foul instrument of the soul in divers lusts; an unclean vessel, stained, polluted, and defiled, with divers kinds of filthy impure lusts; shall rise again with all its impurities cleaving to it, Is. lxvi. *ult. And they shall go forth, and look upon the carcases of the men that have transgressed against me: for—they shall be an abhorring unto all flesh.* It is the peculiar privilege of believers, to have their *vile bodies changed,* Phil. iii. 21. If the bodies of sinners be not cleansed,

cleansed, by the washing with that *pure water*, Heb. x. 22. viz. the blood and Spirit of Jesus Christ: though they be strained in never so minute parts, through the earth in a grave, they will lose nothing of their vileness and pollution, it will still cleave to every part of their dust, and appear again therewith at the resurrection. Then shall they get a new and horrible sight, of the use they made of their tongues in profane swearing, cursing, mocking at religion, lying, reproaching, cruel and unjust threatenings, &c. in undue silence, when God's honour, their own souls interest, and their neighbours good, required them to speak; of the use they made of their bellies, in gluttony, and drunkenness, and pampering of the flesh; of their bodies, in uncleanness, lasciviousness, and wantonness; of their hands, in picking, stealing, unjust beating and abusing their fellow-creatures, immoderately busying them in things of this life, to the neglect of their souls: in a word, of the use they made of their whole body, and every member thereof; with the qualities and endowments thereof, its youth, beauty, comeliness, health, and strength; together with the memorials of dying put into their hands, as hurts, wounds, weakness, sickness, old age; all of them to have been improven for God, the good of mankind, and their own eternal welfare. O, if men could look upon these things now, as then they will appear, the sweet morsel of sin would be accounted as the poison of asps.

3. Their appearance will be frightful and horrible beyond expression, when they come forth of their graves under the curse, and set their feet on the earth again. When, at the sound of the trumpet, the dead shall all arise out of their graves, and the wicked are cast forth as abominable branches, what a fearful awakening will they have out of their long sleep! When they get another sight of this earth, upon which they led their ungodly lives; see their godly neighbours taken out from among them in the same spot of ground where they all lay, and carried away with joy to meet the Lord in the air; and when they see the Judge come to the judgement of the great day, in awful state; and they are going forward to compear before his tribunal: no appearance of malefactors going un-

der

der a guard to the place of execution; no cafe of a befieged city taken, and foldiers burning and flaying, and the inhabitants running and crying for fear of the fword; can fufficiently reprefent the frightful appearance, which men rifen again at the laft day, under the curfe, will make. What ghaftly vifages will they then have! How will the now faireft ungodly faces be black as a coal, through extreme terror, anguifh, and perplexity! How will they fhiver, tremble, their knees fmite one againft another, and their hearts be pierced as with arrows, while they fee the doleful day they would not believe! What roarings and yellings, and hideous noife will then be amongft the innumerable croud of the ungodly, driven forward to the tribunal as beafts to the flaughter! What *crying to the rocks and the mountains to fall on them, and hide them from the face of the Lamb,* but all in vain! Rev. vi. 16. 17. Then will the weight of the curfe be felt to purpofe, how lightly foever men now walk under it.

The condition of natural men compearing before Chrift's tribunal under the curfe.

SIXTHLY, They fhall compear before the tribunal of Chrift under the curfe, like a malefactor in chains before his judge, Matth. xxv. 41. All muft appear there, great and fmall, good and bad; none fhall be a-miffing; Rom. xiv. 10. *We fhall all ftand before the judgement-feat of Chrift.* But they who now receive the bleffing through faith, fhall be in no hazard of the curfe then or there. But it is not poffible, that thofe who lived and died under the curfe, fhould not have it upon them before that tribunal; for after death there is no removing of it. The fearful ftate of thofe under the curfe before that judgement-feat, may be viewed in thefe particulars.

1. In virtue of the curfe, they fhall be fet on the left hand, Matth. xxv. 33. No honour is defigned for them, but fhame and everlafting contempt; no fentence, but what will fix them in an unalterable ftate of mifery: fo there will be no accefs for them to the right hand amongft the bleffed; but they muft be ranged together on the left hand as a company of curfed ones.

2. The face of the Judge must needs be terrible to them, as being under the curse of him, who sits upon the throne, Rev. vi. 16. 17.—*Hide us from the face of him that sitteth on the throne,* &c. When they see him, they shall know him to be he, who with his Father and the Holy Spirit gave that law which they transgressed, made that covenant which they broke, whose voice the curse of the law against transgressors, was and is; the which must needs take effect in their everlasting ruin, by reason of his justice, holiness, and truth. And he will be in a special manner terrible to such as had the gospel offer made to them, and the more terrible, the more plainly, affectionately, and powerfully it was pressed on them to accept it. O how will it strike them through as a dart, when they look towards the throne, thinking with themselves, " Lo, there he sits to judge me now, and destroy me, who so often made offer of life and salvation to me by his messengers, which I slighted! I might through him have obtained the blessing, but now I stand trembling under the weight of the curse. The despised Lamb of God is turned into a lion against me." Consider this, O sinner, while God is on a throne of grace for you; lest it be taken down, and a tribunal of pure justice be set up for you.

3. To clear the equity of the curse, and the execution thereof upon them, their works shall be brought into judgement, Eccl. xii. 14. *God shall bring every work into judgement, with every secret thing, whether it be good, or whether it be evil.* Their whole life shall be searched into, and laid to the rule of the holy law, and the enormity and sinfulness thereof be discovered. Their corrupt nature, with all the malignity and venom of it, against the rule of righteousness, shall be laid open. Their sins shall be set in the light of God's countenance, in such full tale, that they shall see God is true to his word and oath, that he would not forget any of their works. The mask will then be entirely taken off their faces, and all their pretences to piety solemnly rejected, and declared to have been but hypocrisy. Their secret wickedness, which they rejoiced to have got hid, and which they so artfully managed, that there was no discovering of it, while they might have confessed and found mercy, shall then be set in broad day-
light

light before God and the world, when there is no remedy. Conscience shall then be no more blind nor dumb; but shall witness against them, and for God; and shall never be silent any more. The sin and misery brought upon others, by their ungodly courses, taking effect when they themselves were gone out of the world, shall then be pursued in all their breadth and length, and laid to their charge, proven against them: And so the account of their debt to the divine justice shall be fully stated at that day.

4. Their doom shall be pronounced, Matth. xxv. 41. *Depart from me, ye cursed, into everlasting fire, prepared for the devil and his angels.* Thus shall they receive their final sentence, never to hear more from the mouth of him that sits upon the throne. This determines the full execution of the curse on the whole man, soul and body together. The godly shall get their final sentence too: but O the vast difference betwixt *Come ye blessed*, and *Depart ye cursed!* The unspeakable happiness of the saints in heaven, and the unspeakable misery of the damned in hell, will shew the difference. But the weight of both lies, you see, in the state of the parties, as under the blessing, or under the curse. There is the turning point in respect of one's eternal state.

This world burnt with fire, in virtue of the curse.

SEVENTHLY, As they shall be, by virtue of the curse now to be fully executed, driven from the judgement seat into hell; so, in virtue of the same curse of the broken covenant of works, this world shall go up in flames, and so have an end put to it, 2 Pet. iii. 10.—*The heavens shall pass away with a great noise, and the elements shall melt with fervent heat, the earth also and the works that are therein shall be burnt up.* When sin got place in the earth by the breach of the covenant, the curse was laid upon it, and the foundations thereof were shaken; by its relation to man, it came within the compass of the curse for his sin, and so was devoted to destruction, which shall then take its full effect. Yea, the whole frame of the creation having relation to sinful man, was blasted for his sake, being made *subject to vanity*, Rom. viii. 20. 21. And so the heaven, which because it is over the head of the covenant-breaker,

breaker, is therefore now sometimes made brass, shall upon the same account then pass away with a great noise; even as the earth, which is sometimes made iron, because it is under him, shall then be burnt up, Deut. xxviii. 23. with 2 Pet. iii. 10. So the curse is a train laid in the bowels of the creation, which now and then gives it terrible shocks, but will at last blow all up together. And when once it has done that, and so put an end to this stage of vanity and wickedness; all the effects of it that now lie scattered through the creation, shall be gathered together and cast into the place of the damned (Rev. xx. 14. 15.) with them: so that though death and misery are every where to be found now, it shall be no where then, but in that one place; and all that goes under the name of death shall be in that place. The weight comprehended in the curse, lies now on many backs, and so is the more easily borne: but then it shall all lie on the backs of the men of the Lord's curse, and on theirs only; and so shall they feel the full weight of it.

The condition of natural men, lying for ever under the weight of the curse in hell.

LASTLY, They shall lie for ever, under the weight of the curse, in hell, on soul and body together, Matth. xxv. 41. *Depart from me, ye cursed, into everlasting fire, prepared for the devil and his angels.* Here is their misery completed, here is the full execution of the curse. The curse was big with wrath, indignation, and fury of a holy, jealous, just God, against sin, and sinners for sin, ever since it first entered, upon the breach of the covenant: and it has since that time still been bringing forth; yet there has likewise still been some allay in it, and the storm of wrath has not yet come to the height. While men, even the men of the Lord's curse, live in this world, much patience is exercised towards them; and partly through the slenderness of the strokes laid on them, partly through their insensibleness, and partly through the mixture of mercy in their cup, they make a shift to live at some ease; and if their case be at any time disturbed, yet they ordinarily, though not always, find some means to recover it: and even while their souls are in hell, during the time

betwixt

betwixt their death and the last judgement, their bodies lie at ease in the grave; so but the one half of the man is in torment, and a part of him is easy, without any sense or feeling of the least annoyance. But when once the dead are raised again, and the men of the curse have got their last sentence, and time is absolutely at an end, the mystery of God finished, and a quite new state of the creation brought in, to wit, the eternal state; then shall the curse bring forth the threatened death in its full strength and force on the undischarged covenant-breakers; and as Christ standing Surety for the elect, knew by his experience, so shall the men of the curse know by their experience, what was within the compass of the threatening of the covenant of works, Gen. ii. 17.—*In the day that thou eatest thereof, thou shalt surely die.* Many a commentary has Heaven writ upon it unto men, in flaming fire, in blood and gore, in sobs, groans, and swooning of the whole creation: but never a full one yet, excepting in the sufferings of the Son of God on the cross. The elect of God get their eyes opened to read that, and so they make haste and escape out of the dominion of that covenant to which the curse belongs: but the rest are blinded, they cannot read it there. But God will write another full commentary on it, after the last judgement, whence all the men of the Lord's curse shall, in their horrible experience, learn what was in it, namely, in the threatening of the covenant of works. The dregs of the cup of the curse shall then be brought above, and they shall drink them.

1. In virtue of the curse, the pit, having received them, shall close its mouth on them. A fearful emblem of this we have Numb. xvi. 32. 33. in the case of Korah and his company; *And the earth opened her mouth, and swallowed them up, and their houses, and all the men that appertained unto Korah, and all their goods. They, and all that appertained to them, went down alive into the pit, and the earth closed upon them.* Compare that threatening, Psal. xxi. 9. *Thou shalt make them as a fiery oven in the time of thine anger: the Lord shall swallow them up in his wrath, and the fire shall devour them.* They shall be cast into the lake of fire, as death and hell are, to be shut up there without
coming

coming forth again any more, Rev. xx. 14. 15. By the force of the curse upon them, they shall be confined in the place allotted for damned men and devils. It shall so draw the bars of the pit about them, that sooner shall they remove mountains of brass, than remove them. It shall be stronger than chains of iron to bind them hand and foot, that they make no escape, Matth. xxii. 13. yea and to bind them in bundles for the fire of God's wrath, that companions in sin may be companions in punishment, Matth. xiii 30.

2. The curse shall then be like a partition-wall of adamant, to separate them quite from God, and any the least comfortable intercourse with him, Matth. xxv. 41. While on the other side of the wall, the light of glory shines, more bright than a thousand suns, filling the saints with joy unspeakable, and which we cannot comprehend, and causing the arch of heaven to ring with their songs of praise: on their side is nothing but utter darkness, without the least gleam of light; and there shall be weeping, wailing, and gnashing of teeth. For why, God himself is the only true happiness of the creature, and Christ the only way to the Father; but then there is a total and final separation betwixt God and Christ, and them. The day of the Lamb's wrath is come, all possibility of reconciliation is removed, and patience towards them is quite ended, and the curse hath its full stroke: So God, the Fountain of all good, departs quite from them, abandons them, casts them off utterly; and that moment all the streams of goodness towards them dry up, and their candle is quite extinguished. Then shall be known what is in that word, Hos. ix. 12. *Wo to them when I depart from them.* And there is no getting over the wall, no passing of the great gulf for ever, Luke xvi. 26.

3. It shall, hence, be a final stop to all sanctifying influences towards them. While they are in this world, there is a possibility of removing the curse, and that the worst of men may be made holy: but when there is a total and final separation from God in hell, surely there are no sanctifying influences there. The corrupt nature they carried with them thither, must then abide with them there; and they must needs act there, since their being

is

is continued; and a corrupt nature will ever act corruptly, while it acts at all. Matth. vii. 17. And therefore there will be sin in hell after the last judgement, unless one will suppose that they will be under no law there; which is absurd, seeing a creature as a creature owes obedience to God, in what state soever it be. Yea, they will sin there at a horrible rate, in blasphemies against God, and other sins akin thereto, as men absolutely void of all goodness, in a desperate state of misery, Rev. xvi. ult. Matth. xxii. 13. The curse will be a dry wind, not to fan nor to cleanse, but to wither, blast, and kill their souls.

4. It shall be the breath that shall blow the fire continually, and keep it burning, for their exquisite torment in soul and body, If. xxx. 33. *For Tophet is ordained of old: yea, for the king it is prepared, he hath made it deep and large : the pile thereof is fire and much wood, the breath of the Lord, like a stream of brimstone, doth kindle it.* There the worm which shall gnaw them, shall never die; for the curse will keep it in life : the fire that shall burn them, shall never be quenched; for the curse shall nourish it, and be as bellows blowing it, to cause it flame without intermission. The curse shall enter into their souls, and melt them like wax before the fire; it shall sink into their flesh and bones, and torment them in every part. It will stake them down there as marks for the arrows of God, which dipt in the poison of the curse shall be continually piercing and burning them up. No pity, no compassion to be shewn any more, but the fire balls of the curse will be flying against them incessantly; Rev. xiv. 11. *The smoke of their torment ascendeth up for ever and ever : and they have no rest day nor night.*

5. Lastly, The curse shall lengthen out their misery to all eternity, Matth. xxv. 41. *Depart from me, ye cursed, into everlasting fire.* It binds the sinner to make complete and full satisfaction, for all the wrongs he has done to the honour of an infinite God; it binds him to pay, till there be a sufficient compensation made for them all. Now, there being no proportion betwixt finite and infinite, the finite creature can never, by its sufferings, expiate its crimes against an infinite God. Hence, when the sinner has suffered

fered millions of ages in hell, the curse still binds him down to suffer more, because he has not yet fully satisfied: and since he can never fully satisfy, it will bind him down for ever and ever, Rev. xiv. 11. and will bring new floods of wrath over his head, without end; and renew its demands of satisfaction, through the ages of eternity, but never, never say, It is enough.

Thus have I endeavoured to open up unto you, the nature of the curse of the broken covenant of works, and the dreadful condition of those under it, in this life, and after this life. But after all, who knows the power of God's wrath? No tongue can tell, what the frightful experience of those who live and die under it, shall teach them. But thus much may suffice to have shewn you the misery of being under the covenant of works.

Application of the doctrine, That natural men, being under the broken covenant of works, are under the curse.

This doctrine may be improven, (1.) for *conviction*, and (2.) for *exhortation*.

USE I. of *conviction*. What has been said on this awful subject, may serve to fix convictions in the consciences both of saints and sinners.

FIRST, Saints, who are brought from under this covenant, delivered from it and the curse thereof by Jesus Christ, view this curse in the nature and weight, the breadth and length of it; and say in your hearts before the Lord,

1. Do ye suitably prize and esteem your God Redeemer and Saviour? Are your hearts suitably affected with the love of God in Christ, that set on foot your deliverance, and brought it about? Ah! this consideration may afford us a breast-full of convictions. What manner of love was this, that the Father did chuse you from among the cursed children of Adam to inherit the blessing? that the Son died for you, to redeem you from this curse? that the Holy Ghost applied to you the purchase of Christ's death, to the actual removing of this curse from off you? O where is that love, that warm, glowing love to the Lord, that this requires! The Father's love to you while

under the curse, moved him to make his Son to be sin for you, who knew no sin, that you might be made the righteousness of God in him. Christ's love to you made him become a curse for you, and drink the dregs of that cup, which ye should have drunk through eternity in hell. The Spirit's love to you made him watch the moment appointed for your deliverance, and bring you out with a strong hand from the dominion of the law, and transport you into the dominion of grace, where there is no more curse. O look back to the dreadful curse which ye were under; look up to the love in delivering of you; keep one eye upon the one, and another eye upon the other, till these cold hearts of yours warm with love.

2. Do ye suitably prize the new covenant, the second covenant? Do ye pry into the mystery of the glorious contrivance, stand and wonder at the device for bringing cursed sinners to inherit the blessing? Would it not become you well to be often looking into it, and saying, *This is all my salvation, and all my desire?* 2 Sam. xxiii. 5. Ah! why have we not higher and more honourable thoughts of the covenant of grace, of the second Adam the Head, Surety, and Messenger of the covenant, of the gospel the proclamation of the covenant, the Bible the book of the covenant, the promises of the covenant, the matchless privileges of the covenant, and even of the public criers of the covenant too? If. lii. 7. To help you to this, lay the volume of the two covenants before you: open and read the covenant of works in the first place, where ye will find nothing but demands of perfect obedience under the pain of the curse; a promise of life upon conditions impossible to be performed by you, but the curse, wrath, death, hell, and damnation to the sinner. Then turn over to the covenant of grace, and read life and salvation through Jesus Christ by faith; no curse, death, hell, damnation, nor revenging wrath; all these discharged by the Surety. And so raise your esteem of the new covenant in Christ's blood.

3. Do ye walk answerably to the deliverance from this curse? Ah! may not that be applied justly to us, Deut. xxxii. 6. *Do ye thus requite the Lord, O foolish people and unwise? is not he thy Father that hath bought thee? hath*

he not made thee, and established thee? Obedience to all the ten commands is bound on all under the covenant of works, under the pain of the curse, Gal. iii. 10. *Cursed is every one that continueth not in all things which are written in the book of the law to do them.* Obedience to them all is bound on believers too, but by another tie, viz. the tie of their deliverance from the curse by their God-Redeemer, Exod. xx 2. *I am the Lord thy God, which have brought thee out of the land of Egypt,* &c. And this, and not the former, is the way in which the law of the ten commands gets any acceptable obedience, 1 Tim. i. 5. from sinful man. O look to the curse of the covenant of works, from which ye are delivered, and be convinced and humbled to the very dust,

(1) That ye should walk so untenderly, unwatchfully, and uncircumspectly, before the Lord that bought you, and that in midst of cursed children, a crooked and perverse generation. What can more strike a nail to the heart of a gracious person, than when the Spirit of the Lord whispers into his soul, *Have I been a wilderness unto Israel? a land of darkness? wherefore say my people, We are lords, we will come no more unto thee?* Jer. ii 31. And, *Is this your kindness to your friend?* Is that your compassion to the world lying in wickedness, to cast a stumbling-block before the blind? You speak, you act, untenderly: Is that the use of the tongue redeemed from the curse? is that the use of the eyes, hands, and feet, body and soul, delivered from the curse of the broken covenant? I think, a believer looking to the curse, should say, and abide by it, *To me to live is Christ*, Phil. i. 21.

(2.) That ever ye should so dote upon this earth, this cursed earth, that the curse of the broken covenant of works has lien upon these five thousand years, and has sucked the sap out of, and so dried up by this time, that it is near to taking fire, and to be burnt to ashes, by virtue of the curse upon it. Let the men of the Lord's curse, who have their portion in it, set their hearts upon it, go upon their belly, and lick the dust, (it is no wonder they cannot get up their back, on whom the heavy curse of the broken covenant lies): but lift ye up your souls unto the Lord, and hearken to his voice, Cant. iv. 8.

Come

Come with me from Lebanon, my spouse, with me from Lebanon: look from the top of Amana, from the top of Shenir and Hermon, from the lions dens, from the mountains of the leopards.

(3.) That ye should perform duties so heartlesly, coldly, and indifferently; with so little faith, love, fervency, humility, zeal, and confidence. O look to the curse of the broken covenant, with the effects of it in earth and hell, that ye may be stirred up to the performance of duty after another manner. I mean not that ye should look upon it as what ye are actually liable to in case of transgression; for this to a believer, who is never free from sin one moment, may well make his heart die in him like a stone, it will never kindly quicken him; it may well drag or drive him to his duty, like a slave; it will never cause him perform it like a son: but look upon it as what ye are delivered from, and that will draw, melt, and kindly quicken the heart in love, Eph. ii. 11. 12. 13. Luke i. 74. 75.

(4) That ye should bear your troubles and trials so impatiently, as if your crosses were so many curses. Look to the condition of those under the curse in this world, and you will see your heaviest cross is lighter than their smallest ones, which have the weight of the curse in them, that yours have not, however ye cry out under their weight: yea your adversity is better than their prosperity; the frowns of providence you meet with, are preferable to the smiles of providence in their lot; there is no curse in the former, but in the latter there is. Look to the condition of those under the curse in hell, and that duly considered, ye will kiss the rod, and say, *It is of the Lord's mercies that we are not consumed, because his compassions fail not*, Lam. iii. 22. Look how Christ redeemed us from the curse of the law, being made a curse for us, and ye will see the poison taken out of the cup, and the pure water of affliction presented to you in your cup to pledge him in: And why not drink it, and drink it thankfully? bear the cross for him, and take blows and buffets for his sake, and from him for our own good, who has borne away the curse?

4. Have ye due thoughts of the evil of sin? Is your horror of it suitably raised? Rom. xii. 9. *Abhor that which is*

evil, abhor it as hell, so the word may bear. If you duly consider the curse, it may fill you with shame and blushing on this head. There is much blindness in the minds of believers, much hardness in their hearts, and coldness in their affections with respect to spiritual things. The lively sense of the evil of sin is often very small. We dare not own believers to be yet liable to the curse, Christ having, with his precious blood applied to them by faith, freed them from it: but it is of great and necessary use to them as a looking-glass, wherein they may see the evil of sin, the due demerit of it, what their sins do in themselves deserve, what Christ suffered for these sins of theirs, and what they should have suffered for them, if Christ had not suffered it in their stead. Trace the curse in its effects in this life, and after this life, as they have been represented to you: so will you see God's high indignation against sin, the infinite evil that is in the least transgression of the holy law. Behold it in this glass, and you shall conceive a horror of it; and be ashamed, that you have entertained so slight thoughts of it.

5. *Lastly*, Are ye duly affected with the case of those, who being strangers to Christ are yet under the curse? Are ye at due pains for their recovery and deliverance? How natural is it for men, who with difficulty have escaped the greatest danger, to be affected with the case of others who are still in the same danger, in hazard of perishing? But though multitudes are under the curse still, and, it may be, some such as we have a peculiar interest in; yet where is the due care, compassion, and concern for them, that they may be delivered? If it be so with them, why are we thus? They are not concerned for themselves, because they have not yet got a broad view of their hazard: but ah! why are not such concerned for them, as have had their eyes opened in their own case? Sure the case of all men by nature is alike, and therefore the past danger of believers, gives a clear view of the present danger of unbelievers, unless it be out of mind with them, which it should not be, that once they were *without Christ, being aliens from the commonwealth of Israel, and strangers from the covenants of promise, having no hope, and without God in the world,* Eph. ii. 12. The apostle's experience of the

terror

terror of the Lord, ſtirred him up to perſuade others to flee from the curſe, 2 Cor. v. 11.; and it well becomes others who are themſelves as brands pluckt out of the burning, to act with that concern in the caſe of others, as pulling them out of the fire, Jude ver. 23.; and to mourn for the caſe of thoſe who continue inſenſible of their danger, as our bleſſed Redeemer did in the caſe of Jeruſalem, Luke xix. 41. 42.

Secondly, Sinners, ye who are under the broken covenant of works ſtill, not united to Chriſt by faith, and ſavingly intereſted in the covenant of grace, but living yet in your natural irregenerate ſtate, ye may hence be convinced,

1. That ye are under the curſe.
2. That ye are in a very miſerable condition, being under the curſe.
3. That your caſe is deſperately ſinful, while you are under the covenant of works.
4. That while ye remain under that covenant, ye remain under the curſe.
5. That there is no ſalvation for you under that covenant.
6. That there is an abſolute neceſſity of being ſet free from the covenant of works, of being brought into the covenant of grace.
7. That your help muſt come wholly from the Lord Jeſus Chriſt.

Firſt, Sinners, ye who are under the broken covenant of works ſtill, ye may hence be convinced, that ye are under the curſe; ye are they who are the people of the Lord's curſe, under the ſentence of the law actually binding you over to deſtruction. Ye are they who by the breaking of the original contract have fallen under the penalty, and are decerned in the court of heaven to pay it. Againſt you as tranſgreſſors of the law is the ſentence paſſed according to the threatening, Gen. ii. 17. *In the day that thou eateſt thereof, thou ſhalt ſurely die.* Againſt you and every one of you in particular is the curſe denounced. So the condition of thoſe under the curſe, is your condition in particular; and what ſuch are liable to, you are liable to: for your name is in the black roll of the people of the curſe,

of

of those appointed to death, and devoted to destruction, in virtue of the curse of the broken covenant of works.

O Sirs, admit the conviction, and go not about to bless yourselves in your hearts, putting the thoughts of being under the curse far away from you. There is light enough here to convince your consciences in that point, if ye will not shut your eyes against clear light. All who are under the broken covenant of works, are under the curse: but you are yet under that covenant: therefore you are under the curse. If you be not under that covenant, where is your discharge from it? The believer's discharge may be read, Rom. viii. 1. *There is therefore now no condemnation to them which are in Christ Jesus.* Chap vii. 4. *Wherefore, my brethren, ye also are become dead to the law by the body of Christ; that ye should be married to another, even to him who is raised from the dead.* But where is yours? The unbeliever's discharge is no where to be found. It is past dispute that covenant is broken, and that being broken it curseth the breakers: it is undeniable that you are breakers of it, and therefore you must be under the curse.

It is your interest to admit this conviction. What will it avail you to bless yourselves in your own hearts, when God himself in his holy law denounceth the curse against you? It is not by the sentence you pass on yourselves that you must stand or fall, but by the sentence God passeth on you in his word. Nay mens blessing themselves, against whom God denounceth the curse, does but the more expose them to the evils contained in the curse coming on them speedily and furiously; Deut. xxix. 19. 20. *And it come to pass when he heareth the words of this curse, that he bless himself in his heart, saying, I shall have peace, though I walk in the imagination of mine heart, to add drunkenness to thirst: the Lord will not spare him, but then the anger of the Lord, and his jealousy shall smoke against that man, and all the curses that are written in this book shall lie upon him, and the Lord shall blot out his name from under heaven.* The admitting of this conviction is among the first steps to a delivery: and there would be good hopes of one's obtaining of the blessing of the gospel at length, if he were once soundly convinced of his being under the curse

curse of the law. And therefore the curse is preached, not that sinners may perish under it, but that they seeing themselves under it, may stir up themselves to make their escape. The law does its work to prepare sinners for Christ, convincing them of sin, that they are sinners; convincing them of their misery, that they are under the curse: and they that never yet saw themselves under the curse, give a shrewd sign that they were never yet brought from under it. But when once a sinner sees himself concluded under the curse of the law, then he is in a fair way to prize Christ and the blessing of the gospel, and to get himself carefully to inquire, what course he shall take to be saved. And the believing of the curse of the law with a particular application to one's self, must necessarily go before the so believing the promise of the gospel indeed.

Why should it seem strange in your eyes, who yet are not truly united to Christ by faith, that you should be under the curse of the broken covenant of works? That is the common case of all mankind by nature; and the deliverance from under it befals no man in a morning-dream. And sure it is, that most men have never been much in pain to get rid of it; and some there are who striving to get clear of it in a legal way, have but wreathed that yoke faster about their own necks. Do not you know, that Christ himself as the elect's Surety was made a curse? How could that be if they themselves had not been under it, and likewise unable to bear it so as to exhaust it? Now, there is no saving interest in his purchase, till once the soul is brought to Christ by faith, and united to him; which you are not.

It is very consistent with the mercy of God, to lay unbelievers under the curse: for his mercy can never act in prejudice of his exact justice. The covenant being made with Adam for all mankind, the curse behoved to fall on the breakers according to the threatening, by virtue of the truth and justice of God. But mercy indeed has a way made for it towards the miserable under the curse, inasmuch as the prisoners are made prisoners of hope, by having deliverance from the curse proclaimed to them in the gospel; the which may be actually conveyed to them in the way of God's own appointment, namely, the cursed
sinner's

sinner's believing on the name of Christ. But what need were there of either purchasing or proclaming it to you, if you were not under it?

Think not, that you cannot be under the curse, because God has done much for you, has given you many blessings, as health, strength, wit, wealth and prosperity in the world; or because he has wrought many wonderful deliverances for you, has brought you from a low and mean estate to a high one, and mightily increased you, in outward comforts and enjoyments. Remember and consider well, that all these are but left-hand blessings, which one may have poured in upon him in abundance, and yet be under the curse, and they be cursed to him, Mal. ii. 2. —*I will send a curse upon you, and I will curse your blessings: yea, I have cursed them already.* Neither think, that because you are poor and mean in the world, have a hard and afflicted lot therein, that therefore you are certainly possessed of God's blessing, and not under his curse. Nay, these things are in their own nature effects of the curse, and so they are in very deed to all who are not in Christ, but under the first covenant: and the curse may and doth pursue men in this world, as well as in the world to come: and one may be very miserable in this life, and in the other life too, by virtue of the curse. Neither deceive yourselves in this matter, with external privileges which you do enjoy in the fellowship of the church: you may be set down at the table of gospel-ordinances there, and yet be under the curse, and by virtue thereof none of these things doing your souls good, Rom. xi 8.

Wherefore, young sinners and old sinners, yet in your natural unconverted state, be convinced, that ye are under the curse, which has been described. Lay the matter to heart; what the law saith to them that are under it, it says to you; take it home then to yourselves, and believe you are under the curse.

Secondly, From what you have heard, ye may be convinced, that ye are in a very miserable condition, being under the curse. Eph. ii. 3 —*And were by nature the children of wrath.* Whatever your outward lot in the world is, your condition is dreadful in this respect. If you had Samson's strength, Absalom's beauty, Solomon's wit and wealth,

and

and Methuselah's long life-time to enjoy them in; your case is miserable beyond expression, being under the curse of the broken covenant of works. The case of a devoted person, loaded with the curses of a city or country, and so put to death, was lamentable: but whosoever thou art who art under this covenant, and so under the curse, thou hast the curse of the Lord of heaven and earth upon thee, binding thee over to eternal destruction, and so art in a thousand times worse case. Your loss is unspeakable, and the whole world cannot compensate it; namely, the loss of God's favour. This burden is insupportable; for there is that weight in this curse, which will sink thee for ever, though now perhaps thou feelest it not. The curse binds thee to the payment of a debt to revenging justice, which thou wilt never be able to discharge. You have heard your miserable condition under the curse, at large.

To sum it up in a few words: Your condition is miserable here, and will be more miserable hereafter, if you die as you now live. In this world the cloud of wrath hangs over your head, and the small rain of God's indignation is continually falling upon you; in the world to come, the full shower will fall, the floods of wrath will break out and overwhelm you. Your life hangs in doubt every day; and as you live in the most dangerous circumstances, exposed without any covert to the arrows of wrath; so you are not ready to die. On this side death you are in the midst of your armed enemies, and on the other side death you fall into the hands of the living God. O lay to heart your misery, ere it be too late.

Refuse not to admit the conviction of the great misery of your condition, because you do not feel yourself so miserable. Remember, that it is not your feeling, but God's word of truth, which can determine you happy or miserable. The judgement of God is always according to truth: and if you will carry your case to the word, you will see it a most deplorable case; view it in the glass of the holy broken law which you are under, and you must needs be affected with the horror of it: *For as many as are of the works of the law, are under the curse.* You read, you hear the law, with its terrible sentence against the breakers, its fearful curses, and denunciations of wrath: but do you apply them to yourselves? Nay, you entertain them as if they did not concern you, nor were directed to you: and if at any time they are like to take hold of you, and gripe your consciences, you flee from them, and labour to divert your minds from such thoughts. But remember, *what things soever the law saith, it saith to them who are under the law*, Rom. iii 19.; and consequently it saith them to you, as if your name were expressed in what it saith. And if the law speaks to you indeed, it will have its effect on you, however ye may persuade yourself it means not concerning you

What though you do not feel your misery? Many think themselves in good case, who in very deed are in a most miserable and wretched condition, as it fared with Laodicea, Rev. iii. 17. They entertain themselves with dreams of happiness, while ruin abides them; think themselves safe, while they are in the utmost hazard. Nay, there are many who are so far gone under the curse, that they are *past feeling*, Eph. iv. 19 Neither the sinfulness nor misery of their souls gives them any distress, anxiety, or perplexity of mind. And that is a case miserable to a degree, inasmuch as it is so far a hopeless case.

But why are ye not sensible of your miserable case? Though ye feel not the weight of it upon you for the present, yea though ye have all ease and prosperity in the world, being neither under trouble of body nor mind, nor any disaster in your affairs; yet ye ought to remember, that the curse works by silent strokes, as well as by tormenting plagues, as ye have heard; yea and that the most terrible workings of the curse, are awaiting the people of the curse, on the other side death. Surely then ye have reason to believe and be convinced, that your state is most miserable, though for the present you feel not the weight of it: for the curse working like a moth, insensibly, makes a ruinous condition, in which the breaking will at length come suddenly at an instant; and they must needs be in a state of unspeakable misery, whom eternal destruction from the presence of the Lord is abiding, certainly to seize them at the time appointed.

Wherefore, believe the doctrine of the law, concerning the curse, and the misery of sinners under it: believe it

with

with application to yourselves. Believe it, upon the testimony of God, who is truth itself; believe it, because God has said it, though perhaps you do not feel it: so shall you come to be duly affected with it, and by that means be stirred up to a concern to be saved from it, which would be a promising step towards a recovery.

Thirdly, From what has been said, ye may be convinced, that your case is desperately sinful, while you are under that covenant. While sin remains, the root of misery remains, which will spring up; the fountain abides, which will cast forth waters of bitterness; and it must and will remain in its strength, while ye are under that covenant; because being under that covenant, ye are under the curse. Hence says the apostle, 1 Cor. xv. 56. *The strength of sin is the law.* While the law, as the covenant of works, then, hath power over a man, sin will have its strength in him, which he can by no means break. While ye are under that covenant, and so under the curse,

1. The guilt of your sin lies on you, the guilt of eternal wrath; and it cannot be removed. The curse stakes you down under that guilt, it binds it upon you as with bands of iron and brass, that it is not possible you should ever get up your head, while the curse is on it; and the curse will be upon it as long as ye are under that covenant, Gal. iii. 10. The covenant in the threatening of it said, If man sin, he shall die: and so sinning he contracted the guilt of death, he came under debt to vindictive justice. The curse of the covenant says, The sinner must die, he must pay his debt to the utmost farthing, he cannot be freed from it without full payment. This you cannot do. The justice and truth of God confirms the curse of the law on the sinner, that it cannot be balked without an imputation of dishonour on them. And since it is not possible for you to make full satisfaction, and so to exhaust the curse, no not through the ages of eternity; it is evident, that the curse does inviolably bind the guilt of your sin on you, so that while the former remains on you, the latter is immoveable.

Now consider that ye were born sinners under this covenant, and so born under the curse of it; and that the law is most extensive, both as to parts and degrees of obedience, and so condemns every thing you do, because you do nothing in the perfection which it requires. Hence your sins are innumerable, your several pieces of guilt are past reckoning, and you are every day adding to the account: but in the mean time the account never suffers any diminution. The state of a sinner under the curse, is an unfathomable gulf, into which the waters are continually running, but not the least drop goes out from it again: new guilt is still added, but nothing of the old nor new guilt is removed; the curse lets in more, but it lets none out: all is sealed up under the curse, from your sin in the womb, till your sin of this minute.

Ye will say, God forbid! Surely he is a merciful God; I have been troubled about my sins, and I have repented of them, and begged forgiveness, and I hope he has pardoned me: and I hope to do the same for the time to come, and he will pardon me still. *Ans.* Not to speak here of what repentance can be found in one lying under the curse of the first covenant, ye would take notice, that you being still under the covenant of works, God deals with you in the way of that covenant; and that covenant admits of no pardon to them who are under it, Acts xiii. 39. For a pardon under that covenant would render the threatening and curse of it vain, and of no effect; and so fasten a blot and stain on the truth and justice of God, and would indeed quite overturn that covenant, and leave it as little regarded by God himself, as it has been by the sinner. Indeed, if you can bear the curse, so as, by your suffering what it binds on you, to exhaust it, and fully satisfy justice; then your crime is expiated, and even in the way of that covenant, God and you are friends again: but that is as impossible for you, as to lift the whole fabric of heaven and earth out of its place. The truth is, nothing can procure you the pardon of one sin, but what can remove the curse: while you are under that covenant, you have no saving interest in the blood of Christ, so the curse is not taken off you thereby: and certain it is, that your repentance and begging forgiveness can never remove the curse from off you, for they can never be a full satisfaction to offended justice: And therefore, notwithstanding of your pretended repenting and begging pardon,

don, your guilt still remains; there is no pardon in the case; though your guilt is forgotten by you, it is remembered of God still, and is written before him as with a pen of iron, and the point of a diamond.

2. Sin has a reigning power over you; and it neither is nor can be broken, you continuing under that covenant: the apostle writing to the believing Romans, says, chap. vi. 14. *Sin shall not have dominion over you; for ye are not under the law, but under grace;* where he plainly teaches, that they who are under the law, are under the dominion of sin. Man innocent and holy entered into that covenant; but once turning a sinner under it, he could never turn a saint again under it. It furnished strength to man being clean to keep himself clean, but provided no laver for him once defiled, to wash himself clean again. I know, that the men of that covenant do not make, all of them, an alike black appearance in their lives and conversations: some of them bear the devil's mark on their foreheads; others have it in the hollow of their hand, which they can keep from the view of the world. But the whole of them are an unsanctified company, and under the reigning power of sin, which is in them entire and unbroken, Rom. iii. 10. 11. 12. *As it is written, There is none righteous, no not one: there is none that understandeth, there is none that seeketh after God. They are all gone out of the way, they are together become unprofitable, there is none that doth good, no not one.* So that I say your case is desperately sinful as to the reigning power of sin, while under that covenant; ye neither are nor can be holy under it. And think not this strange: for,

(1.) Since you are sinners under that covenant, you must needs be dead men; for so runs the threatening, Gen ii. 17. *In the day that thou eatest thereof, thou shalt surely die.* Your natural life is yet preserved, therefore your spiritual life then must needs be gone, Eph. ii. 1. So all the men of that covenant are dead and buried in trespasses and sins. Death preys on their souls, and bears full sway there. Hence it is called *the law of sin and death,* Rom. viii. 3. sin and death reigning over all that are under its dominion. And therefore Christ, the head of the second covenant, was made a quickening spirit, death reigning under the first.

What though you perform religious duties under this covenant? They are all but dead works, but the carcases of duties, without life and spirit. They have the matter of duty, but they are not done in a right manner: they are not from a right principle, nor are they directed to the right end; they are all selfish, slavish, and mercenary, and can never be acceptable to God.

(2.) Being under the curse, there is a separation betwixt God and your soul, and so the course of sanctifying influences is blocked up, If. lix. 2. *Your iniquities have separated between you and your God, and your sins have hid his face from you, that he will not hear.* While the curse thus stands as a partition wall of God's own making, in the course of justice, betwixt God and you, how can there be any saving communion with him? and without that, how can ye be made holy? Our Lord Jesus Christ, by his death and sufferings, purchased the Spirit of sanctification for those that are his; plainly importing, that there was no access for the Spirit of sanctification to the unholy creature by the first covenant.

You may possibly find an enlargement of heart in duty, under that covenant; but mistake it not for communion with God: for there is no communion with him under that covenant; there is no communion with him but by Jesus Christ, the head of the second covenant, Eph. ii. 18. And for an evidence hereof, you shall observe, that whereas communion with God has a sanctifying and humbling efficacy where it is; these enlargements have no such effect, but on the contrary fill the heart with pride and self esteem, and so render the soul more unholy, 1 John i. 6.

(3.) That covenant is no channel of sanctification to the unholy creature. To a sinner it is *the ministration of death,* 2 Cor. iii. 7. and of *condemnation,* ver. 9. a *killing letter,* exacting obedience to be performed on the strength given at first, but now quite spent; but promising no new strength for duty, but laying on the curse for non-performance. It is the gospel, or covenant of grace, that is the *ministration of the Spirit,* ver. 8. And for this the apostle appeals

appeals to the experience of those who have received the Spirit, Gal. iii. 2. *Received ye the Spirit by the works of the law, or by the hearing of faith?*

It is true, that under that covenant you may have been influenced to reformation of life, and prompted to the performing of duty: but all this amounts to no more in that case, but a change of life, and reaches never to a change of one's nature. Fear of punishment and hope of reward, are here the springs of all; not the love of God: and so the result of it is a form of godliness, without the power of it.

(4.) That covenant, instead of having a sanctifying influence on sinners, has an irritating power on their corruptions. The more close it comes on their consciences, the more their lusts are provoked, as was before explained, Rom. vii. 8. I may herein appeal to sinners experience. Have ye not sometimes found sleeping corruptions awakened by the law's forbidding of them? and weak lusts gather strength by the very sight of the hedge which the law has set betwixt you and them? And have not your hearts, on some particular occasions, finding how their inclinations were crossed by its commands, awed and frighted by its threatenings and curses, even risen against it secretly, and against the God that made it?

Thus under that covenant your case is desperately sinful.

Fourthly, From what has been said, ye may be further convinced, that while ye remain under that covenant, ye remain under the curse; that there is no deliverance from the curse, without deliverance from the covenant. *For as many as are of the works of the law, are under the curse.* It is vain to think one can be under that covenant, being a sinner, and not be under the curse; for in the dominion of the law, the curse will be found to take place, where-ever sin is found. So as long as ye live under the broken covenant of works, so long ye live under the curse; and if ye die under that covenant, ye die under the curse. When innocent Adam entered into that covenant, it did not curse, nor could it curse him or his, while as yet there was no command of it broken: but when once sin entered, the curse immediately took place, and seized on him and all his posterity; and under it they lie, as long as they remain

under

under that covenant, and are not delivered from that original contract.

This is a weighty confideration, and may pierce the hearts of all who have not got their difcharge as to that covenant, who have not got that hand-writing that is fo much againft them, blotted out with refpect to them. Whatever ye do, whatever ye fuffer, whatever change be in your converfation, or in the temper and difpofition of your fpirits, while ye remain under that covenant, the yoke of the curfe remains ftill wreathed about your necks. And to faften this conviction the more on you, confider,

1. Ye being born under that covenant were born under the curfe, *by nature the children of wrath*, Eph. ii. 3. Adam's fin laid all men under it; and as foon as we are Adam's children we are curfed children, bound over to death by the fentence of the broken law or covenant, Rom. v. 18. Now, there are only two ways, how that curfe may be fuppofed to be removed and taken off you, *viz.* either by your own bearing it for yourfelves, fo as to bear it off, or by another's bearing it for you imputed to you: for that it fhould be taken off you in a way of mere mercy, without any bearing it to the fatisfaction of juftice, is inconfiftent with God's juftice, truth, and covenant, as you heard before. But the former way, it cannot be that ye are or fhall be delivered from it: for whatever ye have fuffered in your fouls, bodies, or any other way, or whatever ye may fuffer, is ftill but the fufferings of a finite being, which can never compenfate the wrong done to the honour of an infinite God by your fin; and therefore the fufferings of the damned have no end. The breach made by the creature's fin in the honour of an infinite God, is a gulf which fwallows up all fufferings of the creature, but can never be thereby filled up. As to the latter, it cannot take place, but in the way of the fecond covenant, which is inconfiftent with your continuing under this covenant. The imputation of Chrift's fatisfaction, and the delivery from the curfe thereby, are confequents of the foul's union with Chrift, Rom. viii. 1. which is by one's entering into the covenant of grace, whereby they part with the covenant of works, which they naturally cleave to, Rom. vii. 4. Therefore it neceffarily follows, that

while

while ye remain under the covenant of works, ye remain under the curse, the curse laid on for Adam's sin.

2. Suppose that curse were removed, and no curse were lying on you now for the first breach of the covenant; yet ye cannot refuse, but that, however watchfully you have behaved yourselves, endeavouring to keep the law, you have been guilty of some sins in your own persons: you have, sometimes at least, thought evil, spoken evil, and done evil; some duties ye have omitted, some crimes against God and his law ye have committed. Now these lay you under the curse, since you are under the covenant which curseth the sinner; for it is written, *Cursed is every one that continueth not in all things which are written in the book of the law to do them.* It is not enough to do some things of the law; if all be not done, one is by this covenant staked down under the curse.

3. When you have done the best that possibly you can do to keep the commandments, ye still fall under the curse, while ye are under this covenant: because whatever good ye do, ye do it not well, that is, in the language of this covenant, ye do it not in perfection; for perfection in every point of duty is required under it, Luke x. 27.; and not only so, (for that is required under the covenant of grace too, Matth. v. *ult.*), but it is required under the pain of the curse; for it is written, *Cursed is every one that continueth not in all things,* &c. So that if you should omit no duty, external or internal, consistent with one's continuing under that covenant, and should perform them with all the vigour, zeal, and carefulness ye are capable of; yet even for these the covenant would thunder out its curse against you, for that you fail in them, in any the least measure or degree.

4. Forasmuch as the law requires all perfection, in all things, and at all times; and that at no time, in any action, you attain to that perfection, but are still sinning in all your thoughts, words, and actions: therefore the law is still raining down its curse on you, and binding you over with new ties to death, for your new sins, cursing for every thing done amiss. Wherefore, since you do nothing, but what one way or other is done amiss in the eye of the law, it is impossible you should ever get your head lifted

lifted up from under the curse, while you continue in that covenant.

5. *Lastly*, But put the case, though indeed it is impossible, that you under this covenant could arrive at perfection, so that you should sin no more, either by omission or commission, either in the matter or in the manner of what you do; but that your obedience should be from this moment perfect in parts and degrees, and that you should obey in as great perfection as the angels do in heaven: I say, that, notwithstanding, you remaining under this covenant, should still remain under the curse. For it is evident, that you are guilty of many sins already, and that is done by you which can never be undone: and for that cause you have fallen under the curse already; and your perfect obedience for the present time, and the time to come, being a debt you owe for the time wherein it is performed, can never expiate the former guilt, or be reputed satisfying for the debt before contracted. Yea, suppose you had never sinned in your own persons, but had perfectly obeyed since you were capable of keeping or breaking God's law: yet being under that covenant, you should still be under the curse, as being born under it, on the account of Adam's first sin; which, it is plain, on the former grounds, could not be expiated by that your supposed perfect obedience.

Thus it is evident, that while ye remain under this covenant, ye remain under the curse.

Say not, that, if this rate, all must be under the curse, since in many things we offend all: for the state of sinners under the two covenants is vastly different. By the first covenant, they that are under it are liable to the curse in case of sinning; but by the second covenant, they that are under it, are not liable thereto in any case, but freed from it, Gal. iii. 13. because Christ's bearing it for them is imputed to them. Sin under the former *reigns unto death;* but under the latter, *grace reigns through righteousness unto eternal life,* Rom v ult. In justification the obedience and satisfaction of Christ made for all the sins of all his people, past, present, and to come, are imputed unto believers; and so they are discharged at once of their whole debt to revenging justice, and they can never more fall

fall under the curſe, nor be liable to it for their ſins, more than a man can be liable in payment of a debt already paid and diſcharged. To pretend that believers may be liable to the curſe, and yet not fall under the curſe upon their ſinning, is vain: for if by the law, or threatening, they be liable to the curſe in caſe of tranſgreſſion; the curſe muſt needs ſieze them when they do actually tranſgreſs, in virtue of the truth of God in the threatening; for hath he ſaid it, and ſhall it not come to paſs? Neither is it profitable, in the caſe of the curſe, to diſtinguiſh betwixt groſs ſins and other ſins: for the curſing law makes no ſuch diſtinction in that point, but where it curſeth for one ſin, it curſes for all of what kind ſoever, Gal. iii 10. *Curſed is every one that continueth not in all things*, &c.

So this miſery is peculiar to thoſe under the covenant of works.

Fifthly, Hence ye may be convinced, that there is no ſalvation for you under that covenant: you muſt either quit it, and eſcape out of its dominion, or periſh under it. To be ſaved, and yet be under the curſe, is inconſiſtent: but while ye are under that covenant, ye are under the curſe; and therefore while ye are under it, ye cannot be ſaved, but muſt needs periſh. Therefore, I ſay, if ye abide in that broken ſhip, ye are ruined, ye will be ſwallowed up, ye will never ſee the ſhore of Immanuel's land. O be convinced of this, that you may deſpair of ever entering into heaven by that door; that your hopes and expectations by it may die, being plucked up by the roots; and you may look out for another door of hope. Conſider,

1. It was the door opened to innocent Adam indeed, but by one wrong ſtep miſſing it, he could never make his entry by it any more, but was fain to betake himſelf to another door, even Jeſus Chriſt in the free promiſe, Gen. iii. 15. How then can ye expect to enter by it? He found, that being once a ſinner, he was able no longer to live under the dominion of the law, and therefore did betake himſelf to the dominion of free grace: his garment of fig-leaves which he made for himſelf, he parted with as inſufficient, and took on the coat of ſkins (of ſacrifices)

sacrifices) which the Lord God made unto him. Ye must go and do likewise, or ye perish.

2. Sinners being shut up for destruction under this covenant, the door was bolted with the bar of the curse: so that there is no escaping from death by it for them, Gal. iii. 10. When Samson was shut up for death in Gaza, he took the doors of the gate of the city, bar and all, upon his shoulders, and so got out of the city to the mountain, Judg. xvi. But this bar of the curse is too heavy for the shoulders of angels, they are not able to bear it; far less are ye able. So there is no access to the hill of God that way for you. That gate is like unto that we read of, Ezek. xliv. 2. 3. *No man shall enter in by it; it is for the Prince,* the Lord Jesus Christ, the true Samson, who, when all his elect were shut up for death in the prison of the law covenant, barred with the bar of the curse, put himself in their room; and in his might lifted up the gate, bar and all, and carried them away, and so made a way for them to escape.

Take heed you deceive not yourselves in this matter, with the promises of life you apprehend to be made to your keeping of the commandments of God. It is true, there is a promise of life to obedience, in the covenant of works: but then it is only to perfect obedience; the curse is denounced against the least failure, Luke x. 27. 28. Gal. iii. 10. Now, it is evident you can have no hope by this promise, since you cannot perform the obedience to which it is made. And there is no promise of life in that covenant on any lower condition. Sincere obedience will not entitle you to that promise, though ye could perform it, as ye really cannot; the will cannot be accepted here for the deed: for the law denounceth the curse on every one under it for the least imperfection; and so staves them off from any benefit by its promise. The promise of life and salvation is in the covenant of grace freely made for the sake of Christ, to be received by faith in him: and even in it godliness hath the promise of life annexed to it, but it is made not to the work, but to the worker being in Christ; and not for his work's sake, but for Christ's sake. But you being under the covenant of works, have no saving interest in the promises of the covenant of grace,

and

and so have no part nor lot in the life and salvation there promised. And besides, all your obedience is servile and mercenary, unacceptable to God, so far from having the promise of life, that on the contrary such workers are expresly excluded from it, Gal. iv. 30. *Cast out the bond-woman and her son: for the son of the bond-woman shall not be heir with the son of the free-woman.* So there is no salvation for you under the broken covenant of works.

Sixthly, Ye may therefore hence be convinced, that there is an absolute necessity of being set free from the covenant of works, of being brought into the covenant of grace, and savingly interested in the Lord Jesus, the Second Adam. If you be not set free from the first covenant, ye are ruined; for as many as are under the bond of it, are under the curse. To put the question to yourselves, Whether you had best quit that covenant, or not? is in effect, Whether you had best remain under the curse, or endeavour to escape? This is a point that in reason can admit no more dispute, than whether a drowning man should be willing to be preserved from perishing? or whether a man should cast burning coals out of his bosom?

If you be not brought into the covenant of grace, interested in Jesus Christ by faith, you can never be freed from the covenant of works. No man shall ever get up that bond, but on his instructing full payment both of the principal sum and of the penalty; that is, both of perfect obedience to the law, and satisfaction to justice for the breach made by sin. This you shall never be able to instruct, do or suffer what you will, unless you embrace and unite with Christ by faith in the second covenant, by means of which his obedience and satisfaction shall be counted up on your score.

Here then is the one thing needful; unless you take this course, ye shall never see life or salvation, but perish for ever.

Lastly, From all that has been said, ye may be convinced, that your help must come wholly from the Lord Jesus Christ, and that you can contribute nothing by your own working to your own relief; Hos. xiii. 9. *O Israel, thou hast destroyed thyself; but in me is thine help.* For being

ing under that covenant, ye are under the curse: and what can one do for himself, acceptable to God, who is under these bonds of death? It is true, sinners will not come to Christ, till they be deeply sensible of their sin and misery: but to require such and such qualifications in sinners before they may come to Christ, is to lay a snare before them, keeping them back from Christ, and teaching them to lay some weight upon their qualifications while they are yet under the curse. In a special manner, to tell sinners, that they must truly repent of their sins before they may believe in Christ, or before they may apprehend the remission of sin in the promise, is in effect to say, that they must be holy and repent in a manner acceptable to God, while they are yet lying under his curse, for the curse is not removed but in justification. The truth is, there is a legal repentance agreeing to the state of one under the curse, arising from a legal faith, the faith of the curse, that goes before saving faith and remission of sin; and however necessary it is to stir up the soul to prize Christ, it cannot be acceptable to God, since the man is still under his curse. But no doing, no working, no repenting of ours can please God, till once we are from under the curse, through faith in him who justifies the ungodly. And therefore to effectuate the sinner's passing from the one covenant and its curse, into the other and the blessing thereof, no doing, no working of ours, is required, but only to receive Christ, pardon of sin, deliverance from the curse, by faith, they being all offered and exhibited in the free promise of the gospel to the sinner under the curse. And so the curse being removed, the partition wall betwixt God and the sinner is taken down, and the influences of the Spirit unto sanctification, evangelical repentance, and new obedience, flow into the soul.

Use II. of *exhortation*.

First, Let unbelievers, who are still under this covenant, receive these convictions, and be warned, excited, and exhorted timely to sue to be delivered from under the covenant of works, and for that end to be initated in the covenant of grace, by faith in Jesus Christ. What need is there of further motives than the text gives, in telling us,

The Doctrine applied, for Exhortation.

us, that all under this covenant are under the curse? which has been explained at large to you. Ah! is it safe to go home and sleep another night under the curse? Is it safe to venture more time under it, when ye know not which moment of your time may be the last? As ye have any regard to your own souls, lay this matter to heart, and delay no longer; but haste, escape for your life. Consider, I pray you,

1. The curse is a weight which you will never be able to bear. The weight of God's revenging wrath is in it; and it is a fearful thing to fall into the hands of the living God; on whomsoever this stone falls, it will grind him to powder.

2. It is a growing weight; as your sins grow, the curse grows; Rom ii 5. *After thy hardness and impenitent heart, thou treasurest up unto thyself wrath against the day of wrath.* The evils thou art bound over to are the greater, and the bonds are the stronger.

3. It is a weight that may now be removed from off you, 2 Cor. vi 2. *Behold, now is the accepted time; behold, now is the day of salvation.* Those whom this weight has sunk down into the pit already, it can never be removed from off them: but ye are yet within the reach of mercy, the Mediator is ready to take the yoke off your jaws.

4. If the weight of the curse be not removed from off you, it will be the heavier that deliverance from it was in your offer; Matth xi. 22. *It shall be more tolerable for Tyre and Sidon at the day of judgement, than for you.* The men of that covenant will all feel the weight of the curse, but it will have a double weight to despisers of the gospel.

5. *Lastly*, It will be an eternal weight, Matth. xxv. 41. *Depart from me, ye cursed, into everlasting fire.* There is an eternal weight of glory for the saints in the promise, and an eternal weight of wrath for sinners in the curse, which they shall for ever lie under, and never get clear of.

Let these things then move you to flee from the curse of the broken covenant of works, unto the covenant of grace, where life and salvation is only to be found.

Secondly, Believers in Christ, deliverd from this covenant, (1.) Be thankful for your deliverance, as a deliverance

ance from the curfe. Let the warmeft gratitude glow in your breafts for fo great a deliverance; and let your foul, and all that is within you, be ftirred up to blefs your glorious Deliverer for this unfpeakable blefling. (2.) Walk holily and fruitfully in good works, fince the bands of death are removed, and your fouls are healed. Be holy in all manner of life and converfation; adorning the doctrine of God your Saviour in all things. Let the whole tenor of your lives teftify, that you are not under the curfe, but that you inherit the blefling of eternal life, by living to the praife and honour of Chrift, who hath delivered you from the wrath to come. (3.) Turn not back to the broken covenant of works again, in legal principles, nor in legal practices. The more the temper and frame of your fpirit lies that way, the more unholy will ye be; and the more your duties favour of it, the lefs favoury will they be unto your God. It is only by being dead to the law, that ye will live unto God.

Thus far of the COVENANT OF WORKS.

www.ingramcontent.com/pod-product-compliance
Lightning Source LLC
Chambersburg PA
CBHW020815230426
43666CB00007B/1015